Empire Lost

Empire Lost

France and Its Other Worlds

Edited by Elisabeth Mudimbe-Boyi

LEXINGTON BOOKS

A division of
ROWMAN & LITTLEFIELD PUBLISHERS, INC.
Lanham • Boulder • New York • Toronto • Plymouth, UK

LEXINGTON BOOKS

A division of Rowman & Littlefield Publishers, Inc.
A wholly owned subsidary of The Rowman & Littlefield Publishing Group, Inc.
4501 Forbes Boulevard, Suite 200
Lanham, MD 20706

Estover Road
Plymouth PL6 7PY
United Kingdom

British Library Cataloguing in Publication Information Available

Library of Congress Cataloging-in-Publication Data

Empire lost : France and its other worlds / edited by Elisabeth Mudimbe-Boyi.
      p. cm.
   Includes bibliographical references and index.
   ISBN-13: 978-0-7391-2135-1 (cloth : alk. paper)
   ISBN-10: 0-7391-2135-9 (cloth : alk. paper)
   ISBN-13: 978-0-7391-3224-1 (electronic)
   ISBN-10: 0-7391-3224-5 (electronic)
   1. France—Relations—French-speaking countries. 2. French-speaking countries—
Relations—France. 3. France—Colonies—Intellectual life. 4. France—Intellectual life.
I. Mudimbe-boyi, M. Elisabeth.
   DC33.9.E57 2008
   303.48'2440171244—dc22
2008039292

Printed in the United States of America

♾™ The paper used in this publication meets the minimum requirements of American
National Standard for Information Sciences—Permanence of Paper for Printed Library
Materials, ANSI/NISO Z39.48–1992.

To Roger Barth:
Chief of the Helvètes, Francophone of the Americas

L'objectif, ce n'est pas de construire la société de demain, c'est de montrer qu'elle ne doit pas ressembler à celle d'aujourd'hui.

—Albert Jacquard

The goal is not to build the society of tomorrow, but to show that it does not need to resemble the one of today.

Contents

Acknowledgments for Permission

Jean-Loup Amselle's contribution is chapter 10 of his book, *L'Art de la friche, essai sur l'art africain contemporain*. Paris: Flammarion, 2005. Reproduced here in translation with the permission of Flammarion.

Mireille Le Breton published an abbreviated version of her article in the 2007 edition of *Paroles Gelées*, the journal of the UCLA French and Francophone Studies Department.

Mireille Rosello's maps from Francofffonies /Festival Francophone en France are reprinted with permission from Sophie Lawani, Press Relations Responsible for CULTURESFRANCE.

Introduction

> They ruled over us, ran the country, exploited us, taught us their language, sent us to their schools, and gave us new ancestors called Gauls. That's why we still speak French, love French food, and still like to spend our vacations in France, even if these days it is easier to get a visa to the moon than to that country.
>
> —Emmanuel Dongala, *Little Boys Come from the Stars*

The French colonial empire extended to Africa, Asia, and the Americas. Today, in terms of politics and international relations, decolonization remains one of the major events of the 1960s. In the cultural and social domains, colonization, decolonization, and immigration transformed not only the political relationship between France and its former colonies, but also French literature and the French language itself. In many ways, literature from Africa, from the Caribbean, and to a lesser extent, from Asia, as well as the literature of immigration within France, illuminates these transformations. With the new global promotion of *la Francophonie*, emblematized by the Organisation Internationale de la Francophonie, the relation between the different constituencies of the French-speaking regions of the world needs to be reexamined and debated.

"Lost Empire: France and Its Other Worlds," a conference I organized at Stanford University in April 2006 with Dan Edelstein, was meant to be part of the ongoing debate. The gathering sought to underline the comparative and interdisciplinary perspective of *la Francophonie académique* and to frame in a different manner what, in the academic programs and studies, seems to exclude one from the other: French studies on the one hand, and Francophone studies on the other.

The present collection of essays is not meant to lament the past or the mischief of colonial politics of hegemony. Nor does it constitute an authoritative conclusion about the Empire France lost, nor a solution to the polysemy and the uncertainties of the lexicon that brings France and its other worlds together. Rather, it questions ingrained assumptions and mirrors our contemporaneity, in which the global and the local coexist. It also aims to point out the complexity and the ambiguity of a never-ending relationship between Francophone communities after the Empire. This conversation will, perhaps, consolidate *la Francophonie*, thanks to a lucid examination of its achievements and accomplishments as well as its weaknesses and pitfalls.

At the same time, this volume seeks to continue some of the exchanges that took place during the conference, reflecting on how, despite the loss of Empire, France and its other worlds are—each of four continents in its own way—still bound by a common historical past. The different contributions that came out of the 2006 conference illustrate how textual representations in literature, art, and film do underline, reflect, or actualize the new relationship.

I

In the last chapter of his seminal book, *Portrait du colonisé précédé du portrait du colonisateur*, Albert Memmi alludes to a new kind of relationship between colonizer and colonized as one to be based on new grounds.[1] In his turn, Aimé Césaire suggests an almost friendship between Caliban, the slave, and his master, Prospero, when the latter, at the ultimate moment, renounces any return to Europe, calling Caliban "*mon vieux*," emphasizing "*toi moi, moi toi*" as a new kind of bonding between them.[2] Those literary references actualize a moment of rupture and bring about a new sensitivity to different relations between colonizer and colonized, master and slave—or in other words, between France and its other worlds. This shift could be summarized by Albert Jacquard's words, given as an epigraph to this volume: "l'objectif, ce n'est pas de construire la société de demain, c'est de montrer qu'elle ne doit pas ressembler à celle d'aujourd'hui" ["the goal is not to build the society of tomorrow, but to show that it does not need to resemble the one of today"].

Choosing to entitle this volume *Empire Lost: France and Its Other Worlds*, is in actuality a way to relativize, if not contest, the adjective "Francophone" in "Francophone literatures," "Francophone studies," "Francophone writers," or "Francophone cultures." The adjective is paradoxical in its exclusion of Hexagonal France, which—in good logic and in an obvious manner—is nevertheless the founding site and the originating center of what is Francophone. It is in regard to this self-exclusion that Abdou Diouf, the General Secretary of the Organisation Internationale de la Francophonie, speaks of the "*désamour des Français pour la Francophonie.*"[3]

The adjective Francophone remains problematic in its subtext of an ongoing hierarchical relation, despite all the official discourses of plurality and diversity between France as a center and its other worlds. What is called *Francophonie* today is inscribed in geography and in history. As part of the colonial legacy, it represents a vast, heterogeneous space comprising societies and cultures geographically remote from each other that are shaped by different historical, cultural, and linguistic substrates, which are all brought together through the assimilation of the French colonial culture, as well as the imposition of French language on the colonized and its appropriation by it.

My reluctance about the terminology does not indicate denial of a common legacy of French colonization, language, and culture, nor does it represent a rejection of worldwide Francophonie as a fact of history. The two keynote speakers at the conference were Michel Serres and Assia Djebar. Both Francophone—one a native of France, the other a native of Algeria— today they are both united in the most prestigious institution of the Hexagon in charge of the French language orthodoxy and normativity: *l'Académie Française.*

From the perspective of the colonized or the colonizer, even with the gap in time and space, French colonial spaces share common grounds that allow Assia Djebar—in her intervention featured in this collection as an "Ouverture"— to connect two remote loci of the French Empire, through the intertwined voices of Albert Camus of Algeria and Marguerite Duras of Indochina. Djebar focuses on the autobiographical dimension of Camus's *Le Premier Homme* and Duras's *L'Amant* to highlight their convergence and divergence. The reference to biographies here also signals the relation between self-reflexivity, the way of writing, and the language, as well as the power relation between the dominant French language of the Empire and the local languages: Arabic and Vietnamese. Writing about Camus (who was French of Algeria and did not speak Arabic) and Duras (who was French of Indochina and spoke fluent Vietnamese), Djebar entwines her own voice as a Franco-Algerian writer.

Serres's text, reproduced as the closure to this volume, concerns itself with the language question. Offered as an autobiographical testimony and a personal linguistic itinerary with a glance at the history of the French language,

Serres's account speaks of a forgotten or neglected cartography of *la Fran-cophonie* within the Hexagon itself, from which his maternal language, the *ré-gional* Occitan-Gascon, was excluded. With emotion but also lucidity, Ser-res's narrative revisits the hegemonic relation between French and the "*langues régionales*,"[4] examining the loss that comes with the disappearance of the local: here the mother tongue, in confrontation with the more global and dominant French, his paternal language, which was important to him as well, since it is the language of his intellectual fathers. As Serres points out, Oth-erness and Otherizing also function within the Hexagon: for the Occitan-Gascon speaker he was, French was a foreign language, and he was an Other.

Today, the presence and the settlement in France of immigrants from the former colonies perpetuate Otherness and reproduce the colonial relation. Thus, positing France and its other worlds does not establish rigid di-chotomies.[5] In bringing France and its other worlds together, I chose to em-phasize the conjunction "and," considering the constant contact and inter-twined relationship that bears testimony of historical facts: from centralization to colonization to immigration, as well as their consequences and lasting legacy. If the Empire was lost with decolonization, there are still sequels, substrata, and crosscurrents to which one could add the emergence of new sensitivities and new ways of thinking; all of that makes *la Francoph-onie* a project embedded in ambiguity and, sometimes, contradiction.

Two anecdotes provide an illustration of apparently contradictory charac-ters of Francophonie. In 2005, as I do during each of my stops in Paris, I went to the Montparnasse Rue de Rennes FNAC: one major bookstore in Paris. As usual, I wandered the book floor and looked at "littérature Francophone," where I used to find books by African and Caribbean writers. To my surprise, only works by French writers from France were under this label. After some searching, I found the writers I was looking for under the rubrique "littéra-ture étrangère." It was unclear to me how what was considered Francophone literature only a few months before had become foreign literature.

The second anecdote is about African scholars. Although they are Fran-cophone and natives of former French colonies, they are regularly denied en-trance visas to France. They frequently get tied up in bureaucracy, even when the goal of their trip is to attend professional conferences, including confer-ences on Francophone literatures. Among these scholars, one was the recip-ient of the *Palmes Académiques*, a French honorific award bestowed by the French government to writers and scholars who have distinguished them-selves in the promotion of French language and culture. This scholar-writer, in danger and fleeing his country, was denied a visa for France, despite his *Palmes Académiques*, while the United States of America, an English-speaking country, granted him the visa! He has since settled in the United States, and, still writing his novels in French, he is considered a Francophone writer. The ironic quotation opening my introduction is from one of that writer's novels. It offers another example of the ambiguity in which *la Francophonie* is embedded.

Anecdotes tell stories, which might be part of a history that translates the fluctuant, sometimes evading the character of the adjective Francophone, the complexity and ambiguity conveyed in the multiple layers of a terminology tied to history, culture, and politics, or they might also represent the uncertainties of *la Francophonie's* contours. They point to the mobile position of the Hexagon between self-inclusion and self-exclusion, as well as the exclusion and inclusion of France's other worlds from *la Francophonie*: necessary and strategic inclusion perhaps, if France needs to maintain a global presence and visibility of the French language that might be overshadowed today were it not sustained by the use and the vitality of the French language outside of France by all its other worlds.

The adjective Francophone carries a multiplicity of references, varying according to context, subtext, and sites of enunciation from which discourse is produced in its name. The same term covers different geographical, cultural, political, social, and economic spaces. Sometimes Francophone designates only the world outside of France, as if France itself were not Francophone.

One such example could be seen in the United States, in the denomination of some departments as French and Francophone Studies. For some, this distinction indicates a hierarchical relation between the Hexagon and the rest of the French-speaking world. As for my part, I chose to read this distinction, paradoxical at first glance, as the assertion of a nonmarginal and autonomous existence outside the Hexagon, or the affirmation of a difference from the centrality of France. Again, emphasizing the "and," I prefer to read "French and Francophone" as a desire to subvert the hierarchical relation between the two terms. I consider the coordination marker to be erasing the vertical relation and, implicitly, defining what *la Francophonie* ought to be and how it ought to function: not only as an unifying factor but also, at the same time, as an affirmation of diversity and pluralism, a recognition and a genuine acceptance of difference between the Hexagon and its other worlds.

As for the collective substantive *la Francophonie*, it raises a challenge for both the French Empire and its other worlds. Its denomination and project call for questions: How do contemporary France and its former Empire relate to each other today? How do we conciliate a *Francophonie plurielle* with a still persistent Jacobin conception of the Republic and the assertion of an *exception française?*[6] These questions might point in two directions. First, to a vertical relation represented by a binary model, posing a Center and a Periphery; second, to a horizontal relation that calls for an inclusive model and a comparative approach to Francophone studies, taking into consideration the differences of the historical trajectories of each constituent, but also their relations with the meaning given to the word by Édouard Glissant in his *Poétique de la Relation*.

In the absence of an adequate terminology or fixed meaning of what is labeled as *Francophone* or *la Francophonie*, I acknowledge my own ambiguity in keeping with these words. The ambiguity that characterizes *la Francophonie* might not necessarily and immutably be construed as negative. Witness to a history of contact and relation, even unequal relation, ambiguity constitutes the fabric of *la Francophonie*, which has, nevertheless, been productive and fruitful in some cases.

This has been accomplished through the existence of a literary *Francophonie* (writers and their literary production) and an academic *Francophonie* (the study and criticism of the writers' productions). The major contribution of the literary and academic *Francophonie* is the recognition of a non-France-centered literature in French produced outside of Europe. Their teaching and promotion by academic institutions, at least in the United States, is exemplified by the introduction and the consolidation of Francophone studies in many academic departments.

This newness has opened academia to a better knowledge and appreciation of the diversity and the pluralism of cultures that constitute France's other worlds. On the other hand, these developments have generated challenging interrogations regarding the relation between French and Francophone, Francophone and the postcolonial, and have led to revisiting the traditional model of French studies as shown by recent publications.[7] To avoid redundancy, I will, for my part, summarize with a few questions I raise elsewhere in different terms: Has the institution of a "language community" erased or significantly changed the relationship between the Center and its Periphery—that is, France and the non-Hexagonal Francophonie? How do we confront or reconcile the tension between a global perspective carried through the French language and the specificity of each of the Francophone areas of Europe, Africa, Asia, North America, and the Caribbean? Francophone Studies has emerged as a field that transgresses geographical and racial boundaries. Does a more global, transcultural, transnational, or transcontinental Francophonie, as practiced in the academic space, allow for escaping the rigid and reductive binaries such as Self and Other, Center and Periphery? Regarding literary production, what in the writers' imagination translates a consciousness of belonging both to the global and the local?

If there is no perfect or definitive answer to these theoretical questions, the anecdotes told earlier in this introduction highlight the inscription of the terms *la Francophonie* and *Francophone* in a historical trajectory. Both terms bear the imprints of history, as well as the epistemological and ideological marks of different periods and changes in mentalities. Accordingly, one could choose to see the frontier between France and its other worlds as an unshakable geographical, political, and cultural limit, which, it seems, goes against the grain of a globalizing world and the official discourses promoting "la Francophonie." One could also consider that frontier as a line that has become mobile, fluctuant, and permeable, across which currents, ideas, sensitivities, and creativities are expressed, bearing testimony to vitality and diversity but also to the cross-fertilization of cultures and societies (re)crossing or meeting at that line.

This conclusion allows for an understanding of the adjective Francophone as an autonomous, separate entity focusing outside of France but also as inclusive of France. Positioning one as separate from the other would assert an absence of history or a denial of a historical moment.[8] The present volume illustrates, with texts and contexts, the colonial contact and its palimpsest: how, in France and in its other worlds, that contact, its repercussions, and its memory[9] are lived, expressed, and actualized today through a variety of disciplinary and textual representations.

II

The contributions in the first part of this volume translate the complexity of a postempire context *mise en abyme* within the Hexagonal center, changing its demographic landscape, awakening new sensibilities and cultural presences that transform France in a lieu of diversity and newness, which leads to investigating the Republic and some of its fundamental principles.

In her article, Mireille Le Breton echoes current interrogations and France's revisitation of republican claims for *laïcité* in relation to "*le port du voile islamique*" ("wearing of the Islamic veil"), which, seen as a religious symbol, perturbs the homogeneous landscape of a secular republic.

Jocelyne Dakhlia interrogates the "*mise sous le tapis*" ("putting under the carpet") and occultation of Islamic presence, while in actuality, given the historical context, Islam has become an undeniable presence in contemporary French society.

Alec Hargreaves examines a novel dimension of the subversion of French homogeneity by opening the conversation to cultural currents and manifestations from the Anglo-American world, showing how Anglo-American models have been "appropriated and renewed by their incorporation in Francophone cultures."

Tyler Stovall also speaks of the Anglo-American component, focusing on the African American presence in France. Taking as a point of departure the 2005 *banlieues* riots to compare the societies of France and the United States, he underlines their differences and commonalities. He argues that the 2005 *banlieues* riots in France reveal the disappearance of the mythical image of a color-blind France, which, in the past, has attracted African American expatriates fleeing a racist America to find a haven in France: a country that, for them, embodied the ideals of *liberté, égalité, fraternité*. Stovall's conclusive statement is that Paris "no longer constitutes a refuge from racism, but rather the frontlines of diasporic and global debates about what it means to be black."

Mireille Rosello reverberates parts of my introduction, as well as Michel Serres's intervention regarding what constitutes a "community of language" and the relation between accepted languages and "barbaric" ones—a term from which she evacuates the usually negative connotation. Rosello disrupts the homogeneous space implied by "Francophone" and "la Francophonie" as tied only to the colonial context, reminding us of the existence of a European *Francophonie* independent from colonization. She also points out a variety of contexts in which French is spoken: as a daily or occasional language, the interlocutors involved, and the circumstances from which emerge what she calls "Francophone moments." Finally, she introduces a novel aspect of "la Francophonie," demonstrating how Internet networks create a Francophone map outside the officially promoted *Francophonie*, thus challenging its homogeneity to display a fragmented and disjointed contour that questions what a linguistic community is.

The second part of this volume exemplifies the ways in which the aftermaths of historical contact between France and its other worlds has given birth to new kinds of cross-cultural expressions in the arts, in literature, and in aesthetics. It emphasizes interrelations and appropriations from both sides of the Hexagon frontier, highlighting the fluidity and the permeability of its borders, as I mentioned earlier in this introduction.

Yvonne Hsieh, who has written on the West-East cultural relations, uses Édouard Glissant's theory of *la Relation* to show a "rencontre entre la langue française et la langue classique chinoise," through a commentary of Victor Segalen's remarkable poetic work *Stèles*, which contains poems written in French that are structured according to Chinese poetics. Hsieh's analysis clearly illustrates what she considers a "creolized" aesthetic that illuminates a process of cross-fertilization, with the West borrowing from the East and appropriating.

Kathy Richman's essay, without forsaking the question of identity and Otherness woven in Jacques Roumain's novel, *Gouverneurs de la rosée*, connects the Haïtian rural novel to nineteenth-century French social novel tradition, as exemplified by George Sand. More importantly, Richman implicitly discusses the relationship between *langue dominée* and *langue dominante*. In effect, she emphasizes the presence or the shadow of the Creole language and its specific turnings throughout the novel, demonstrating the imbrications of French and Creole in the novel thus embedded in a linguistic diglossia. Using such an angle of analysis, she demonstrates how Roumain, emulating Sand as a social novelist, was concerned about translating the voices of the major actors of his narrative—the Haïtian peasants—and making them present in his work.

André Benhaïm uses movement as a trope to analyze Assia Djebar's work, illuminating movement and mobility that engage different orders, directions "between Orient and Occident, between France and Algeria, between Berber, Arabic, and French, [. . .], writing and orality." If Benhaïm describes weaving as a form of feminine aesthetic, his reflection underscores the cross-cultural dimension of Djebar: creativity, nurtured by an encounter of diverse sources and origins, in which the resonance of local languages and cultural signs merge with those of this other appropriated language—"le français comme butin."

While Benhaïm focuses on the aesthetic of mobility, Jean-Loup Amselle considers movement in time by retracing the genesis of contemporary African art. This genealogical perspective stresses how change in conceptions as well as in mentalities impacts the conditions of the production of the arts and their circulation. The perception of African art linked to Africa as a land of adventure and experimentation progressively grants room to its greater autonomy, but it also provides for interaction with the Western world, mostly France. This new vision offers a "Franco-African cultural fermentation" and "métissage," as exemplified by some of Maurice Béjart's works or the journal *Revue Noire*, leading to coin the term "Françafriche" as an actualization of a cross-cultural exchange.

The larger picture of Karl Britto's reflection revisits the ambiguity of "la Francophonie," through his study of fiction and films featuring colonial soldiers, or *tirailleurs*. They are considered "Same," thus French and having to fight for France. Yet, at the same time, they are also perceived as Other, because their uniforms clearly distinguish them and make their Otherness visible. At a closer angle, Britto's analysis focuses on the body of the *tirailleur indochinois*. Cultural assimilation brought by the *mission civilisatrice* made the colonized subject to cross the line of separation between him and the colonizer, so to speak. In the colonial novel and the Vietnamese Francophone novels examined, Britto shows how Otherness staged through external signs, such as the military uniform, renders evanescent the possibility for a cross-cultural encounter. The body wearing a different uniform remains an external body, foreign to the body of the nation the *tirailleur* has fought for in that uniform.

The aesthetic of mobility brought to light by Benhaïm in his reading of Assia Djebar posits her "like a fugitive, an eternal exile"—that is, without frontier, crossing lines back and forth, reproducing the elusive character of "la Francophonie" and the indeterminacy of its contours. Djebar thus mirrors what a true Francophone literature or a real *Francophonie* ought to be: a site without borders, dynamic, "poreux à tous les souffles du monde," as the poet Aimé Césaire puts it. In other words, *la Francophonie* should be a space embracing, containing, and expressing the diversity of cultures and of other languages—paternal and maternal—through a common French language.

III

The success of the conference was the result of institutional interest and support; it was a friendly collaboration between several people. Dean Arnold Rampersad graciously accepted the task of giving the allocution at the opening of the conference. I thank him and Provost John Etchemendy for their support and generous funding of the conference. I would like to acknowledge and thank the co-organizer of the conference, Dan Edelstein; Mireille Le Breton, who served as the coordinator of the conference; Zoé Bower, who designed and regularly updated the conference Web site; Audrey Calefas, who served as a benevolent and trustful chauffeur for the keynote speakers, Assia Djebar and Michel Serres.

My thanks also go to the colleagues who came to speak at the conference. Some of their papers appear in this volume. I am grateful to my Stanford colleagues who served as chair panels or took part in the roundtable on the *exception française* that concluded the conference: Robert Harrison, Chair of the Department of French and Italian; Jean-Marie Apostolides, Josh Landy, and Laura Wittman from the same department; Richard Robert from the History Department; and Sarah Sussman, Curator of the French and Francophone section of Green Library. Special thanks go to Mr. Julien Kilanga Musinde, Director of la Langue française et de la diversité linguistique at the Organisation Internationale de la Francophonie in Paris—he made simultaneous translation during the conference possible.

Several Stanford Centers, Programs, and Departments cosponsored the conference: the Abbasi Program in Islamic Studies; the Center for African Studies;

the African and Afro-American Program; the Center for the Comparative Study of Race and Ethnicity; the Department of Comparative Literature; the Division of Literatures, Languages, and Cultures; the department of French and Italian; the Forum on Contemporary Europe; the History Department; the Program in Modern Thought and Literature; the Religious Studies Department; the Taube Center for Jewish Studies; and the Stanford Humanities Center.

As usual, the support of copy editors and book production is invaluable. Julie Kirsch, editorial director at Lexington Books, Maera Winters, and Lynda Phung deserve my warmest thanks for working with such diligence and patience. Through books and conversations, over dinners and meetings, Dr. Roger Barth of Menlo Park has been for me a father, a big brother, a friend, and a continuous Francophone presence since I settled in California in 1995. It is with affection and immense gratitude that I dedicate this book to him.

Elisabeth Mudimbe-Boyi
Schacht-Audorf (Germany), July 2008

Notes

1. Albert Memmi, *Portrait du colonisé précédé du portrait du colonisateur*. Paris: Payot, 1973.

2. Aimé Césaire, *Une Tempête, d'après* La tempête *de Shakespeare*. Paris: Seuil, 1969.

3. Abdou Diouf, "La Francophonie, une réalité oubliée." *Le Monde*, March 19, 2007. Actually, several scholars and writers resist the label of Francophone (see the most recent document published by a collective of writers: "Pour une 'littérature-monde' en Français: le Manifeste des 44," *Le Monde des livres*, March 15, 2007). Abdou Diouf's text quoted here comes as a response to this collective (see also Michel Le Bris and Jean Rouaud, eds., *Pour une littérature-monde*. Paris: Gallimard, 2007).

One could exercise irony by saying that the so-called Francophone writer, at best, should be a "francographe": a person writing in French (see *Magazine littéraire* devoted to "Défense et illustration des langues françaises," 451, March 2006, p. 37). Without renouncing my critical stance, for practical reasons and in absence of any other more adequate terminology, I will be using the official terminology current in academia. I will be using quotation marks around "Francophone" and "Francophonie" where the term is contested or used with irony, to differentiate it from neutral usage with the term in italics. On the other hand, further in this introduction, I propose to recuperate somehow the term "Francophone" and to read it as positive process of differentiation and self-identification.

In her contribution to this volume, Mireille Rosello also discusses the adjective Francophone and mentions such writers as Amin Maalouf's reaction to the label of "Francophone writer." After the completion of this introduction, I came across a reflection on "Francophone" versus French by Jacques Coursil, "Le Paradoxe Francophone" in *Montray Kréyol*, online publication, accessed July 25, 2008.

4. See J. B. Marcellesi, "Les 'langues régionales' de France, langues minorées," in Wolfgang Bandhauer and Robert Tanzmeister, eds., *Romanistik Integrativ: Festschrift für Wolfgang Pollack*, *Wiener Romanistische Arbeiten*, Wien, Wilhelm Braumüller, 13, 1985, pp. 363–71. Marcellesi distinguishes "langues minoritaires," "langues dominées," et "langues minorées."

5. Elisabeth Mudimbe-Boyi, ed., *Beyond Dichotomies: Histories, Identities, Cultures, and the Challenge of Globalization*. Albany: SUNY Press, 2002. See also *Essais sur les cultures en contacts. Afrique, Amériques, Europe*. Paris: Karthala, 2006.

6. The conference "Empire Lost: France and Its Other Worlds" concluded with a roundtable about the *exception française*.

7. See for example, Alec Hargreaves, "Ships Passing in the Night? France, Postcolonialism and the Globalization of Literature." *Francophone Postcolonial Studies*, 1, 2, 2003: pp. 64–69; Françoise Lionnet and Dominic Thomas, eds., "Francophone Studies: New Landscapes." *Modern Language Note*, 118, 4, September 2003; Tyler Stovall and Georges Van Den Abbeele, eds., *French Civilization and Its Discontents: Nationalism, Colonialism, Race*. Lanham: Lexington Books, 2003; Farid Laroussi and Christopher Miller, eds., "French and Francophone: The Challenge of Expanding Horizons." *Yale French Studies*, 103, 2003; Jean-Marc Moura, *Littératures Francophones et théorie postcoloniale*. Paris: Presses Universitaires de France, 1999; and Anne Donadey and Adlai Murdoch, eds., *Postcolonial Theory and Francophone Literary Studies*. Gainesville: University of Florida, 2005.

8. See the position of colonial historians Ann Laura Stoler and Frederick Cooper, "Between Metropole and Colony: Rethinking a Research Agenda" in Ann Stoler and Frederick Cooper, eds., *Tensions of Empire: Colonial Cultures in a Bourgeois World*. Berkeley and Los Angeles: University of California Press, 1997, pp. 1–56; and Matthias Middel, "Francophonia as a World Region?" *European Review of History*, 10, 2, 2003, pp. 203–20. See also the special issue of the *Francophone Postcolonial Studies*, 5, 2, Autumn–Winter 2007 centered on "France in a Postcolonial Europe: Identity, History, Memory": particularly, Charles Forsdick, "Colonial History, Postcolonial Memory: Contemporary Perspectives," pp. 101–18; and Adlai Murdoch, "Making Frenchness Plural: How France Contends with Its 'Others,'" pp. 41–68.

9. See Alec Hargreaves, *Memories of Empire and Postcolonialism: Legacies of French Colonialism*. Lanham: Lexington Books, 2005.

Works Cited

Césaire, Aimé. *Une Tempête, d'après* La Tempête *de Shakespeare*. Paris: Seuil, 1969.

Collective, "Pour une 'littérature-monde' en Français: le Manifeste des 44." *Le Monde des livres*, March 15, 2007.

Diouf, Abdou. "La Francophonie, une réalité oubliée." *Le Monde*, March 19, 2007.

Donadey, Anne, and Murdoch, Adlai, eds. *Postcolonial Theory and Francophone Literary Studies*. Gainesville: University of Florida Press, 2005.

Forsdick, Charles. "Colonial History, Postcolonial Memory: Contemporary Perspectives." *Francophone Postcolonial Studies*, 5, 2, Autumn–Winter 2007, pp. 101–18.

Forsdick, Charles, and Murphy, David, eds. "France in a Postcolonial Europe: Identity, History, Memory." *Francophone Postcolonial Studies*, 5, 2, Autumn-Winter 2007. Special issue.

Hargreaves, Alec. "Ships Passing in the Night? France, Postcolonialism and the Globalization of Literature." *Francophone Postcolonial Studies*, 1, 2, 2003: pp. 64–69.

———. Memories of Empire. *Legacies of French Colonialism*. Lanham: Lexington Books, 2005.

Laroussi, Farid, and Miller, Christopher, eds. "French and Francophone: The Challenge of Expanding Horizons." *Yale French Studies*, 103, 2003.

Le Bris, Michel, and Rouaud, Jean, eds. *Pour une littérature-monde*. Paris: Gallimard, 2007.

Lionnet, Françoise, and Thomas Dominic, eds., "Francophone Studies: New Landscapes." *Modern Language Note*, 118, 4, September 2003.

Marcellesi, Jean-Baptiste. "Les 'langues régionales' de France, langues minorées," in Wolfgang Bandhauer and Robert Tanzmeister, eds. Romanistik Integrativ: Festschrift für Wolfgang Pollack. *Wiener Romanistische Arbeiten*, Wien, Wilhelm Braumüller, 13, 1985, pp. 363–71.

Memmi, Albert. *Portrait du colonisé précédé du portrait du colonisateur*. Paris: Payot, 1973.

Middel, Matthias. "Francophonia as a World Region?" *European Review of History*, 10, 2, 2003, pp. 203–20.

Moura, Jean-Marc. *Littératures Francophones et théorie postcoloniale*. Paris: Universitaires de France, 1999.

Mudimbe-Boyi, Elisabeth, ed. *Beyond Dichotomies: Histories, Identities, Cultures, and the Challenge of Globalization*. Albany: SUNY Press, 2002.

———. *Essais sur les cultures en contacts. Afrique, Amériques, Europe*. Paris: Karthala, 2006.

Murdoch, Adlai. "Making Frenchness Plural: How France Contends with its 'Others.'" *Francophone Postcolonial Studies*, 5, 2, Autumn-Winter 2007, pp. 41–68.

Stoler, Ann, and Cooper, Frederick, eds. *Tensions of Empire: Colonial Cultures in a Bourgeois World*. Berkeley and Los Angeles: University of California Press, 1997.

Stovall, Tyler, and Van Den Abbeele, Georges, eds. *French Civilization and Its Discontents. Nationalism, Colonialism, Race*. Lanham: Lexington Books, 2003.

~

Ouverture

Writing Loss—Indochina, Algeria—Voices Entwined

Assia Djebar, Member of L'Académie Française

My keynote speech is a literary text. When I first accepted to speak on "Writing Lost Empire," I seized the opportunity to plunge deeper into the work of Marguerite Duras. When I first began thinking of "entwined voices," I imagined a dialogue between Marguerite Duras, a French voice from "Indochina," writing in France, and Linda Lê, a Franco-Vietnamese voice in exile from Vietnam, writing in exile from France. I anticipated the differences between the voices of a French Indochinese writer and a young Vietnamese Francophone writer.

I also toyed with the idea of a dialogue face to face between two Algerian writers. I would take up the French Algerian Albert Camus and the Algerian Francophone Kateb Yacine, just as I have done in past university seminars, and analyze Camus's *L'Etranger* or *Le Premier Homme* counter to Kateb Yacine's *Nedjma*. By alternating French and Francophone voices—voices entwined—I introduce Francophone literature for my students.

Then, as I began gathering biographical background details on Marguerite Duras, I realized Marguerite Duras was Albert Camus's contemporary. Camus born in 1913, Duras in 1914. Duras publishing her first text *Les Impudents* in 1942, Camus publishing *L'Etranger* in 1943. If it hadn't been for the brutal interruption of Camus's literary career in 1961, the two could have continued along their route as contemporaries awhile longer, giving us the first full dialogue as intertwined voices of a lost French empire.

Introduction

I will begin like in the olden days, taking my time to adjust the lantern on the oak table, at dusk, in anticipation of a long night of writing . . . Illuminating my way is the light from the great contemporary poet Jacques Dupin:

> A ses crimes, l'écriture est liée, malgré son exécration, par le double fil lâchement tressé, de sa dépendance et de sa dissidence.[1]

> To its crimes, writing is tied, despite its execration, by the double cord loosely entwined, of its dependence and its dissidence.

In this verse's inner progression, I see the perfect "frame" for opening up my comparison of two contemporary writers: Marguerite Duras and Albert Camus. In this excerpt from Dupin's *Dehors* (1975), or to be more precise, this poem "Le soleil substitué," I also found this magnificent verse to reserve for my conclusion:

> Et gronde dans le sous-sol. Qui hurlerait sans le sable qui l'étouffe.

> And rumbles in the basement. What would howl without the suffocating sands.[2]

You see, writing always has a basement with something rumbling below. On that note, I will conclude my approach to two children of the former French colonies, Albert Camus and Marguerite Duras.

To ask what "writing loss" means—or, as the title of this conference invites, what "writing the loss of the French colonial empire" means—let's hold on "par le double fil lâchement tressé, de sa dépendance et de sa dissidence" entwining two voices, those of Marguerite Duras and Albert Camus.[3] But I have also included a second duo in my title, Indochina and Algeria. I will start by tracing the lives of two premier novelists of their time, from colonial childhood to final published texts, thus following two literary works whose strong ties to their homeland are ties to two lost French colonial lands disappearing one after the other from the Imperial map: Indochina after the War for Indochina, from 1945 to 1954, then Algeria after the violent seven-year Algerian war from 1954 to 1962. Officially the Algerian revolution began after the Indochinese revolution ended in 1954, but Algeria's struggle for independence began the day of the first popular insurrection, and the first violent repression, on May 8, 1945. If I remember the exact date of the Sétif insurrection, it is not because I am a colonial historian, but because the date was engraved in my literary memory by the first major Algerian Francophone novel by Kateb Yacine, *Nedjma*. At age seventeen, Kateb was a student marcher swept up in the excitement of the demonstrations and then a victim swept up in the widespread arrests and detentions. If it hadn't been for Kateb's experience being locked up with other Algerians in prison, he probably wouldn't have written his superb masterpiece *Nedjma*. But after Sétif, Kateb never got his normal life back again . . .

Meanwhile, back in Algeria, Albert Camus, world-renowned French author since his hit novel *L'Etranger* (*The Stranger*) in 1943, found himself under mounting pressure to respond to the violent fever racking Algeria's body. The French author Camus ever since was condemned—and I believe unjustly so—by all the other Algerian intellectuals for his apparent silence during the Algerian war.

Thus, I confront two writers, Marguerite Duras, born in Indochina, and Albert Camus, born in Algeria. I draw from Duras's autobiographical writing set in Indochina from *Le Barrage contre le Pacifique* in 1950 and thirty-four years later in 1984, *L'Amant*, an autobiographical novel crowning Duras's career with her greatest commercial success ever. From Camus's life works, I choose over Camus's *L'Envers et l'endroit*, in limited circulation in Algeria, *Les Noce à Tipasa* from 1950, and over *L'Etranger*, the 1943 international best seller which catapulted Camus to celebrity overnight, *Le Premier Homme*, Camus's last unfinished novel published posthumously by his daughter in 1994. But from the outset, without any real *a priori*, I let the subject of this conference "Lost Empire"—a rather socioliterary one at that—be my only guide through these works by Marguerite Duras, from Indochina, by Albert Camus, from Algeria, being read side by side. For both authors *lost empire* means lost childhood territory or nostalgia for those left behind. Voicing one's loss of childhood territory, or impossible return for Marguerite Duras, sets in motion a narrative or poetic structure around absence, for absence is consubstantial to any desire to write, whether that desire engenders a poetic or narrative form . . .

Part One

I must admit this surprising match made by Marguerite Duras and Albert Camus started as a series of coincidences between two birth dates, birth places, and two literary careers. A couple of biographical parallels between two "first landscapes" began linking the destinies of two otherwise vastly different writers because of their genders and their almost diametrically opposed conceptions of writing. Marguerite Duras and Albert Camus were born a year apart,

1914 and 1913, in colonial Cochinchine and Algeria respectively. Both spent all of childhood and adolescence in French colonial territory; both grew into young adults in French colonial territory. Both childhoods were shaped by the premature loss of the father and a strong maternal presence to compensate. Camus was raised by two women: an authoritarian and virile grandmother and his gentle-spirited mother who was partially deaf and illiterate. Duras's mother taught the "native" class at school, applied for a plot of land, and spent her life fighting the local river's annual flooding to cultivate her own garden. She was a self-supporting single mother who favored her elder son over Duras and her other brother . . .

The first time either Camus or Duras set foot in metropolitan France was to attend university. At age eighteen, Duras spoke Vietnamese so well she could pass for a *métisse* in Paris. Meanwhile Camus, though also a poor child from the French colonies, would never have learned "the other tongue" let alone speak this other language as well as his French mother tongue. In Algeria, at that time a French colony territory for over a century, such was the norm in the European community. You would hear Algerians speaking Spanish or bad French before you heard them express themselves in Arabic in front of Europeans. There were exceptions, of course, such as Camus's close writer friend Jean Pelegri, who grew up on a farm in the Algerian countryside.

Camus and Duras came to France children of poor *pieds-noirs* (literally "black feet," a name the French from France called French colonists from Algeria and the Maghreb). Therefore, we can say their success once in Paris—at the heart of the French literary intelligentsia—is a true reflection of each one's literary talent. Camus rose to fame and fortune almost overnight with *L'Etranger* in 1943; Duras's ascension was slower but nonetheless stunning at the finish. Each one is a pioneer in the eyes of future French and Francophone writers. Their works tackle themes of lost childhood, lost territory, breakdown, and poverty, and thus resist the prevalent ideal in elite literary circles of a sort of abstract perfection, or immobility. Again, Jacques Dupin's verse—"And rumbles in the basement"—comes to mind: what roars below, what hidden fury grumbles within, or what force needs to be constantly disciplined? Even in Camus's transparent drought where we sense he is struggling to get the best of something beneath . . . With Dupin's verse in mind, let's return to the two authors whose progression as a duo is beginning to surprise even myself . . .

At one point in her career, Duras's name got linked to the literary movement *le nouveau roman*. Duras published with Editions de Minuit the apparently all-exclusive publisher of the novelists of the new wave or *le nouveau roman*: Claude Simon, Nathalie Sarraute, and Alain Robbe-Grillet himself. Acting a bit like a schoolyard bully, Alain Robbe-Grillet dubbed Marguerite

Duras "*the nouveau roman's* Edith Piaf." But the nickname really sticks to the multiple feminine personae streaking through Duras's novels, each driven to the brink of madness by an uncontrollable passion.

Starting in texts like *Moderato Cantabile* in the early 1960s, this theme of feminine unrequited passion takes over all of Duras's love stories. The pathetic voices belong to vagabond, hallucinating women living out impossible desires, trying to get out the *unspeakable* but doomed to repeat, over and over, like incantations, their loss of love like an obsessive rite. By then, Duras had moved beyond the usual landmarks in a writer's career such as a conventional love novel and a first novel based on childhood memoirs (*Le Barrage contre le Pacifique*, a commercial success, would have won the Prix Goncourt were it not for Duras's ties to the Communist Party). After *Le Barrage contre le Pacifique*, in each and every successive novel, Duras sets loose figures of lost women condemned to live out, heart emptied, a passionate love affair or sometimes a love triangle. From time to time, she lets us glimpse the strings behind her melodramatic figures . . .

If these lost heroines move us so, it's because the authorial voice supporting them from behind moves us. Her rhythmically repetitive sentences, her alternation of slow cadences with abrupt stops, then sudden revivifying verbal cymbal clashes when a word suddenly just bursts out . . . Out of a raw emotional material—which at any moment could collapse into soft putty-like sentimental filler—emerges a suffering figure who cries out. This vagabond figure along her way crosses several books, then over to films, but always turns up somewhere in Asia. She weaves her way from place to place, from India through Indochina, even to Hiroshima, without ever leaving Asia behind, in order to search for the irreparable point of no return, the rupture wearing away the couple at its seams, stretching further and further, back to the first childhood wound on colonial soil.

In Duras's return to a painful childhood trauma, there was bound to be a face-to-face confrontation with the mother. The mother who had always favored the other child, the older brother . . . Come to think of it, the suffering figures encountered on the road to solitude are all female. The higher she proclaims her loss, or her unbearable envy, of another's love, the farther we move in colonial backgrounds, in Cochinchine, the Indochinese provinces where the Donnadieu family lived or around Cambodia, or India, or even Hiroshima. We are reliving the primitive pain against the first background or against all of Asia refashioned around the obsessive structure being built up to the first sentimental loss . . . By prolonging her staggering march across novels, novellas, scripts, scenarios, it's as if Duras hoped to transform her heroine's abandoned plaints, from Lol V. Stein to the Beggar from Vinhlong, into her enchanting leitmotif. So beginning in *Le Barrage contre le Pacifique*, moving on in *Dix heures du soir en été*, then suddenly hitting full stride in *Moderato Cantabile*, where the passionate, stylized climate congeals into a metallic and orchestral substance, she is recycling once painful incantations into a bold and earth-shattering chant. At long last, yet quite abruptly, the author launches into an overt practice of textual confession in *L'Amant*. She moves from the pathetic mode to an authorial voice of razor-sharp sincerity, gleaming in the harsh light of inwardly turned cruelty. Thirty-four years later, Duras takes back up all the autobiographical elements composing *Le Barrage contre le Pacifique*, but this time digs at the source of the other desire, the stranger by race.

After writing and publishing *L'Amant*, Marguerite went public to play the part of the author, mask and makeup off, under the harsh studio lights of the Bernard Pivot show. *L'Amant* plots the episodes of a young preteen white girl's slow surrender to a Chinese lover right under the nose of her family and the "White" colonial society. In the background, the Mekong River flows under lighting harsh and brutal like a Francis Bacon painting . . .

All along, Duras's multiform work was really one long confession partly nourished by guilt, partly pure infantile bravado. Her exhibition and theatrics of sexual and racial transgression defies the silent laws of the colony society of yesterday. In 1950, when the plot functioned from the mother's point of view, Duras plotted the story of a woman struggling to survive against an exotic and powerful landscape. . . . Thirty-four years later, Duras looks at everyone peopling her childhood space through the lens of her former adolescent self and in the first-person "I" singular. She sets her narrative at the heart of her aroused body, or rather, her aroused Chinese lover's desire for her teenage body, alongside her family's complicity in the matter . . . and suddenly her plot snaps into a political message. The act of a child-woman, rewritten, reenacted, relived four decades later, becomes an act of decolonization as the narrating adolescent "me" of autobiographical confession, abruptly, slips over to the other side. She is allured by the beautiful car, the record player; she is a lure for the marriage her mother hopes will save her family from ruin . . . in exchange the lover only asked to see her in the nude. Was that all?

In *Le Barrage contre le Pacifique*, Duras brought all these biographical details, and power relations, even the singular tension running through all the characters (the mother and brother using the adolescent sister as bait), under the control of classical narrative conventions but the rising river, swelling close by in the distance, would not be contained permanently . . .

In 1984, *L'Amant* strips—pardon my expressions—down to the raw/flood. The same biographical elements from before now flow from the source of the first-person "I" of autobiography. Set at the heart of her desire, or the adolescent's troubling sense of empowerment on seeing the Chinese's lover's arousal, the author, age seventy, at last relives her first love scene from two sides . . .

Dans la limousine, il y a un homme très élégant qui me regarde, ce n'est pas un Blanc. Il est vêtu à l'européenne, il porte le costume de tissu clair des banquiers de Saigon. Il me regarde. J'ai déjà l'habitude qu'on me regarde. On regarde les Blanches aux colonies, et les petites filles blanches de 12 ans aussi.

In the limousine, a very elegant man sits watching me, he is not White. He wears a European suit, the light, silky costume of a Saigon banker. He is staring at me. I'm already used to their stares. They stare at Whites in the colonies, and little twelve year-old white girls too.

Later on page 49 she describes the Chinese lover . . .

La peau est d'une somptueuse douceur. Le corps, le corps est maigre, sans force, il pourrait avoir été malade . . . Il est imberbe, sans virilité autre que celle du sexe.

The skin is sumptuously soft. The body, the body is skinny, limp, he may have been ill . . . No facial hair, no signs of virility except his penis.

While promoting *L'Amant* through the live, powerful effects of oral confession for a live television audience, Duras turned the same harsh spotlight on her mother and brothers, explaining to her audience:

Nous étions dans la brutalité, le naturel, l'animalité. Nous étions des animaux nobles.

We lived in a state of brutality, nature, animal instincts. We were noble animals.

Part Two

Before I approach Camus as an Algerian writer or "Camus, l'Algérien" (as he referred to himself in notes for *Le Premier Homme*), I have a confession, or perhaps digression, of my own to make as an Algerian.

In 1975, I went to Tipaza to scout out terrain for my first feature film *La Nouba des femmes du Mont Chenoua* (1978). I took my time, and at the end of my long, fruitful search decided without hesitating to rent one-half of a peasant family's farm—a farm formerly owned by French *pieds-noirs*—for my actors, my camera crew, and myself. On the outskirts of Tipaza, the farm lay between the foot of Mont-Chenoua and a long deserted shoreline along the Mediterranean Sea. I began shooting right away in December 1975 and stayed on until the film's wrap-up in the spring of 1976. But during my entire stay in Tipaza, never, no not even once, did the thought of Albert Camus's *Noces à Tipasa* (1950) cross my mind.

In the first two decades of Algerian independence, when criticizing Albert Camus for not putting any Arabs in his novels became the vogue in Algerian universities, I didn't join in. Whenever my colleagues academically aired their grief with Albert Camus (especially professors of European origins—those were the ones who tended to go overboard), I would stand back in uncomfortable silence. Had I stood up for Camus back then, so early along in my own literary career, I would have countered their attacks with: "But look at my novels, there are hardly any *pieds-noir* characters in my first four novels. So what?" Criticizing a text for what isn't inside, to my mind, is not good literary practice. Once you find a good angle into an author's work, why criticize it for what it is not? Like in cinema, why would you judge the composition of a shot for what lies off screen?

Filming on location in Tipaza, I immersed myself, daily, in my solo visual quest. A visual quest for new images, naturally, but one anchored in the house's shoreline and mountain views . . . Here I was, aged forty, debuting in cinema in Tipaza and just a half-hour drive from my family's ancient port city of Cherchell. Tipaza became like "home" for me. I must have passed through the same farm valleys and plains and village markets hundreds of times as a child. My ancestral roots towered above me at the summits of Mont-Chenoua in the distance and on the other side the open sea was ever present with me. I was in my element. Then and there, I totally forgot about Camus's novel set in Tipaza from 1950.

I was in search of my Tipaza, or I was back in Tipaza in search of the Tipaza I could imagine long before my birth, long before Camus's birth thanks to the oral memory passed down from great-grandmothers to grandmothers to me as a child. I have a thread of entwined voices linking my body's memory back to the 1871 revolt lead by my mother's ancestor, Malek el Berkani, against France. Of course, you can read the French version of the insurrection in books. But I was bent solely on capturing images for my oral living memory connecting me to the past.

So I confess. I did not read *Les Noces* until the 1980s and I did not think of Camus in Tipaza in the 1970s. What is stopping me today, after a slight delay, I admit, from approaching Camus "the Algerian" in Tipaza? I cite this excerpt from his novel *Les Noces à Tipasa* in 1950:

Tipasa m'apparaît comme ces personnages qu'on décrit pour signifier indirectement un point de vue sur le monde. Comme eux, elle témoigne. Et virilement.

Tipaza is like one of those characters you describe to indirectly signify a point of view of the world. Like them, she testifies. And virilely.[4]

Camus's Tipaza witnesses the world "virilely." In the same light so dazzling for Camus, I was gathering images for an uninterrupted chain of women testifying from the shadows. I was working from the shadows where women once stayed behind, but I was filming outside. I was seeing through my camera, for the first time in 1973 and 1975, women out walking on the dirt roads, heads held high, walking on the road to school or coming from the market balancing giant baskets of victuals on their heads like crowns—even girls barely out of adolescence! Other women were standing outside on the thresholds watching these colorful passers-by.

On the other hand, after leaving Indochina for good, Duras wrote almost exclusively about her mother and two brothers, along with her lost heroines the Beggar from Vinhlong, or Lol V. Stein. To represent Indochina from the other side, the "native" Indochina, there is only the sole figure of a naked Chinese lover projected behind a laminated screen which makes his tetanized silhouette appear even more mysterious. Besides the beggar-woman from Vinhlong, Duras leaves no(one) back there to speak of . . . oh here I go, doing just what I reproached others for doing before me: noting only those absent on screen.

Maybe we should blame Duras's choice of theatrics, or her obsessive incantation, for her overwhelming and overflowing need to spill the desire tearing the two lovers, lover and teenager, apart . . . Yes, maybe Duras was trying so hard to stage the scene of the young Chinese man and his white teenage lover's passion that she ended up masking her childhood landscape and its segregated colonial scenery behind her fantasized love story. The colonial land, far back, serves only as background decor for a heroine's roaming desire . . . Never once returning to her native land, Marguerite Donnadieu goes there in every story—if not to India, then to Cambodia, or touring all of Asia, even Hiroshima—to the Extreme-Orient or should we just say she "goes to all extremes." "Going to extremes" becomes the only permanent place or motif for Duras's memory and writing. It's as if the lost childhood land, really lost, enables long pent-up emotional and sensual barrages to break down . . .

While reliving Duras's intimate scenes with her Chinese lover through the eyes of the fifteen-and-a-half year old adolescent, I remembered another love story Guy de Maupassant wrote in 1881 called *Állouma*. I went back to *Állouma* and was surprised to find this love story set in nineteenth-century colonial Algeria was not as *exotic* as you would expect. In *Állouma*, a young voyager falls under the spell of a beautiful and elusive nomad girl . . . Only Maupassant does not stop his story of seduction there, but converts the duo's influx of sensual energy into a larger discovery for the young colonist. The lover on his voyage discovers an entire nomadic people, the beautiful Állouma's kin . . .

I return to Camus, in spite of his stiff, classical, even Roman posture, for his last novel posthumously published ten years after Duras's *L'Amant* in 1984, *Le Premier Homme*. Long suspended and left unfinished by the author's premature death, this text long concealed the author's secret reason for his silence during the Algerian war. I would like to personally salute Camus's daughter and express my gratitude for her decision to publish her father's unfinished manuscript, notes and all, in 1994: she gave Camus back to his childhood territory, or to Algeria.

From a literary standpoint, Camus's daughter brought new evidence to light. On the road that day, tucked in his satchel, then strewn out in the mud of his fatal car wreck, were Camus papers bearing a new style of writing. I imagine Camus that day, solitary and solar, leaving us proof that his style, his form, and his sentence structures—thus the core of his inner literary being— were undergoing a profound mutation. In the end, his generous nature, his profound concern for the new Algeria being born, or breaking away, was present in Algeria, chronicling the unresolved drama between his solidarity with his people and his love for Mediterranean space, but accelerating toward a shattering wide-open of himself against an immutable background.

Another point of convergence for these two authors, each molded socially and sensually by both the French metropolitan and the colonial culture, lies in their haunted backgrounds. It is time we consider how both works conceal their haunting colonial backgrounds or reveal the *first* landscapes haunting their writing.

First I turn to Camus, and exclusively *Le Premier Homme*, just as it was when interrupted by his fatal car accident on January 4, 1960. One thing is certain in this text. If Camus betrays his "Algerian" origins (as he called himself in his book notes), it is by his mastery of the Algerian "landscape," geographic and human, in Algiers, in Tipaza, and Djemila. He captures landscapes just by the way he passes through them, rolling with a procession of thoughts and sensations and associations running through his head as he moves, it's in his eye always on the lookout for perspectives. And above all—like Saint-Augustin in *Confessions*—it's in his way of drinking in the intense, untapped splendor of Algeria's light . . . Rarely, though, does he stoop to watch from the shadows, or from the only perspective allotted an entire people, mostly women folk, in colonial Algeria.

What can we learn new from *Le Premier Homme?* Or more precisely, what does this text say differently about the "loss of Algeria"? Algeria's French colonial period lies behind us now, like the time frame in which this text written from 1957 to January 1960 (date of the author's premature death). We learn from this book, conserved thanks to the notes recovered at the scene of the accident, that Camus was experimentally "stretching loss out" to see how far it goes. Groping along his way toward an unknown conclusion, or back to the sources of the colonial knot, the author was so focused on inscribing the loss of Algeria he didn't heed other intellectuals' calls to take political action and engage himself intellectually, loudly, precipitately in their rapid-fire succession of manifestos and signed petitions sent to press every morning. Camus—stretching loss out—was narrating all the way-stations along the road to loss. He saw Algeria's body disappearing progressively, irreversibly in the background, and he saw that there was nothing he as a writer could do. His mother, brother, uncle, would stay behind in Belcourt (on the same popular Boulevard Cervantès I knew from visiting my maternal aunt who still lives there today).

At the heart of this gradual distancing from Algeria, or thanks to the unfinished text's posthumous publication, we imagine the author was in the process of constructing the first text between Algeria and Paris. Camus was seeking a balance between those staying back there (with the image of a living, weakened, dependent mother, childlike, etched in his mind) and Paris ahead of him. He was groping for a way to reenact the nineteenth-century past against his present day, 1958 and 1959, breaking away from the nineteenth century. Indeed, this book does have something new to tell us: Camus was heading toward a complete deontology of the French colonial period. He consecrated entire passages of his unfinished book, and prepared copious notes, on the arrival of the first nineteenth-century revolutionaries, or deported revolutionaries and expatriates, in this other place. While his historical reconstitution through the new settlers' eyes of the colonial past spare no concrete details, he is also looking from the other's point of view. Camus had realized while working in the French Algerian archives the greatest lie at the heart of the colonial enterprise was that the land had been unsettled, uncultivated territory when really it was stolen from rebellious tribes. We see scenes denouncing the sequestration of Algerian's native land and developing the theme "Give them back their land." Completed, this book would have been magnificent.

Conclusion

The final point of convergence between these two authors—born and raised on colonial soil, both witnesses inscribing its loss—leads back to the body in their texts. This meeting point can only be summed in one word: DESTRUCTION.

In Duras's autobiographical hit novel *L'Amant*, all the threads of her colonial childhood memory move together in a vibrant, pulsating style. After, Duras would rather adeptly re-enact this scene live for Bernard Pivot's television audience as if looking for more witnesses of the birth of this novel. In the opening mirror scene of the novel, Duras describes a scene about her face towards the end of her life:

> Un jour, j'étais âge déjà, dans le hall d'un lieu public, un homme est venu vers moi. Il s'est fait connaître et il m'a dit: "Je vous connais depuis toujours. Tout le monde dit que vous étiez belle lorsque vous étiez jeune, je suis venu pour vous dire que, pour moi, je vous trouve plus belle maintenant que lorsque vous étiez jeune, j'aimais moins votre visage de jeune femme, que celui que vous avez maintenant: dévasté!" (9)

> One day, I was already old, in the entrance of a public place, a man came up to me. He introduced himself and said, "I've known you for years. Everybody says you were beautiful when you were young, but want to tell you I think you're more beautiful now than then. Rather than your face as a young woman, I prefer your face as it is now. Ravaged." (9)

So, we hear what sounds at first like one of the best comments a woman could receive. You are beautiful but wait, you are even more beautiful than you were when in youth when you were . . . ravaged. That's a hard one to swallow. And then she continues with her commentary:

> Très vite dans ma vie, il a été trop tard.

> Very early in my life, it was too late. At 18, it was already too late . . .

And so we witness Duras transforming the common theme of a woman's face over time in the mirror—a common theme shared by all women without exception—in that direct, brutal, and even musical cut-and-dry rhythmic way of hers. She goes on, and here strikes me as particularly masochistic:

> A 18 ans, j'ai été vieille. . . . le vieillissement a été brutal. . . . J'ai un visage lacéré de rides sèches et profondes, à la peau cassée [etc . . . etc.] et le final, toujours sur le visage dans le miroir. "Il ne s'est pas affaissé comme certains visages très fins, Il a gardé les mêmes contours mais sa matière est détruite. J'ai un visage détruit."

> I grew old at eighteen . . . And I've kept the new face I had then. It has been my face. . . . It's covered with deep, dry wrinkles, the skin is cracked. But my face hasn't collapsed . . . It's kept the same contours, but its substance has been laid waste. I have a face laid waste.

That's how *L'Amant* begins. Duras delineates the destruction inscribed in her body. In English she has a "ravaged" face or a face "laid waste." In the French version, it's the word "destroyed" *(détruit)* we hear. Further along, Duras uses this figure of a destroyed young body to describe all children of the colonies. Using the same direct, brutal tone of voice for the other children, she remembers:

> Les enfants-vieillards de la faim endémique, oui, mais nous, non, nous n'avions pas faim, nous étions des enfants blancs, nous avions honte, nous vendions nos meubles, mais nous n'avions pas faim, nous avions un boy.

> Children grown old from chronic hunger, yes, but not us, we never went hungry, we were white children, we were ashamed, we sold off our furniture, but we never went hungry, we even had a boy.

Meanwhile in *Le Premier Homme*, we get to witness Camus on his way to "stretching out loss." Here, we relive a scene through the eyes and ears of Jacque Cormery—Camus's alter ego—while visiting the Algerian farm where his father worked before Camus was born. The scene takes place on the road between Bône and Mondovi. Jacques Cormery is asking everyone—even old farm hands who would only vaguely remember—if they remember working with his father before the war. In vain.

But, on the domain Saint-Apôtre that day, we catch the last glimpse of the old colonial farmer running the farm since the day he took over the vineyard after World War I. The region by that time was paralyzed by a widespread campaign of terror. No longer able to secure the population against daily terror attacks, the French soldiers call all European settlers to evacuate. The author or hero, on his quest to recover traces and souvenirs of the father's identity, suddenly turns into a journalist reporting live at the scene of destruction. This is not a tale of the destruction of a woman's face over time. Cormery—or Camus—witnesses the devastation of a land and its vineyards. From a dramatic point of view, this passage is truly beautiful. I can't help but imagine how I would film this scene from Le Premier Homme:

Quand l'ordre d'évacuation est arrivé, le vieux colon n'a rien dit. Ses vendanges étaient terminées, et le vin en cuve. Il a ouvert les cuves. . . . [je saute deux pages] puis il a équipé un tracteur en défonceuse. Pendant trois jours au volant, tête nue, sans rien dire, il a arraché les vignes sur toute l'étendue de la propriété . . . tout cela du lever au coucher du soleil, et sans un regard pour les montagnes à l'horizon, ni pour les Arabes vite prévenus et qui se tenaient à distance le regardant faire, sans rien dire eux non plus.

When the order to evacuate came, he didn't flinch. The year's harvest was over, and all the wine in vats. He opened the vats . . . [A few pages later] [. . .]
    Then he put a pitchfork on his tractor. For three days straight behind the wheel, baldhead exposed, silently determined, he dug up vines of the entire vineyard . . . from sunrise to sunset, never once looking up at the mountains on the horizon, or over at the Arabs who had come to observe at a distance, silently.

Here is how the documentary scene ends. A young French captain, on hand to oversee the evacuations, approaches the old man and asks him why he is destroying his vineyard:

Jeune homme, puisque ce que nous avons fait ici est un crime, il faut l'effacer!
    Puis il a traverse la cour trempée du vin qui avait fui des caves et il a commencé à ses bagages. Un de ses ouvrières ouvriers? arabes lui demande:
    —Patron, qu'est qu'on va faire?
    — Si j'étais à votre place, a dit le Vieux, j'irais au maquis. Ils vont gagner. Il n'y a plus d'hommes en France.

Young man, since what we did here is a crime, we must erase it!
    Then he walked across the courtyard, still drenched in wine flowing from the vats, and began to pack his bags. One of his Arab workers asked him:
    —Boss, what about us?
    —If I were you, said the old man, I'd join the Resistance. They're going to win. There are no good men left in France.

Camus is writing historical tragedy down as it unfolds before him. He delves into the emotions of his characters, or his own, as he watches tragic scenes.

Meanwhile in her scene on a woman's face "laid waste," Duras's French brutally draws a face destroyed over time. However, I turn to Duras for my closing remarks.

In an interview with one of her closest friends, Duras remembered her first sighting of the Beggar woman from Vinhlong when only eight years old. She had been frightened by the Beggar running about half-mad outside. On that fleeing, hollering woman returning in every one of her texts after, Duras concluded:

L'histoire peut être perdue, la perte ne peut se perdre.

The story can be lost, loss can't get lost.

This beautiful conclusion returns us to Jacques Dupin's beautiful verse for my conclusion:

Et gronde dans le sous-sol. Qui hurlerait sans le sable qui l'étouffe.

And rumbles in the basement. What would howl without the sand suffocating it. (Translated from the French by Jennifer Williams)

Notes

1. Dupin, Jacques, *Dehors* (Paris: Gallimard, 1975), p. 30. The complete sentence reads: "A L'Institution, à ses crimes, l'écriture est liée malgré son exécration, par le double fil lâchement tressé, de sa dépendance et de sa dissidence." In English, I translate approximately: "To its crimes, writing is tied, despite its execration, by the double cord loosely entwined, of its dependence and its dissidence."
2. Dupin, *Dehors*, p. 29.
3. Dupin, *Dehors*, p. 29.
4. Camus, Albert, *Les Noces à Tipaza* (Paris: Folio), p. 23.

PART ONE

HOMOGENEITY SUBVERTED

~

CHAPTER ONE

Laïcité in the French Public School System

In the Name of the Law!

Mireille Le Breton, Nazareth College of Rochester

The book *Une République, des Religions*,[1] which takes the form of a witness account, shows how the perennial French antagonism between Church and State (that is, the Catholic Church) no longer stands, and how a dialogue between various religions has emerged on French soil. It is true that inter-religious dialogue has long been established and remains ongoing, but the relationship between the newly emerging form of Islam and the State suffered significant blows in the aftermath of the 2004 law that banned wearing visible religious signs in public schools. Indeed, many intellectuals commented on the apparent rift between Church and State. Some interpreted this law as the French state's punishment of a specific "church" (Islam) affirming too great a visibility through the *hijeb*, in a country that had not dared face up to the part of her own multiculturalism.[2] Many denounced the "fear factor," which they saw as the silent motive for passing the law.[3] To some extent, these two points are well founded. What was the reasoning behind passing of the 2004 law? What historical and political changes led—over a period of thirty years—to the "dead-end" reached in 2003 within the French public school system, and to the subsequent passing of the law? What positive solutions could be envisioned for the future of the French educational system, and for its pupils?

Two elements need to be mentioned here. In the late 1970s, after the Glorious 30s, France was in a transition period. The challenge was to adjust to her newly emerging ethnic and religious communities and the struggle to recognize herself as a multicultural country. France and its Others were involved in a heated dialogue, trying to find a common ground for all to live peacefully under the laws of the Republic. A difficult task, when inequality regarding housing, job opportunities, and access to social benefits was rife among immigrant communities. In 2003, the way to reach this common ground in a newly self-recognized, multicultural France was first and foremost to reassert within the public school system the principles at the basis of the constitution and democracy itself: the *laïc* ideal. Secondly, a nationwide dialogue on teaching religious history within public schools had begun in the early 1980s, and had timidly started to be implemented in an interdisciplinary way. Mireille Estivalèzes in her 2005 book *Les Religions dans l'enseignement laïque*[4] gives a thorough historical analysis of the development of religious studies, thus highlighting the reality of the efforts developed since the 1980s. Even though the 2005 "Nouveau contrat pour l'avenir de l'école"[5] does not envision the creation of courses dealing with the history of religion, the report nevertheless states that the French educational system will dispense this teaching for the first time:

> Il convient donc, dans le respect de la liberté de conscience, et des principes de la laïcité et de neutralité du service public, d'organiser dans l'enseignement public la transmission des connaissances et des références sur le fait religieux et son histoire.[6]

I will argue in this chapter that this interdisciplinary approach to teaching the history of religions, from a rational, even scientific perspective, is not sufficient. Should, and could, a new course on the history of religions be taught in France today?

Paradoxical France, as one might name her: reasserting the ban of all religious symbols from schools, on the one hand, and yet installing the interdisciplinary "teaching of the religious fact" in public schools, on the other. One may also ask whether or not France is living a difficult and schizophrenic beginning to the twenty-first century. In the context of the 2004 law, this paper discusses the tensions at work within the *laïc* idea/l and its institutional implementations in today's French public school system, in a country that seems to be oscillating between being "une et indivisible" and "plurielle et divisée."

This paper starts by defining the principles of *laïcité*, analyzing them in their historical context, and showing how these work in public schools today. This paper then studies the protective/preventive character of the law on visible religious signs. In doing so, we will analyze the political and religious tensions at the origin of the revival of the debate around *laïcité* in public schools in order to see if it is possible, and how it is possible to reconcile the tensions between the ideal of *laïcité* and its institutional implementation, from a judicial perspective. A pedagogical dimension is given to this paper, which finally considers the importance of creating new classes within the Education Nationale (the French State Department for Education), for teaching the "history of religions."

The Defining Principles of *Laïcité* and Its Ideal Implementation in Public Schools

Laïcité is the outcome of a long historical, philosophical, and political evolution in France. This evolution did not go without trouble, revolutions, and bloodshed. *Laïcité* in this sense is not an *exception française*, as other European countries and America have gone through the separation of churches and State in their own peculiar ways. During the first part of the twentieth century, *laïcité* embodied the violent opposition between the free, public, and non-Christian Republican school and the religious Christian schools. It emerged as a means to diminish the power and control of the Catholic Church in politics and was embodied in the law of 1905. *Laïcité* must be understood in its historical, judicial, and philosophical dimensions, but we also need to bear in mind that it is an abstract principle,[7] a direct consequence of the "Déclaration des Droits de l'Homme et du Citoyen."

Laïcité is not a word in the English language. Etymologically speaking, it comes from the Latin word *laicus* and from the Greek *laicos*, which itself is derived from *Laos*, for people. Its basic meaning is: "someone who is not part of a sacerdotal body." *Laïc* is thus a state, which differentiates the cleric from the noncleric. Interestingly enough, the word first appeared at around the same time as the term *clericalism*. These are almost twin words, whose meanings are exactly opposed.

What is to be found at the roots of *laïcité*? The philosophical concept precedes the word itself. Two ideas are related to this concept, as Daniel Beresniak succinctly describes in his book *Laïcité, Pourquoi?*:

1. Every Man has the right (or duty) to choose his/her Gods and to practice the rites that please him/her, in so far as it does not disturb other men and does not interfere with public tranquility.

2. Knowledge is acquired by a personal effort, and no one possesses it in its totality. Thus no one can pretend to be psychopompos (leader of souls).[8]

These two ideas are very old. Older yet is the concept of *laïcité* found in the Gospel, at a time when Jesus said to the Romans who were invading Palestine: "Give to Cesar that which is Cesar's and to God that which is God's." *Laïcité* is also an expression of the eighteenth-century Enlightenment philosophy related to tolerance and to the respect of the Other in that which is most intimate to him/her, that is to say in his/her beliefs, philosophy, and convictions. The word itself does not figure in the law of 1905, but the concept is clear, and thus *laïcité* rests on two conditions:

1. The freedom of the individual to believe or not believe, to think as s/he wishes, and therefore to express him/herself freely.
2. The submission under the laws of the Republic.

As of 1905, *laïcité* became the main idea at the origin of a law, written to ensure, through education, "freedom of conscience and separation of churches and state."[9] The notion of law is key to the idea of *laïcité*, as it is impossible to envision a state of law without *laïcité* guaranteeing it. Indeed, the principle of *laïcité*, whose emergence is intimately connected to that of the judicial field,[10] grants every individual equal treatment with his/her neighbor and also prevents a specific religion from becoming more important than another or excluding the right of atheism. Henri Péna-Ruiz explains that *laïcité* ensures: "l'égalité des droits de l'individu, incompatible avec la valorisation privilégiée d'une croyance ou de l'athéisme."[11] *Laïcité* is invaluable to the child within public schools, as s/he is in the process of "learn[ing] how to learn," and developing a critical mind in such a context of neutrality. Within public schools, "neutrality" is an important concept: from the Latin *neuter*: "Neither . . . nor." The public school system in France plays the important role of neither promoting religious beliefs nor atheism.

How then, does *laïcité* work in the public school system, for pupils, teachers and . . . infrastructure? The implementation of this neutrality is an *exception française*. From 1937 until 1989, pupils as well as teachers were forbidden to wear religious or political signs or clothes within schools. Indeed, in 1937, two decrees were passed by the Minister of Education (*Instruction publique*) Jean Zay. Not only did these involve teachers and pupils but buildings too. Teachers had (and still have) to abide by religious neutrality in their function as teachers. Moreover, as they served the State, they were (and still are) required not to discuss their religious preference (*devoir de réserve*). For pupils, the principle was also straightforward: school was free and open for all to study the achievements of human culture, but the school space was closed to all that could mirror the tensions present in civil society. This meant a lot in the midst of the Popular front at the time. Schools could not be left to perpetuate the conflicts of civil society, where religious or ideological lobbies may have been trying to dominate or fight for power and may consequently have been trying to censor or influence the educational programs. The values of the Republic were carried here, along with gender equality, equality between people(s), and freedom of the individual. No visible manifestation of belonging to a group or of submission to a group could curb these values. In public high schools, chaplaincies[12] were created on December 10, 1802, to preserve freedom of religion. The 1905 law kept this measure to ensure the free practice of cults. In 1905, chaplaincies thus continued to expand in boarding schools and in public places such as asylums, old people's homes, and prisons. Today, these chaplaincies are regulated by the decree of April 22, 1988, which states that secondary public school buildings, including daily schools, can be granted the service of a chaplain if parents ask for it. This request is subject to the commissioner of education's final authorization.

Today in France, about 3,800 public buildings have Catholic chaplaincies. At their heads are *laïc* people, who are nominated by the commissioner of education, and also by a letter of mission from the bishops. A priest visits them once a week. They are open to all pupils, independently of their creed, and about 150,000 to 200,000 pupils attend these chaplaincies.[13] While in theory every religion has the right to request such a service, most of them today remain Catholic, with a couple of exceptions for the Protestant and Jewish faiths, but it seems that none exist for Muslims. With Mireille Estivalèzes, we can say here that "laïcité" in the public school system is a complex reality, often not very well known nor understood but which preserves both the neutrality of the public space and the religious freedom. The public school system is therefore often thought of as a sanctuary, where pupils, in the long process of becoming adults, are offered a unique opportunity. Once they push open its doors, they leave behind the pressures exerted by society. They enter into a neutral space in which to study and learn. Endowed with the same rights as their schoolmates, they keep their religious beliefs in their hearts, but their critical mind is ready to operate. Thus no exterior social, religious, or ideological forces can disturb their learning process. Three founding principles in this context best apply to *laïcité*:

1. Freedom of conscience.
2. Full equality among atheists, agnostics, and individuals of various religious beliefs.

3. Neutrality in the public sphere, where common law must promote what is common to all.

According to Henri Péna-Ruiz, as he states in his 2005 *Histoire de la laïcité, genèse d'un idéal*, the ideal of *laïcité* prevents all sorts of lobbies (*dérives communautaristes*) within the public sphere, as it enables implementing law and order for the general common good, as it allows men to "jouir de l'égalité des droits pour s'affirmer sans tutelle extérieure."[14] Transposed in the context of the schoolroom, the tensions which emerged as a consequence from wearing signs of religious belonging have been real and numerous, and many have led to acts of violence. Neither the teachers nor the pupils can favor one religion over the other, as all religions are, by law, exactly on the same equal footing. In light of this, the principle of *laïcité* is a direct consequence of the 1789 "Déclaration des Droits de l'Homme et du Citoyen," the French Bill of Rights, which guarantees every human being the freedom of conscience and equality in rights within the *Res Publica*. The role of public authorities is to guarantee these freedoms and rights by ensuring neutrality.

Historically speaking, the quest for *laïcité*, the founding principle of the French Republic, started in French public schools at the beginning of the twentieth century with Jules Ferry's laws, among others. The separation of churches and State put an end to Napoleon's "Concordat" regime,[15] thus re-assigning religion to the private sphere. And it was within the public school system, three decades ago, that the debate around *laïcité* resurfaced, at a time when the principles of *laïcité* and its institutional implementation were no longer in agreement with one another. In 2003, a point of no return was reached, and teaching staff in French schools as well as pupils could no longer handle religious-related acts of violence.

The Protective/Preventive Character of the 2004 Law on Religious Visible Signs, or the Failure of Governmental and Educational Institutions in the Face of "Local" Decisions

The discrepancies between the ideal and the institutional implementation of *laïcité* within schools have been an issue that has been stifled for more than twenty years. The passing of the 2004 law came at a time when the only solution to a situation, which had been ignored for years, seemed to be the use of the blade of justice to cut to the core of the problem.

Within the Republic, French citizens are all equal before the law, since the Republic grants the same rights and duties to all. One justice for all, and all equal under the same law. Yet public schools, since the Conseil d'État's (the

French Supreme Court) 1989 deliberations, had to deal with the question of religious signs on a local basis, which even if "exceptional," could work so long as national order was not disturbed.[16] In the late 1980s, teenagers had been demanding—in the name of their freedom of religious expression—to be allowed to wear a scarf within *laïc* buildings. Over twenty years, these decisions led on many occasions to outbursts of violence and to judicial decisions that varied from place to place. Faced with local decisions, both the government and the Education Nationale had a very difficult time resolving conflicts efficiently. From the moment school order had been disturbed by the wearing of religious signs, a law needed to be passed. And when the media got involved in the story, the question whether or not the veil, or other religious signs, were to be worn took on gigantic dimensions. In 2003, the highly publicized question of *hijeb* was suddenly propelled onto the national scene. Not since the Affaire Dreyfus at the beginning of the century had France witnessed such a passionate debate at the national level than the one surrounding the "Islamic scarf" in public schools. The principles of *laïcité* were being shaken and questioned again by the issue of wearing—or not wearing—signs of religious belonging. *Laïcité*, taken for granted for a long time, suddenly stopped being the federating link to a common culture within the educational world and within French society at large.

Alma and Lila Lévy, two sisters who adopted the Muslim faith, were on the front cover of the newspaper *Le Monde* on October 17, 2003, after being expelled from school for wearing *hijeb*. Reported as unjust—shouldn't everyone in France be granted the right to study, whether they wear a Gap cap or a *hijeb*?—this event generated an epiphenomenon which led the Republic to suddenly realize that Islam was the second most popular religion in France.[17] The conditions of using religious signs in public schools forced France to question its *laïcité* principles. The question also set off a wider national debate, which further opened the breach within French social and political bodies. After the 2003 media frenzy, what then needed to be done? How was the complex situation faced by public schools going to be handled? To whom should the government turn in trying to assess the situation and foresee positive outcomes? What solutions might be envisioned?

One way of bridging the gap between the principles of *laïcité* and the institutional implementation of *laïcité* was to solve an important rights issue: that which makes all citizens equal under the same law and no longer depends on local decisions. Two important points need to be stressed at this juncture. First of all, the complex mechanisms of local rights and their excesses often left violent race- or religion-related acts unpunished—exacerbated by displaying or wearing religious signs within schools.[18]

Second, the controversy around the Conseil d'État's decisions of 1989 and the role played by intellectuals in the debate created a lot of confusion within the institution of Education Nationale, which seemed unable to ensure respect of the law and order in the same way for all. Teachers, along with school directors and other staff members, had to deal with racist, anti-Semitic, xenophobic, and sexist aggression (be they verbal or physical) on a regular basis, often being isolated by the institution that directed them.[19] To solve the conflict they could rely only on local rule, and in some cases, schools failed to address the issues in order to avoid dealing with the complex and "exceptional" system of local justice.

This situation seemed to freeze society at both educational and political levels: it was no longer possible for educators in school districts to deal locally with recurring outbursts of violence related to religion, nor unaided with the issue of wearing the *hijeb* in schools. The lack of homogeneity in decision-making was obvious. Why should some schools expel female students while others were more understanding and accepted their outfits? Politicians would more or less ignore the questions at stake. Lax was the word used many times to describe the situation, or the image of a government closing its eyes in front of a situation which seemed too intricate to address. Indeed, between the late 1980s and the 2003 Stasi Commission[20] and its resulting 2004 law, about fifteen years had passed without any real institutional support to schools and high schools. Over the course of almost two decades, the Education Nationale, relying on governmental action, had been unable to take steps to solve a complex and urgent issue.

The three following examples[21] illustrate the defeat of the institutions against the problem of religious signs pervading the public school system and show how the different sanctions against pupils depended on local decisions. On the 18th of September, 1989, in Creil, three young Muslim girls were excluded from high school because they showed up with scarves on their heads. The director of the school had recently banned Jews from wearing the Kippa in his school in the name of *laïcité*. He had justified his exclusion by saying: "It is a disgrace to *laïcité* and the neutrality of public schools, and it plays a role of ideological pressure on the other students while at the same time perturbing the relationship with the teachers."[22] What would happen to these teenagers who suddenly were expelled from their school for expressing their personal beliefs? Monique Canto-Sperber and Paul Ricoeur, in an article in *Le Monde*, mentioned that "a *laïcité* of exclusion is the best enemy of equality."[23]

The media became involved in the case. It appeared that Creil was not an isolated phenomenon, but that this type of incident had been recurring from time to time throughout the country. Lionel Jospin, then Minister of Education, chose to bring the case before the Conseil d'État, the judicial institution in charge of solving issues between individuals and the administration. The famous recommendation of November 27, 1989, was immediately reproduced in a decree addressed to the Education Nationale, and for more than fifteen years it became the rule that would have to be applied in schools. It stated that: "wearing the signs to express religious belongings is not in itself incompatible with *laïcité*," except if it constitutes "an act of peer-pressure, of provocation, of proselytism or of propaganda."[24] From this date, the pupils were no longer submitted to the same *laïc* behavior as their teachers. To some, the principle of *laïcité* within public schools was betrayed. Indeed, many intellectuals, and teachers, then firmly made their voices heard to reaffirm the principle of *laïc* neutrality of the school space, invoking Jean Zay's decrees,[25] which had ruled in favor of forbidding displays of religious signs in schools since 1937. The decisions of the Conseil d'État were putting an end to these 1937 rules. What would be the determining factor in assessing what act would be considered crossing the border between "normality" and "peer-pressure, provocation, proselytism, or propaganda"? Some intellectuals were strongly united in affirming that the school environment should be open to all to study the achievements of human culture in a calm and peaceful environment, but that religious discords and strifes would reappear within the public schools if schoolchildren were allowed to wear religious signs, leading schools to be the mere reflection of already existing societal conflicts and breaking apart its role as a sanctuary for *laïcité*. They were not only defending the neutrality of public schools but also the democratic values of the Republic: equality between genders, freedom of the individual to believe or not believe. They were also stressing the dangers of displaying one's belonging to a particular community within the school system, which had already, and would ultimately, lead to more tensions.[26]

Since the events of 1989, and until 1994, about 400 cases of *hijeb* controversy were counted each year. The numbers increased to 3,000 in 1994.[27] While 1989 showed the firm belief in *laïcité* of a school headmaster who expelled students who were either Jewish or Muslim, in 1994 the irrationality of the arguments trying to justify the expulsion a Muslim female teenager showed the failure of the rule passed by governmental decision in 1989, and it exemplified the defeat of the French judicial and educational institutions in dealing with religious issues in public schools, as we shall see in our second example.

In 1994 religious tensions within schools started to be very high once again. Letters from teachers were sent to the government in a cry for help, and the tribunal of Clermont-Ferrant in 1994 confirmed the exclusion of a girl, mentioning in its explanatory report that the *hijeb* was "a sign of identification marking the belonging to a religious extremism from Foreign Origin; this obedience has international views and claims to belong to an orientation that is particularly intolerant."[28]

In this second example, the reason for being expelled was far more extreme, based on fear and a fantasist view of Islam. The "fear factor" of the international Islamic terrorism was the reason for a little girl to be expelled.

It is worth noting that the 1989 decree passed by the Conseil d'État was the only set of rules which could enable schools to deal with their day-to-day issues. The rules thus supposed pragmatic implementation on a case-by-case basis to solve conflicts related to wearing visible religious signs. To give justice, administration judges thus faced the difficult task of:

> À arbitrer entre, d'une part, le principe de la laïcité de l'enseignement posé par les lois scolaires des années 1880 et conforté par le préambule de la Constitution de 1946 intégré à celle de 1958, et, d'autre part, le principe, également constitutionnel, de liberté de conscience consacré par la Convention européenne des droits de l'homme.[29]

The task of applying justice under these rules was extremely complex. It is understandable, in this light, to see why the Education Nationale should have asked her staff, in a veiled manner, to make as little noise as possible when dealing with religious signs. "Hush" with a finger on the mouth, was the attitude to take, which leads us to our third case.

Emmanuel Brenner's book *Les Territoires perdus de la République* published in 2002 is the first collection of witness accounts written by teachers working in ZEP areas ("ghetto" areas, ZEP standing for *Zone d'Éducation Prioritaire*). While the first part of the book is devoted to showing how "lax" the government is in intervening to help stop "religious" outbursts of violence, the second part gives first-hand accounts of the reality of violence, discriminations, racist, and anti-Semitic verbal or physical aggressions in schools. The attitude to adopt, Brenner says, was "not to provoke," in a word, to behave as if the reality of the violent situations did not exist:

> De tous côtés parviennent les mêmes échos sur l'attitude globale des autorités: on tend à adopter un profil bas, à ne pas faire de vagues, à ne pas "provoquer inutilement," à faire en un mot comme si l'on ne voyait pas.[30]

Emmanuel Brenner provides statistics to show how punishments tended to be kept quiet, as they would probably have resulted in the intervention of administrative judges on the scene. Reports of the Minister of Education for the region Ile-de-France show, for instance, that at the beginning of 2002, some 70 percent of violent acts were the responsibility of students. These happened mostly in secondary schools (76 percent). Only 10 percent led the students to the disciplinary committee. In 44 percent of cases, violent acts, of which the authorities had been aware, remained unpunished.[31] We can see that the first steps taken by the judicial authorities were not punitive ones but consisted rather in silencing and covering up violent acts. Brenner also gives evidence of the fact that teachers themselves were the last people to be made aware that race-related and religious violence had been taking place in their school. Insults, as well as psychological or even physical aggressions, would remain unpunished. These politics revealed the failure of the governmental and educational institutions. Brenner's book added fuel to the fire. As long as the religious signs worn at schools were not disturbing the peace of the learning environment, it was possible to deal with such events on a local, case-by-case basis. Yet, when the order was significantly disturbed, then protective and preventive measures needed to be taken.

To break the status quo over the question of allowing or not religious signs in public schools and the public sphere, on July 3, 2003, President Chirac launched a national public debate. For this purpose, he created a commission, led by Bernard Stasi, which would meet twice a week to discuss and reflect upon the implementation of the principles of *laïcité* within the Republic. The quest for *laïcité* was to be put to the table, and once again, with specific relation to public schools.

The Stasi Commission invited witness accounts selected to provide a wide array of social, religious, and political representations. There were members of political parties, representatives of all religious and philosophical beliefs and opinions, trade union leaders, leaders of associations involved in the defense of human rights. The commission also comprised local representatives, directors of schools and high schools, directors of hospitals and prisons, and company leaders. Finally, high school pupils were also invited to take part in the debate, along with members of the European Union. The entire country seemed to be involved in this public debate, which was televised "live." Numerous letters were received, demonstrating the massive interest French citizens had in this issue. This way of questioning *laïcité* was very democratic, and decisions would be taken after all parties were heard. This Referendum had a social dimension, and it led to passing the 2004 law banning religious signs from schools. When the Stasi Commission delivered its final report, it almost unanimously opted for passing of a law,[32] which was soon to be implemented. And on March 15, 2004, in the name of the principle of *laïcité*[33] and to "reassess it,"[34] the Parliament (made up of the Assemblée Nationale and Sénat) passed a controversial law forbidding "students from wearing distinctive signs or clothing by which they would ostensibly manifest their religious belonging, within public primary, secondary, and high schools."[35]

In his *Lettre de Mission* opening the report of the Stasi Commission, and just before promulgating the 2004 law, Jacques Chirac stated that:

> La France est une République laïque [. . .]. Elle s'est imposée comme une garantie de neutralité des pouvoirs publics et des respects des croyances [. . .]. Elle accueille l'adhésion de toutes les confessions religieuses et de tous les courants de pensée, qui y voient la meilleure défense de la liberté de croire ou de ne pas croire.[36]

This law was thus reaffirming the principles of *laïcité* translated in the ban on wearing religious signs. But it was also the best way envisioned at the time to put an end to the disorders raised due to religious tensions within public schools and the public sphere. This new law was the only way to cancel the decision taken by the Conseil d'État in 1989, and to put an end to local decisions, which were contrary to the Republican "one justice for all."

Yet, to many, this law was denounced for stigmatizing the Muslim population. Seen from a judicial perspective, nevertheless, the law was the way to reimplement order, in a law against force battle. It is uncertain whether the law will put an end to the question of religious tensions in schools or not. Pupils are no longer allowed to express their religious beliefs in French public schools today. Banning religious signs does not teach tolerance and respect for the creeds of other. It does not help pupils to recognize that today's France is multicultural. What pedagogical ways could be applied to teach respect and tolerance? What could be done to help pupils to recognize the reality of "multicultural France" today? What new ways would allow pupils of each religious creed to feel at ease within the Republican *laïc* public school system? What could be envisioned and still be in touch with the principles of *laïcité*?

A Pedagogical Dimension to *Laïcité*: The Teaching of the History of Religions

Since the tragic 2001 attack on the World Trade Center in New York, we are exposed to religious data everywhere, all the time, mostly through the media. This is not necessarily to say that the twenty-first century is going through a revival of faith, but rather that media coverage exposes us to religion in unprecedented proportions. To make sense of the world, to avoid falling into stereotyping and generalization, a personal effort is thus required to go deeper in the analysis of the history of the different religions practiced on the planet. A small space has recently been created in the French public school system for teaching the history of religions. Would it be possible to implement a full course on the subject? And if so, with what aims in mind?

Teaching the history of religions has been a "taboo" in public schools in France since the very first implementation of *laïcité*. Though the question was raised at the beginning of the twentieth century, when Durkheim asked, for instance: "Comment enseigner au collège l'homme, et les choses humaines?,"[37] such a course was never implemented. The idea of creating a course dealing with religions has faced strong opposition from the very beginning, which we can divide into two groups: the militant *laïc* group,[38] and the religious group. The militant *laïc* group is an antireligious group who strongly opposes any discourse on religion. They are a minority in French schools today.[39] Firmly positioned against a religious discourse dealing with catechism and faith, this first group also strongly refuses any "objective" and rational approach to the history of religion. Just like the militant *laïc* group, the religious group, on the other hand, seems to be unable to accept an intellectual approach to the history of religions because it cannot dissociate the intellectual method of dealing with religious facts from the faith-based method.[40] The fear that one group would exploit the teaching of the history of religions to further its own interests has also dominated the debate over the course of the twentieth century. It was feared that the militant *laïc* group might want to use religions as a means to "preach" secularism, while the religious group would use religion as a means to preach catechism. These oppositions, divisions, and fears are still a problem today. They have been a social taboo for almost a century. In the same way as it took a long time to introduce sexual education classes in French public schools over the course of the twentieth century, the taboo against teaching the history of religions has been tenacious. Because of its nature, when a "taboo" is verbalized, its sacred aura is taken away. The fear of what is forbidden, and dangerous, slowly stops governing people's minds, as the taboo is turned into an object of reflection. Mireille Estivalèzes, Jean Baubérot, Régis Debray, Jean-Pierre Willaime, among others, have begun to break through the "taboo" barrier which is still overshadowing the teaching of the history of religions.

It was not until the 1980s that new possibilities emerged to create a course dealing with the history of religions. In 1986, teachers used the press to express their worries. They were deploring the fact that their students' knowledge of religions had decreased radically. Ignorance with regards to religious matters was sharply denounced. The Joutard report written in 1988, when Lionel Jospin was Minister of Education, made an analysis to assess the situation of three courses: history, geography, and social sciences. The report recommended that the history of religion be taught in those fields, in an interdisciplinary way. The implementation within the Education Nationale slowly took place ten years later, in 1996. The main goal of the new program was to enrich courses of history, French language, philosophy, foreign languages, and arts with some elements of the history of religion, without creating a new course. After the 9/11 terrorist attacks, Jack Lang, then Minister of Education, asked the philosopher Régis Debray to write a report, which would account for the ways these new programs had evolved since 1996, and to formulate new hypotheses. Once more, the Debray report did not encourage the creation of a new course, but recommended the development of this type of teaching within the French, history, and philosophy curricula. The Debray report emphasized a "culture against cult" approach to teaching and stressed the importance of transmitting a cultural heritage to pupils. It also focused on the necessity of teaching the history of religions to understand our contemporary world. It finally recommended the creation of the European Institute for the Sciences of Religions.[41]

Yet, with Mireille Estivalèzes, I would like to warn against the limitations of an interdisciplinary way of teaching the history of religions. If this conception is necessary, especially for the training of teachers, as it is done today, it is not sufficient for pupils. Mireille Estivalèzes shows in her book *L'Enseignement du fait religieux à l'école laïque* that this interdisciplinary approach leads most teachers to skip the part of their programs devoted to the history of religions because their syllabi are too full.

The possibilities for implementation of a full course have recently been developed, through new research and educational institutes and through the university level, which now exist to train students in the field of the history of religions. The European Institute for the Sciences of Religion, for instance, was created after the Debray report in 2002; two Masters Programs were created in 2005, in Strasbourg, through the IFER (Institut de Formation pour l'Etude et l'Enseignement des Religions).[42] As the pedagogical structures are now ready to train future teachers, it would be important to create a new course, which would teach the history of the three monotheisms (Christianity, Islam, Judaism) without focusing almost exclusively on Christianity, as is the case in the classroom today. This course would also devote time to the religious systems of Greece and Rome, to atheism and agnosticism, and to the spiritual values of the African societies and of Asian societies (India and China, including Animism, Buddhism, Hindouism, Chinese spiritualities).

Many more goals are to be achieved should this course be implemented. The first goal is related to cultural heritage. This course would give the pupils the tools for understanding the cultural and religious heritage not only of France, as is the case today, but also that of other civilizations, legacies of the past and of humanity. The second goal is aesthetic: teach the critical tools used to understand and analyze the artistic expressions of the various civilizations of the world. The third goal is civic. The course would allow pupils to be less ignorant in matters related to religion and therefore would lead them to recognize the reality of cultural and religious pluralism. The Debray report stated that it would help them understand the world in which they live: "en leur donnant les moyens supplémentaires de s'échapper du présent-prison, pour *faire retour, mais en connaissance de cause, au monde d'aujour-d'hui.*"[43] Civic also in the sense that it would foster dialogue and, as stated in the Stasi report, develop the mutual understanding of the various contemporary cultures and religions: "une meilleure compréhension mutuelle des différentes cultures et traditions de pensées religieuses est aujourd'hui essentielle."[44] Intellectual maturation is the fourth goal, since the pupils would be armed with intellectual tools to understand the world. These intellectual, civic, aesthetic, and cultural goals aim to foster tolerance and respect. This new course, breaking away from the old ethno-euro-centrist way of teaching history, would not only teach pupils to become citizens but also citizens of the world.

Although today reforms are taking place to implement the teaching of the religion from an "objective," "scientific" point of view in an interdisciplinary way, more work needs to be done. Even though the opponents to this idea have radically diverging opinions, be they the "ultra *laïc*" minority or the "ultra religious" group, they seem nonetheless to be united against the possibility of a *laïc* historical analysis of religion in schools. Jean-Pierre Willaime explains:

> Entre la critique réductionaliste des rationalistes, qui dissout l'objet religion au motif qu'il s'agit d'une pure illusion entretenue par les prêtres, et l'approche spirituelle, qui dissout l'objet religion au motif qu'il s'agit d'une réalité seulement accessible au langage de la foi, il y a une convergence objective pour interdire toute analyse historique des phénomènes religieux.[45]

If the radical opinions of different groups are united against this approach, there must be a precious lesson to be learned from it.

Conclusion

To conclude this paper on *laïcité* within the French public school system, let us keep in mind that democracies can die. As Jacques Myard[46] points out, democracy is constantly being reinvented. The same goes for *laïcité*, which is cosubstantial to it. It belongs to every generation to question, to understand, and to explain. The respect of two conditions has to be followed in order for *laïcité* to be implemented:

1. The respect of human freedoms.
2. As they are regulated by the laws of the Republic, and of democracy.

If the 2004 law on visible religious signs in public schools was often regarded as a controversial law, it was, from a judicial perspective, the only possible way to bridge the gap between the ideal of *laïcité* and its institutional implementation, by bringing to an end a complex system of local rights, which had ruled chaotically for two decades almost. A new conception of *laïcité* could be envisioned here, a "*laïcité* en mouvement" which would no longer approach religion at school from a preventive/protective point of view but from an educational one as well. To this end, creating a course on the history of religions in schools would replace the logic of exclusion, the "neither . . . nor" which forces religions to remain in the domain of what is forbidden and taboo in schools, by a logic of inclusion and intelligence, where all pupils would be in full possession of their rights to understand. Would this violate the principle of neutrality of the school space? Not as long as the course would deliver an "objective" and rational teaching. *Laïcité*, rather than being an obstacle to this teaching, would thus become one of its conditions. Not only would this course provide French pupils with critical tools for life but it would also form them as world citizens. Pupils would consequently be prepared to start life with the appropriate tools of knowledge. Germany and Great Britain have already started to develop such courses. France can become, with Germany and Great Britain, today, one of the "laboratories" for Europe.

Acknowledgments

A shorter version of this article appeared in *Paroles Gelées*, UCLA Press, Spring 2007.

I would like to thank: Trevor Merrill for being the best research partner one can ever rely on; Scarlett Baron for her careful editing and for her enthusiasm, even in the most difficult times; Steph and Juli for their caffeinated effects, their patience and attention in hearing me explain the *laïc* differences between France and America, for their advice and above all, for their friendship; Lorenzo Giachetti for his kindness, comments, and close reading, thanks for being here . . . always, Lorenzo!; Lo, for being himself and for bringing sunshine to my life; Elisabeth Mudimbe-Boyi for giving me the opportunity to be part of this wonderful experience. "De belles et grandes choses sont devant nous, sur ce continent ou bien sur un autre . . . Que la vie nous donne le loisir de les saisir et de les faire fructifier . . . "

Notes

1. Guy Bédouelle, ed., *Une République, des Religions. Pour une laïcité ouverte* (Paris: L'Atelier, 2003).

2. Numerous articles written by intellectuals and activists in France and worldwide were published in 2003 to express indignation in face of the possibility of the passing of a law that would ban religious signs from public schools. The question of expelling pupils from public schools, which will be approached in this paper, was one of the recurring arguments put forth by the opponents of the law.

3. Alain Badiou writes: "En vérité, la Loi foulardière n'exprime qu'une chose: la peur. Les Occidentaux en général, les Français en particulier, ne sont qu'un tas frissonnant de peureux. De quoi ont-ils peur? Des barbares, comme toujours. Ceux de l'intérieur, les 'jeunes des banlieues'; ceux de l'extérieur, les 'terroristes islamiques.' Pourquoi ont-ils peur? Parce qu'ils sont coupables, mais se disent innocents." Alain Badiou, "Derrière la loi foulardière, la peur," *Le Monde*, 22–23 March 2004.

4. Mireille Estivalèzes, *Les Religions dans l'enseignement laïque* (Paris: Presses Universitaires de France, 2005).

5. François Fillon for Jean-Pierre Raffarin, "Nouveau Contrat pour l'Avenir de l'école," *Assemblée Nationale*, 12 January 2005, <http://www.assemblee-nationale.fr/12/projets/pl2025.asp>, (2 May, 2008).

6. Monsieur Brard, "Avenir de l'école, no 2025, amendement no 136, article 8, rapport annexé," *Assemblée Nationale*, 14 February 2005, <http://recherche.assemblee-nationale.fr/amendements/visualiser.asp?k2dockey=http percent3A percent2F percent2Fwww percent2Eassemblee percent2Dnationale percent2Efr percent2F12 percent2Famendements percent2F2025 percent2F202500136 percent2Easp percent40AMDT&serverSpec=localhost:9920&querytext= percent3CAND percent3Epercent282025 percent3CIN percent3ENUM percent5FINIT percent29&OrigQuery=&QueryParser=Simple&logTitle=&dtype=2&collection=AMDT&allsite=&ResultStart=111&ResultDocStart=116&maxDocs=500&ResultCount=10>, (2 May, 2008).

7. Jean Baubérot, "Débat Public: la laïcité," *France*, 5, <http://www.france5.fr/actu_societe/W00137/9/103209.cfm>, (2 May, 2008).

8. Daniel Beresniak, *Laïcité, pourquoi?* (Saint-Estève: Cap Béar éditions, 2005), 9.

9. 1905 Law, Article 1, <http://www.assemblee-nationale.fr/histoire/eglise-etat/1905-projet.pdf>, (2 May, 2008).

10. Jules Ferry stated in his famous "Letter to the teacher" that: "la loi du 28 mars [. . .] affirme la volonté de fonder chez nous une éducation nationale et de la fonder sur les notions du devoir et du droit que le législateur n'hésite pas à inscrire au nombre des premières vérités que nul ne peut ignorer." Jules Ferry, *Circulaire*, 17 November 1883, <http://s.huet.free.fr/paideia/paidogonos/jferry3.htm>, (2 May, 2008).

11. Henri Péna-Ruiz, *La Laïcté* (Paris: Domino Flammarion, 1998), 7.

12. Estivalèzes, *Les Religions dans l'enseignement laïque*, 15.

13. Estivalèzes, *Les Religions dans l'enseignement laïque*, 15.

14. Péna-Ruiz, *La Laïcté*, 92.

15. On July 14, 1801 (26 messidor an IX), Napoléon Bonaparte recognized Catholicism as the "religion de la majorité des Français." The spiritual authority of the Pope over his bishops was still valid, but bishops were no longer chosen by the Pope, but by the Head of State. Christian privileges were restored, and the old alliance "du trône et de l'autel" reestablished. Four religions over time would be recognized and would receive financial privileges: Catholicism, Lutheranism, Calvinism, and Judaism. Napoléon would contribute, nevertheless, to "laïciser" civil society with the 1804 "Code Civil," which he wrote. Alsace-Moselle still follows Concordat rules in France today.

16. Jean Baubérot, "La Laïcité," *Embassade de France aux Etats-Unis*, <http://www.ambafrance-us.org/fr/aaz/laicite.asp>, (2 May, 2008).

17. This data is just an estimation. Indeed, since the 1978 law "Informatique et liberté" it is forbidden to survey ethnic origins or religious belongings in France. The last cult-related census took place in France in 1872. Five million Muslim people are estimated to be living in France today, which makes Islam the second most practiced religion. Source: Ministère de l'emploi et de la solidarité, Ministère de l'Intérieur, Agence pour le développement des relations interculturelles, *L'Islam en France* (Paris: La documentation française), 20–21.

18. Emmanuel Brenner, ed., *Les Territoires perdus de la République* (Paris: Mille et une nuits, 2002), 117.

19. Brenner, *Les Territoires perdus*, 57.

20. The Stasi Commission was proposed by President Chirac in order to discuss the question of "laïcité." It was organized around a series of public debates, which gathered numerous intellectuals, teachers, pupils, and public employees of diverse ethnic origins and cultural backgrounds.

21. My first two examples are the summary of a detailed analysis to be found in the book by Henri Péna-Ruiz, *Histoire de la Laïcité, genèse d'un idéal* (Paris: Découvertes Gallimard, 2005), 85–86, and 88.

22. Quoted in Péna-Ruiz, *Histoire de la Laïcité*, 86.

23. Monique Canto-Sperber and Paul Ricoeur, "Les Philosophes en parlent," *Le Monde*, 10 December 2003.

24. "Le port par les élèves de signes par lesquels ils entendent manifester leur appartenance à une religion n'est pas lui-même incompatible avec le principe de laïcité dans la mesure où il constitue l'exercice de la liberté d'expression et de manifestation de croyance religieuse; mais cette liberté ne saurait permettre aux élèves d'arborer des signes d'appartenance religieuse qui, par leur nature ou les conditions dans lesquelles ils seraient portés individuellement ou collectivement ou par leur caractère ostentatoire ou revendicatif, constitueraient un acte de pression, de provocation, de prosélytisme ou de propagande, porteraient atteinte à la dignité ou la liberté de l'élève ou d'autres membres de la communauté éducative, compromettraient leur santé ou leur sécurité, perturberaient le déroulement des activités d'enseignement et le rôle éducatif des enseignants, enfin troubleraient l'ordre dans l'établissement ou le fonctionnement normal du service public." Avis du Conseil d'Etat, *conseil-etat*, 27 November 1989, <http://www.conseil-etat.fr/ce/missio/index_mi_cg03_01.shtml>, (2 May, 2008).

25. In 1937, two ministerial decrees ("circulaires") were passed by the Minister of Education ("instruction publique"), Jean Zay, forbidding clothes or religious or political signs within schools. Contrary to the common held belief, not only did it concern teachers and buildings, but pupils too.

26. Hanifa Cherifi, member of the Stasi Commission, and mediator for the Minister of Education Nationale, gives a terrifying account on the extremes that can be reached when dealing with the question of religious signs. She relates the murder of a young girl who did not want to wear the veil and for this was burnt alive in a trashcan, in a poor suburban area.

27. Péna-Ruiz, *Histoire de la Laïcité*, 86.

28. Quoted in Péna-Ruiz, *Histoire de la Laïcité*, 88.

29. Philippe Bernard, "La règle actuelle suppose une appréciation pragmatique de chaque cas," *Le Monde*, 10 December 2003.

30. Brenner, *Les Territoires perdus*, 57.

31. Brenner, *Les Territoires perdus*, 57.

32. One of the members of the Commission, Jean Baubérot, who was against the law, chose not to vote.

33. The first Article of the 1946 Constitution reads: "la France est une République indivisible, laïque, démocratique, et sociale." "Constitution du 27 octobre 1946," *Conseil Constitutionnel*, 27 October 1946, <http://www.conseil-constitutionnel .fr>, (2 May, 2008).

34. President Chirac said in an address at L'Élysée, after the Stasi Commission handed in their report: "Nous devons réaffirmer avec force la neutralité et la laïcité du service public." Jacques Chirac, "Discours Prononcé par Monsieur Jacques Chirac, Président de la République, relatif au respect du principe de laïcité dans la République," *Elysée*, 17 December 2003, <http://www.elysee.fr/elysee/interventions/ discours_et_declarations/2003/decembre/discours_prononce_par_m_jacques_chirac _president_de_la_republique_relatif_au_respect_du_principe_de_laicite_dans_la_ republique-palais_de_l_elysee.2829.html>, (2 May, 2008).

35. The first article of the 2004 law reads: "Dans les écoles, les collèges et les lycées publics, le port de signes ou tenues par lesquels les élèves manifestent ostensiblement une appartenance religieuse est interdit." "Loi n° 2004-228 du 15 mars 2004 encadrant, en application du principe de laïcité, le port de signes ou de tenues manifestant une appartenance religieuse dans les écoles, collèges et lycées publics," *Légifrance*, 15 March 2004, <http://www.legifrance.gouv.fr/WAspad/UnTexteDeJorf? numjo=MENX0400001L>, (2 May, 2008).

36. Jacques Chirac, "Lettre de Mission du Président de la République à Mr. Bernard STASI, président de la commission de réflexion sur l'application du principe de laïcité dans la République," *Elysée*, 3 July 2003, <http://www.elysee.fr/elysee/ francais/interventions/lettres_et_messages/2003/juillet/lettre_de_mission_du_ president_de_la_republique_a_m_bernard_stasi_president_de_la_commission_de_ reflexion_sur_l_application_du_principe_de_laefcite_dans_la_republique.1037.html>, (2 May, 2008).

37. Quoted in Estivalèzes, *Les Religions*, 2, in Émile Durkheim, *L'Évolution pédagogique en France* (Paris: Puf Quadrige, 1999 [1ère ed. (posthume), 1938]), 368.

38. Estivalèzes, *Les Religions*, 63.

39. Estivalèzes, *Les Religions*, 63.

40. Estivalèzes, *Les Religions*, 27.

41. Régis Debray, "L'enseignement du fait religieux dans l'École laïque," *Rapport*, February 2002, <http://lesrapports.ladocumentationfrancaise.fr/BRP/024000544/ 0000.pdf>, (2 May, 2008).

42. Esther Benbassa, "la République doit admettre qu'elle est multiculturelle," *Le Monde de l'Éducation*, May 2005.

43. Debray, *Rapport*, 6.

44. Bernard Stasi, *Rapport*, 3 July 2003, <http://lesrapports.ladocumentationfrancaise .fr/BRP/034000725/0000.pdf>, (2 May, 2008).

45. Quoted in Christian Bonrepaux, "L'enseignement du fait religieux: au nom de la loi," *Le Monde de l'Éducation*, May 2005.

46. Jacques Myard, *La Laïcité au cœur de la République* (Paris: L'Harmattan, 2003), 8.

Works Cited

Baubérot, Jean. "Débat Public: la laïcité." *France*, 5. <http://www.france5.fr/ actu_societe/W00137/9/103209.cfm> (10 November 2006).

———. *Laïcité 1905–2005, entre passion et raison*. Paris: Seuil, 2004.

———. "La Laïcité." Ambassade de France aux Etats-Unis. <http://www.ambafrance -us.org/fr/aaz/laicite.asp> (10 November 2006).

———. *Vers un nouveau pacte laïque?* Paris: Seuil, 1990.

Bédouelle, Guy, ed. *Une République, des religions. Pour une laïcité ouverte*. Paris: L'Atelier, 2003.

Beresniak, Daniel. *Laïcité, pourquoi?* Saint-Estève: Cap Béar éditions, 2005.

Brard. "Avenir de l'école 2025, amendement no 136, article 8, rapport annexé." *Assemblée Nationale*. 14 February 2005. <http://www.assembleenationale.fr/12/amendments/2025/202500136.asp> (2 May 2008).

Brenner, Emmanuel, ed. *Les Territoires perdus de la République*. Paris: Mille et Une Nuits, 2002.

Chirac, Jacques. "Discours Prononcé par Monsieur Jacques Chirac, Président de la République, relatif au respect du principe de laïcité dans la République." *Elysée*, 17 December 2003. <http://www.elysee.fr/elysee/interventions/discours_et_declarations/2003/decembre/discours_prononce_par_m_jacques_chirac_president_de_la_republique_relatif_au_respect_du_principe_de_laicite_dans_la_republique-palais_de_l_elysee.2829.html> (10 November 2006).

———. "Lettre de Mission du Président de la République à Mr. Bernard STASI, président de la commission de réflexion sur l'application du principe de laïcité dans la République." *Elysée*. 3 July 2003. <http://www.elysee.fr/elysee/francais/interventions/lettres_et_messages/2003/juillet/lettre_de_mission_du_president_de_la_republique_a_m_bernard_stasi_president_de_la_commission_de_reflexion_sur_l_application_du_principe_de_laefcite_dans_la_republique.1037.html> (10 November 2006).

Constitution. "Constitution du 27 octobre 1946." *Conseil Constitutionnel*. 27 October 1946. <http://www.conseil-constitutionnel.fr> (10 November 2006).

Debray, Régis. "L'enseignement du fait religieux dans l'École laïque." *Rapport*. February 2002. <http://lesrapports.ladocumentationfrancaise.fr/BRP/024000544/0000.pdf> (10 November 2006).

Estivalèzes, Mireille. *Les Religions dans l'enseignement laïque*. Paris: Presses Universitaires de France, 2005.

Ferry, Jules. *Circulaire*. 17 November 1883. <http://s.huet.free.fr/paideia/paidogonos/jferry3.htm> (10 November 2006).

Fillon, François. "Nouveau Contrat pour l'Avenir de l'école." *Assemblée Nationale*. 12 January 2005. <http://www.assemblee-nationale.fr/12/projets/pl2025.asp> (10 November 2006).

Gruson, Luc, ed. *L'Islam en France*. Paris: la documentation française, 2000.

Law. "Loi du 15 mars 2004 encadrant, en application du principe de laïcité, le port de signes ou de tenues manifestant une appartenance religieuse dans les écoles, collèges et lycées publics." *Légifrance*.

Law. "Loi concernant la séparation des Eglises et de l'Etat." *Assemblée Nationale*. <http://www.assemblee-nationale.fr/histoire/eglise-etat/1905-projet.pdf> (10 November 2006).

Myard, Jacques, ed. *La Laïcité au cœur de la République*. Actes du Colloque du 23 mai 2003. Paris: L'Harmattan, 2003.

Péna-Ruiz, Henri. *Histoire de la Laïcité, genèse d'un idéal*. Paris: Découvertes Gallimard, 2005.

———. *La Laïcité*. Paris: Domino Flammarion, 1998.

Stasi, Bernard. *Rapport*. 3 July 2003.

CHAPTER TWO

~

Muslims in France

History under the Carpet

Jocelyne Dakhlia,
École des Hautes Études en Sciences Sociales, Paris

The great debates taking place in France and across Europe over Muslim "integration" reveal as never before just how tricky the term "integration" is.[1] Planning a group's "integration" excludes them from the status quo *already*; marginalizes them *already*; keeps them off the national construction site, acts like these men and women were not *there already*. The very notion of integration, consequently, has as its prerequisite a full body forced to "ingest" a second body into its system, or digest a series of individual bodies one by one.

In the case of Islam and Muslim immigration, we're seeing a repeat of what happened to the Jews, and what drove some to Theodore Herzl's Zionism: the prediction, even from within the Jewish community, that the Jewish were ultimately "inassimilable" and entitled to their own separate territory, *apart*. Postcolonial France, like the rest of Europe, like the rest of the Western world, but also like the Muslim populations, or some among them, are today grappling with the "inassimilable" nature of Islam. But behind this open investigation lies a radical historical illusion, the illusion that the West's first contact with Islam is a current event, at most a colonial byproduct, and represents a major crisis of our time. Consensually, we accept the Muslim presence in France as the consequence of colonial expansion or the former imperial enterprise. *Almost, but not quite.*

Even in the colonial context, Islam was *unthought of*—an *impensé*. Protected, but also under close watch, in the Muslim provinces of Empire, it was banned from sight in metropolitan France. In the colonies, especially in Algeria, the French built their religious policy around an obsequious deference for Islam or (some of) its religious leaders. The best illustrator of this policy was Lyautey by ostensibly banning non-Muslims from entering Muslim mosques in Morocco then banning French citizens from decorating Casablanca with posters of the Declarations of the Rights of Man on Bastille Day. He assumed such principles to be contrary to Islam.[2] This open deference covered up the real intention to assign Muslim and non-Muslims to separate territories so there could be no confusion between cultures and religions belonging to separate territories. Social sciences today—even if theories of a *Third space* do not fly in France—strongly favor the phenomena of cultural hybridization resulting from colonization, but such theories should not make us forget that the origin of all colonial hybridizations, acculturations, or melting pots, is the primal, radically divided colonial power relationship. The first and primal phenomenon is the dichotomy of territories and cultures. Multiple hybridizations resulted from this divided reality, but these hybrids are secondary realities.

Effectively, the separation was so radical that in metropolitan territory Islam as an officially recognized religion was unimaginable, in direct opposition with the policy implemented in predominantly Muslim territories of total deference to Islam. The first wave of North African immigration arrived in France at the end of the nineteenth century, mostly at the behest of French industry heads, but at this time, it was unthinkable for the French society to conceive of these immigrants as *Muslims*.[3] In the midst of the separation of Church and State, it was a given that the migrants' religious faith, if they had one, stay private. The hold of this *impensé* has been so powerful and deeply entrenched in collective consciousness that even research specialists on the first wave of Muslim immigration continued to ignore the issue of the migrants' religious beliefs, their daily practice—even the problem of burial rites or the existence of separate cemeteries for immigrants—until only just recently.[4]

We know the massive enlistment of colonial subjects in World War I, composed mostly of West-African and Maghribi Muslims, revealed the loyalty of colonial subjects for the empire and obliged France to recognize Islam on their territory as a token of eternal gratitude. But the first official Mosque of Paris, and the first mosque in French metropolitan territory, did not go up until in 1926.[5] Actually, the first official French mosque was built in 1905 in the city of Saint Denis on the French island of Réunion, a fact only further illustrating a general consensus to refuse Islam on French *metropolitan* territory. A new territorial logic was dawning with the idea that Islam required territorial concessions, an idea we still find in the vague and striking saying: "Territoires perdus de la République," or "Lost Territories of the Republic."[6]

Meanwhile all this hush-hush around Islam is not the sole fault of official policy. The same silence perforated the discourses of Algeria's partisans and sympathizers to the anticolonial struggle in France. Not one "porteur de valises" ("baggage porter") was conscious of helping a *Muslim*. The religious undertones behind key terms for the Algerian liberation movement, such as *chahid,* or martyr, or *moujahid,* a warrior of faith derived from the Arabic word for holy war *jihad,* totally escaped the minds or perceptions of auxiliary actors.[7] Algerian militants may have also been only semiconscious of the Muslim dimension of their cause, but the Muslim dimension was real, and some fully assumed their Muslim identity.

Pierre Bourdieu himself, whose analysis during the fight for Algeria's liberation were so incisive, left out the issue of Islam. The issue of Islam is barely broached in his works with the sole exception of *Sociologie de l'Algérie* where he takes on the role of Islam head on. Bourdieu explains that if Islam appears to pervade every aspect of Algerian society, it is a sign of natural and deep structural affinities between the message of Islam and the Algerian society's natural way of life. Algerian society sees itself reflected in Islam: "la force de l'Islam algérien tient en effet à ce qu'il est, dans son esprit, en harmonie avec l'esprit de la civilisation algérienne. Le message coranique enferme des prescriptions conformes au style de vie traditionnaliste et le système de normes qu'il propose s'accorde aux structures profondes de la société algérienne."[8]

That's like saying, in so many words, that Algerian society pre-exists Islam and could exist without Islam, or without this language of Islam. He sees the Koran as the justification for keeping a traditionalist lifestyle in his discussion, or denunciation, of a widely influential notion at the time: Muslim fatalism. But in general, if we refer to his theory of praxis laid out in *Esquisse d'une théorie de la pratique* or *Le Sens pratique,* we find Islam absent most of the time. I once heard Bourdieu describe this apparent lack of interest for the question of Islam in his autobiographical defense: his belief in a strong laïc and even antireligious culture lead him to downplay or *minoritize* the Muslim religion.[9]

It was *a fortiori* ignorance. Essentially, for the Enlightened and progressive leftists, religion *itself* was an archaic element and Islam figured the most backward of all of them. It was an element behind Algerian society's underdevelopment, whose backward ways naturally would have to be emancipated little by little. Otherwise, Islam was a religion preaching submission and a religion keeping its subjects dominated. Many would scoff at the flattened Muslim prayer position on the floor, superimposing the image of the faithful man bent over in prayer over the colonized man's prostrate position under his Master. It's no coincidence that Primo Levi, in his tragic memoirs *Se questo è un uomo* (*If It's a Man*), remembers the word Muslim as the name given broken, submissive, vanquished men in the concentration camps.[10] *That* signals a similar colonial schema, one we tend to forget, fully operative in colonial Italy too in those years. In the interwar period, or during the first half of the twentieth century, a widespread prejudice against immigration in metropolitan France disdainfully called the Muslim a carpet vender, caricatured as a poor peddler knocking door to door, a carpet slung over his shoulder. "Prayer carpet," "the magic carpet," the "carpet vender" . . . this caricature or derisive poke at the Muslim grew around the image of a carpet, instilling the image of a culture in horizontality, in self-flattening abasement, but in a cloister.

Of course, a scholarly vision of Islam was also developing at this time, but these studies did not concern the Islam "of France." Jacques Berque offers diverse and sophisticated analyses on the tapestries but ultimately partakes in the same cultural rupture. Berque delineates a *hypercoherent* vision of Islam from the tapestry patterns, a Muslim culture whose artisan's handiwork echoes high culture just like the geometrical motifs woven into the tapestry, particularly the famous "layered five point star" (*polygone étoilé*), reflect mystical elaborations of utmost hermeneutic and rarefied strains. But his metaphor of a weaver's loom, however inspiring, does not pass one thread from one side to the other Mediterranean shore.[11]

So why this denial? Why this refusal to *see* Islam in public space as soon as we touch ground on metropolitan territory? There has been a lot of speculation, in postcolonial France, about an "underground Islam" or "cave Islam," with a tinge of indignation and disdain (who would accept to live and pray in a cave?). Only a few Christian groups evoked the primitive Christians' forced to congregate in "catacombs" with empathy. This comparison only lent the migrants' Islam a temporary air of novelty, the irruption of a previously unknown cult.[12]

The idea of a "cave Islam" reflects, in reality, the idea of a repression, in the psychoanalytic sense of the word, or a hidden truth swept under the carpet, or dare I say, buried down below the consequences of a colonial past or its consequences for present-day France. Islam has been present in France since the Middle Ages, from the Middle to Modern ages, and thus long before France expanded to become a colonial power.[13] We know little of its public visibility down the centuries though. Islam doubtless was barely visi-

ble despite the fact that hundreds of thousands of Muslims, from the medieval to modern times, lived in France and Europe, on a temporary or permanent basis, free or in the majority of cases, as captives or slaves.[14] Europe
"assimilated" as many baptized Muslims into its history as the Muslim
Mediterranean "assimilated" Christians into theirs (the famous "renegades")[15]; but one-half of this circular symmetry is far less pregnant in our
memories. It weighs less on our conscience, either because Islam was barely
noticeable (we think most Muslims were baptized, at least in name, the moment they set foot on Christian soil), or because we have repressed these historical taboos for so long.

Held captive or converted into Christianity by force or partly by force, do
you automatically cease to be a Muslim? And free, like the Muslim merchants trading in Marseille and Toulon, Livorno or Venice, to openly worship and if so, under what conditions? It's easier to put these questions to the
Muslim scullers who occupied 20 percent of the ship galleys. They would
spend the winter months at port working odd jobs in town or temporarily
employed in Provencal soap factories.[16] Muslims would have been a familiar
site in these urban landscapes long before the Siege of Algiers and the first
waves of migrations under the colonial empire. We also know for a fact that
as early as the seventeenth century, for example, at Marseille and Toulon, the
problem question of religious practice and separate burial grounds was formally entered into the public registers.[17]

Such historical records, so far removed from our present-day consciousness, lead us back to the role writing played behind the colonial enterprise.
These imbrications of colliding histories serve as a constant reminder, whatever the fluctuating rhythms and their historical amplitude, that cultural
mixing happened first. The violence of colonial historical writing does not
stop at depicting the Other as a savage, as Edward Saïd and others have successfully argued since his book *Orientalism*, or since T. Todorov's *La Conquête
de l'Amérique*. Colonial written violence lies in the denial of a commonly
shared past, woven back and forth from shore to shore of the Mediterranean,
and even when these intricate links and fusions came at the high price of a
violent, antagonistic history.[18] Picturing Algeria, or the Maghrib, we have
stuck in our head, from a purely fictive model of conquest, the conquest illustrated in Todorov's *Conquête de l'Amérique*, or the theme of a mythical *first
contact*, the shocking discovery of the Other. *Almost, but not quite.*

Bugeaud's cave fumigations were real, those men and women who sought
refuge in the grottos were really sacrificed, and we must keep such real acts
of colonial violence alive in our memory so that our memory can resist suc-
cumbing to a nostalgia for colonialism out there today. At the same time, our

evocation of colonial violence must not vehicle a second misleading image.[19] The image of Algerians holed up in grottos primitivizes Algerians and comforts the theme of the shocking discovery of *alterity*. If the conquest was a shocking revelation of the Other, it was for the other side on the receiving end of our violence.

These societies had been in constant interaction, in perpetual actions and counteractions, since antiquity. Never underestimate the intellectual operation of reduction the French army, the French state, put in place before deploying their military forces. The French conceptually had to distance this country to refashion "Algeria" from afar decked out in signs of savagery. Assia Djebar tells how the French renamed Algiers's streets after species of wild animals; literally rebaptizing Algiers under the sign of savagery.[20] Inversely, Napoléon Bonaparte's expedition of Egypt was doomed to fail from the start. His violent expedition of Egypt, but under the banner of recognition of Egyptian's culture and civilization, met with patent defeat.

We can see the fundamental role amnesia, or the negation of a preexisting *already shared* history or culture, plays in setting up the colonial relationship. The balance of power between the two societies, previously antagonist yet relatively balanced, is henceforth destroyed to make way for a radically unequal and unprecedented basis for power relations: acculturation. For this reason, we can see how the recent resurgence of interest for the historical leader Abd al Kader is really quite ambiguous. Abd al Kader, first historical leader of Algeria's anticolonial resistance, at first incarnated the noble enemy in the eyes of the French, but at the end of his life gained widespread public support for protecting the Damas Christians from Muslims.[21] Today we celebrate the universal spirit in this Freemason Abd al Kader as the incarnation of a rare form of cultural mediation.[22] In an interview for the Enlightenment exhibition at the French National Library, the writer and essayist Abdelwahhab Meddeb went so far as to attribute the Emir's Freemasonry and reception of its "masonic message of salvation" to his prior adherence to a mystical deist immanent branch of Islam, and thus implies his "proximity" to the philosophy of Spinoza had helped prepare him to "receive the Masonic message" and become a Freemason. In other words, this noble and enlightened combination of faiths reposes upon a select "deist" form of Islam having nothing to do with the common man's Islam or "ordinary" Islam. Another elitist way of simultaneously finding what is "assimilable" in Islam for the West, or in the eyes of its enlightened elite, while comforting the idea of a literally "undigestible" reality.

I prefer to imagine the men and women filling the pages of Assia Djebar's novels and essays, most notably *Vaste est la prison*. Cervantes, captive in the city of Algiers for five years, and his character Zoraïdé who leaves Alger and Islam after secretly converting to Christianity[23]; Thomas d'Arcos in *Vaste est la prison*, rebaptized Osman in Tunis.[24] Each of these real-life historical characters or their kind, verifiably authentic, would have had their equivalents across Europe. Even better, I believe the time has come to move past the singular destiny of "renegades" symbolized by Léon l'Africain, main character of one of Amin Maalouf's fictions, but acting as a veritable intercultural mediator in Natalie Zemon Davis's historical readings, to experience the massive and anonymous past presence, free or captive, left by Muslims in Europe before 1830.[25] Four thousand Muslims counted in eighteenth century Paris according to Arlette Farge . . . How much would it be in Livorno or Venice . . .

The colonial lock on historical narration must be forced open, its knots unsnarled— without ever trying to reevaluate the colonial enterprise itself, I must insist . . . An introspection about our historiographic perspectives, how they came into play or get us into trouble, does not need to turn into a euphemization of the colonial past.[26] Colonization in France, to a greater degree than any other European or Western nation, structures historical schemas and our idea of what the first contacts of Islam looked like. But the *impensé* of Islam predates the Siege of Algiers and the colonial period; its invisibility in public space, its reduction to a larval practice, quasi-clandestine, predates our nineteenth- and twentieth-century colonial heritage. Why do we deny all this? Why have we conserved the faces of medieval and modern synagogues in Bordeaux, Rouen, or even Provence, in the Comtat Venaissin, while no mosques dot the French urban landscape, or stir our urban memory?[27]

Our denial of Islam owes its force to more theological arguments than we are prepared to handle. Many of the intellectuals who pronounce ideas hostile to Islam, based on their Enlightenment heritage or the assumed incompatibility between the two traditions (Enlightenment and Islam), hold their line unaware of their position's debt, at bottom, to inherited Christian anti-Muslim theological polemics. The spectacular reappearance, on the French public stage, of an anti-Muslim critique of polygamy, or of the "polygamous Prophet," brandished by Hélène Carrère d'Encausse following the 2005 riots in the suburbs, the stance taken by the philosopher Robert Redecker in 2006, falls under this polemical tradition.

According to polemical anti-Mahomet rhetoricians in the Middle Ages, Islam, as an avatar of Christianity, is a heresy, that is to say, an *internal* deviation. It is unacceptable because it claims to surpass Christianity; conversely, the Judaic faith was surpassed by the advent of Christ. We would have to tailor our methods to study how the modes of thought challenging the Muslim world's supposed mimicry of Judeo-Christian European principles, or its supposed incapacity to fully reproduce, implement, and fully embody them, dwell on old Judeo-Christian values and institutions (this last term has reemerged as of late in the French civic debates). C. Castoriadis, for one, could not stop denouncing Muslim's incapacity to partake in the Greek heritage of which they too are recipients.[28]

But if we refer to past theological arguments, even our latent religious unconscious, as the basis for explaining France's constant and deep-seated hostility to Islam, and our strong denial in France, does this make the colonial factor, in this case, secondary? And does this shatter the national framework, the French specificity, to pieces? The Danish caricature crisis appeared to confirm so given that Denmark is not known for its colonial past (with the exception of Greenland). My only response can be to continue affirming the theological heritage should not in any way relativize the colonial heritage. First of all, only the colonial disdain for Islam can explain why Muslims have waited so long to receive equal civic rights in public space or the right to worship as Muslims in decent conditions on metropolitan soil. Their visible presence and increasing statistical proportions in the country's public and political demographics do not suffice . . . The first French Muslims to be officially recognized as a community, the Harkis, were physically and socially pushed to the margins of postcolonial France, lodged in isolated *Cités* or out of the way forest campgrounds . . . [29]

Second of all, the idea that national histories of Denmark, Sweden, or Northern Europe are exempt from all "colonial" contacts, the idea then that they discovered Islam with the Kurdish, Afghani, or Moroccan contemporary immigration movements in the twentieth century—this idea is just another historical fallacy. We do not have to go all the way back to the Norman occupation of Sicily to prove it wrong. We have only to recall how the vehement waves of reaction to the Danish bombing of Alger in 1770 are still recorded in hostile anti-Danish songs.[30] In the eighteenth century, Denmark deployed a diplomatic political campaign supporting an exploitive commercial enterprise throughout the entire Muslim Mediterranean basin. In the opposite direction, expeditions of Maghribi pirates sailed up to Iceland and took hundreds of Icelandic hostages as booty from their coastal raids in 1627 back to North Africa.[31] A number of Icelandic prisoners converted to Islam while the rest were ransomed and returned speedily to the north of Europe. This event was so traumatic that Iceland began holding annual *alla turca* ceremonies to conjure it from happening again.

The illusion that Islam is a "contemporary" conflict must continue to be examined; the past undercurrent of contacts, fusions, and conflicts, even the recent mutual inflammation of passions set off by the Danish then Swedish caricatures of the Prophet should all play an integral part in our studies. And if the term *colonial* cannot too broadly and retrospectively be exploited, thereby diluting its specificity, we must reintegrate the full story "buried under the carpet" when speaking and reformulating the relationships between the Christian West and Islam. We must have in mind the constellation of interlacing ties where exchange, however violent, was at the foundation of truly coextensive identities, the one for the other. We must loosen the reductive grip.

Translated from the French by Jennifer Williams.

Notes

1. This text was especially written for the conference "Empire Lost: France and its Other Worlds," held at Stanford University, Stanford, California, in April 2006 at the French and Italian departments of Stanford University. I would like to thank Elisabeth Mudimbe-Boyi for including me in this conference. The first version of this text appeared in the journal *Multitudes* in October 2006.

2. Belal, Youssef. *Le Réenchantement du monde: autorité et rationalisation en Islam marocain*, PhD thesis (Paris: Sciences Po, 2005).

3. Dirèche-Slimani, Karima. *Histoire de l'immigration kabyle en France au XXe siècle: réalités culturelles et politiques et réappropriations identitaires* (Paris: L'Harmattan, 1997).

4. Chaïb, Y. *L'Islam et la mort en France. Introduction à l'islam en France: le rapatriement des dépouilles mortelles entre la France et la Tunisie*, thèse doctorale, Aix-en-Provence, 1992; *L'Emigré et la mort: la mort musulmane en France* (Aix-en-Provence: Edisud, 2000).

5. The film *Indigènes*, by Rachid Bouchareb, 2006, recently introduced the theme of "loyalty" into French civics debates on colonialism. M. Michel. *L'Appel à l'Afrique. Contributions et réaction à l'effort de guerre en AOF (1914–1919)* (Paris: Publications de la Sorbonne, 1988).

6. Brenner, E., ed. *Les Territoires perdus de la République: antisémitisme, racisme et sexisme en milieu scolaire* (Paris: Mille et Une Nuits, 2002).

7. Dakhlia, J. *Islamicités* (Paris: PUF, 2005) and "Islam et nationalisme: la fin des Etats de grace," "Le Religieux dans le politique" in *Le Genre humain* (mai 1991), pp. 19–32.

8. Bourdieu, Pierre. *Sociologie de l'Algérie* (Paris, PUF, 1958), 98.

The force of Islam's hold on Algeria is its kindred spirit with the spirit of the modes of life in Algerian civilization. The message of the *Qu'rân* literally enforces a traditionalist life style and moral normative prescriptions in concordance with the deep structures of Algerian society.

9. Oral commentary transcribed from Fanny Colonna's thesis defense.

10. Levi, Primo. *Si c'est un homme (Se questo è un uomo)* (1947).

11. Dakhlia, J. "Du 'tapis maghrébin' au 'polygone étoilé': retour sur le motif," *Revue des Mondes musulmans et de la Méditerranée* (no. 83–84, 1997/1–2), pp. 125–34.

12. Ibid.

13. Despite its remarkable amplitude, the collective works edited by M. Arkoun on French Muslims barely touches upon the dimension of deep roots, and instead focuses on the modern period, or the circulations of embassies, for example. M. Arkoun. *Histoire de l'Islam et des Musulmans en France. Du Moyen Age à nos jours* (Paris: Albin Michel, 2006).

14. We have found the most information on the practice of Muslim capture and enslavement in Europe in the Southern European archives. A project currently is in progress, based at the EHESS in Paris, attempting to deepen our knowledge foundation of practices occulted by a stronger historical cover-up, it would seem, than the attempt to dissimulate the transatlantique slave trade in France ("Le temps long de l'intégration entre l'Europe et l'Islam").

15. Bennasser, B. and L. *Les Chrétiens d'Allah. L'histoire extraordinaire des rénégats (XVI et XVIIe siècle)* (Paris: Perrin, 1987).

16. Zysberg, A. *Marseille au temps des galères (1660–1748)* (Marseille: Rivages, 1983); *Les Galériens, Vies et destins de 60 000 forçats sur les galères de France (1680–1748)* (Paris: Seuil, 1991).

17. Bertrand, R. "Les Cimetières des 'esclaves turcs' des arsenaux de Marseille et Toulon au XVIIIe siècle" in *Revue des Mondes musulmans et de la Méditerranée* (no. 99–100, 2002), pp. 205–17.

18. Todorov, T. *La Conquête de l'Amérique, la question de l'autre* (Paris: Seuil, 1982).

19. In and around 1840, Bugeaud and his officers executed a brutal colonial policy to repress tribal uprisings and especially killed hundreds of civilians seeking refuge in caves in their "fumigations." These tragic events have recently come up again in official Algerian cultural memory.

20. Djebar, Assia. *Villes d'Algérie au XIXème siècle* (Paris: Centre Culturel algérien, 1994).

21. For more on the Emir Abd al Kader, I recommend the recent bibliography or at least one of the most current and considerable bibliographies on his subject by B. Etienne, *Abdelkader* (Paris: Hachette, 2003).

22. Benmakhlouf, A., ed. *Routes et déroutes de l'universel* (Rabat: Le Fennec, 1998).

23. Cervantes and Zoraïdé both appear in the essay titled "L'Algérienne fugitive de Don Quichotte," 2005.

24. Djebar, Assia. *Vaste est la prison* (Paris: Albin Michel, 1995) or in English *So Vast the Prison*, transl. Betsey Wing (New York: Seven Stories Press, 2000).

25. Davis, Natalie Zemon. *Trickster Travels. A Sixteenth-Century Muslim between Worlds* (New York: Hill & Wang, 2006).

26. Dakhlia, J. "L'Historien, le philosophe et le politique" in *La Colonisation, la loi et l'histoire*. Liauzu, Cl. and Manceron, G., ed. (Paris: Syllepse, 2006), pp. 145–150.

27. Bertrand, R., op. cit.

28. Castoriadis, C. *Une Société à la dérive. Entretiens et débats, 1974–1997* (Paris: Seuil, 2005).

29. For more precise examples see Jordi, J-J and M. Hamoumou, *Les Harkis, Une mémoire enfouie* (Paris: Autrement, 1999).

30. Deny, J. "Chansons des janissaires turcs d'Alger" (Mélanges René Basset, 1925).

31. Helgason, D. "Historical Narrative as a Collective Therapy: The Case of the Turkish Raid in Iceland," *Scandinavian Journal of History* 22, (1997), pp. 75–289.

~

CHAPTER THREE

Beyond Postcolonialism

Globalization and Postcolonial Minorities in France

Alec G. Hargreaves, Florida State University, Tallahassee

The colonial period was marked by significant population flows from Europe to the overseas empires in America, Africa, Asia, and Oceania together with forced migrations from Africa to the Americas. One of the unexpected consequences of European empires and their dissolution has been a reversal of those original North to South migratory flows. Since the end of empire, there have been growing population flows from South to North, i.e., from formerly colonized territories to Europe, leading to the rise of postcolonial minorities within the heartland of the former colonial powers. Postcolonial migrants and their descendants constitute new minorities in Europe not only in a demographic sense but also in their social, political, and cultural status. Unlike the United States, which from 1965 onwards gave priority to skills-based criteria in selecting migrants, in Europe during the same period the majority of immigrants from former colonies were unskilled and often illiterate. Not surprisingly, the languages they brought with them have generally remained highly marginalized in relation to the national languages of the countries in which they have settled.

Among these culturally hybrid minorities, especially second- and third-generation members born in Europe, the languages of migrants have been steadily displaced by those dominant in their adopted countries. Yet although these minorities have in many ways acculturated to the lands in which they have settled, in majority ethnic eyes they are often perceived as outsiders. In

France, writers originating in former colonies are often classified as "Francophone" rather than "French," even when they are born in France and have French citizenship. As "Francophone" is generally applied to authors who write in French but are perceived as standing outside the national community of France, this label serves in many ways to position minority ethnic writers outside the society in which they live (Hargreaves 1996).[1] Among English-speaking scholars, it is more common to categorize these writers as "postcolonial," thereby highlighting the political dynamic within which their cultural hybridity is imbricated. What both the "Francophone" and the "postcolonial" approaches have in common is the framing of the cultural production of these minorities within an essentially bipolar center-periphery model, positioning them between the cultural heritage of formerly colonized spaces on the one hand and between the national language and dominant culture of the former colonial power on the other. This bilateral model misses out a whole gamut of other cultural forces rooted in spaces which are neither European on the one hand nor African or Asian on the other. The most important of these additional cultural forces are located primarily within what may be broadly called the dynamic of globalization.

Globalization is itself a highly contested term. For some, the phenomena which it denotes are heterogeneous in nature, spreading, for example, different varieties of world Englishes, while others equate globalization with homogenization and more specifically with the global hegemony of the United States, mediated through American English. In France, it is the second view of globalization that predominates, certainly among political elites, who tend to see globalization as U.S. imperialism. In this new historical phase the old colonial powers in Europe, certainly in countries such as France, now often see themselves as the victims of a new imperial power, namely the United States. During the last forty years, extensive efforts have been made by French political elites working in tandem with the Francophonie movement to resist the global domination of English. Those elites have been far less concerned with promoting cultural—and more specifically linguistic—diversity within France. Where language policy within France is concerned, their main preoccupation has been to keep English out rather than to promote internal diversity in the form of immigrant, or for that matter regional, languages.

These ambiguous (some would say hypocritical) aspects of French cultural policy reflect a deep ambiguity in France's position in the global political system since the end of the nation's formal overseas empire. If France is today a postcolonial nation in the sense that it is still struggling to come to terms with the loss of empire, French policy-makers may arguably also be seen as postcolonial in a radically different, if not indeed contrary, sense to the extent that they strive to resist the hegemonic tendencies of the United States within France and across the globe more generally. The official language policies pursued in France have not prevented large parts of the population from embracing very enthusiastically many aspects of Anglophone and more specifically American popular culture. This is true not only of the majority ethnic population but also of the minority ethnic groups originating in former French colonies, the largest of which originate in former French North Africa, i.e., Algeria, Morocco, and Tunisia. It is on the relationship between language policies, minority cultural practices, and globalization that the present chapter focuses with particular reference to North African minorities in France. My analysis is divided into two parts. The first of these examines language policies in France and their implications for postcolonial minorities. The second part of the paper looks at the role Anglophone influences among these minorities.

Language Policies in France

The mid-twentieth century was marked by what, in a memorable phrase, Toynbee called the dwarfing of Europe.[2] There were two main strands in this process: the loss of Europe's overseas empires and the rise of a new world order dominated by the United States and the Soviet Union. A new term, *Superpower*, was coined to reflect this quantum leap in the global status of the United States and the U.S.S.R., superseding an international system long dominated by European states which had been accustomed to thinking of themselves as great powers. Nowhere were these trends resisted more fiercely than in France. While Britain divested herself more or less voluntarily of her empire, beginning with the jewel in the crown, India, in 1947, France engaged in a series of bloody and ultimately futile military campaigns, most notably in Indochina and then in Algeria, in unsuccessful attempts to resist decolonization. Returning to power amid the political turmoil provoked by the Algerian imbroglio, de Gaulle resolved to cut France's losses and liquidate the overseas empire so as to better reassert the national independence and international standing of France in the face of American hegemony. While the nomenclature of empire disappeared, behind the new vocabulary which replaced it—*coopération, Francophonie*, etc.—lay a neocolonial project through which France was to retain considerable visibility and power in formerly colonized regions. At the same time, France pursued a range of policies designed to limit American power. The two strands in this strategy, offensive and defensive, overlapped in the field of language policy.

While the language policies adopted by successive French governments have addressed a number of other matters, including the languages of regional and immigrant minorities, these have always been a secondary consideration compared with the protection of French from American linguistic hegemony and the global promotion of French. These twin imperatives have often been thinly disguised in official discourses, the latest versions of which champion the notion of "diversité culturelle" [cultural diversity]. In February 2003, for example, President Jacques Chirac announced that he would press for the adoption through UNESCO of "une convention mondiale sur la diversité culturelle" [a world convention on cultural diversity].[3] At first sight, it might appear that such a convention would bring benefits to linguistic and other minorities who are currently marginalized or repressed in many countries. Yet far from weakening the power of the state over such minorities, the central feature of Chirac's proposal was the strengthening of the state in the field of culture, above all by permitting national governments to retain protective measures over the circulation of cultural goods and services while liberalizing international trade in other respects. Although the United States was not explicitly mentioned by Chirac, it was abundantly clear in this and other official pronouncements that "la diversité culturelle" was essentially a coded way of referring to the perceived need to resist American cultural hegemony and protect the national culture of France.

Since the establishment of the Haut Comité pour la Défense et l'Expansion de la Langue Française in 1968, there have been countless government initiatives in pursuit of those twin objectives. Framed initially in the context of France and her former colonies, these measures have increasingly included a European dimension, with France pressing her EU partners to back protective trade measures in the field of culture, notably through a system of quotas designed to limit American audio-visual imports. Chirac's proposal for a UNESCO-backed world convention was simply an extension of this policy.

France has been far less active in promoting the languages of regional and immigrant minorities. It was not until 1999 that France signed the Council of Europe Charter for Regional or Minority Languages, which had been drawn up seven years earlier. France's signature was hedged around with important conditions guaranteeing the primacy of the French language, and implementation was to be limited to only selected parts of the Charter. Even this was considered to be a bridge too far by France's Constitutional Council, which ruled that the Charter could not be ratified without a constitutional amendment, which Chirac refused to facilitate. While some of the Charter provisions have been implemented without a constitutional amendment, and the main official body responsible for coordinating language policy, the

Délégation Générale à la Langue Française [General Delegation for the French Language], has been renamed as the Délégation Générale à la Langue Française et aux Langues de France [General Delegation for the French Language and the Languages of France], regional languages in France continue to receive very little state support. According to official statistics, in 1997 less than 3 percent of the nation's children were learning regional languages at school.[4] In the same year, France 3, the principal public channel responsible for regional television broadcasting, aired a total of only 324 hours of programs (less than one hour a day) in regional languages; the rest were in French or foreign (mainly English-language) programs subtitled in French.[5]

At first sight, the languages of immigrants may appear less marginalized. In 1998, almost a fifth of children eligible for lessons in immigrant languages under a program known as Enseignement des langues et cultures d'origine (ELCO) were receiving them. But the numbers were falling. In 2002/2003, only 70,000 schoolchildren were enrolled, compared with 140,000 twenty years earlier. The number of teachers supporting the program had also been halved.[6] Moreover, the French state did not contribute a cent to the cost of these lessons. The ELCO program is paid for entirely by the governments of countries from which migrants come. An important consequence of this is that the languages in the ELCO program are often other than the mother tongues of the children to whom they are taught. This is because the governments concerned are prepared to fund only their official national languages, whereas many migrants and their children speak regional dialects or completely different languages. Thus many children of North African origin learn Berber from their parents, rather than the official language of their home country, Arabic. For them, the ELCO program is in effect an encounter with a foreign language rather than support for their mother tongue. And as the program provides only a few hours of tuition each week, often for only a year or two, the competence acquired by pupils is very limited.

Not surprisingly, French has generally displaced their mother tongue as the principal language of most young people of immigrant origin.[7] Very few are able to read and write in Arabic or Berber, making French the only practical option for those with literary aspirations. Most retain at least fragmentary oral competence in the parental language, which is therefore in principle available to them in cultural forms such as music and film which are less centrally dependent than literature on the written word. A smattering of Arabic and/or Berber is certainly present in the films, songs, and indeed novels produced by second- and third-generation North Africans, popularly known as "Beurs," but except for performers of raï (a popular musical form originating in Algeria) it is rare for them to write and/or perform entire pieces of work in a language other than French. Moreover, borrowings from English are at least as much in evidence as Arabic or Berber and not uncommonly these outweigh the mother tongue. It is to these Anglophone borrowings that I now turn.

Anglophone Influences

The growing influence of cultural forces rooted in the Anglophone world is complicating and eroding some of the basic assumptions which have traditionally structured Francophone studies and their Anglophone counterpart, postcolonial studies. There are of course significant differences between the postcolonial paradigm and the theoretical leanings of *Francophonie*. While students of postcolonialism emphasize disparities of power between (ex-)colonizers and (ex-)colonized, scholars of *Francophonie* are seemingly more concerned with cultural processes. Yet both schools of thought are built on what is a root a bipolar distinction between the colonial center and the colonized periphery. Moreover, "Francophone" cultures have often been analyzed in terms of the political tensions which subtend them, while the cultural politics of postcolonialism have been examined primarily in texts which compete over a shared language, namely English. Within both theoretical approaches, therefore, the relationship between language and power is viewed in terms of a tension between the former colonial center and the periphery, albeit nuanced by varying shades of hybridity. The encroachment into the Francophone space of cultural forces drawn from the Anglophone world complicates and arguably transcends this binary model.

This encroachment has been incremental rather than sudden. The earliest writers of French expression to emerge in the overseas empire were overwhelmingly preoccupied with the cultural and political relationships between colonizer and colonized. For a considerable period after independence, the process of nation-building in the wake of colonial rule provided the dominant framework for Francophone writing. In the later stages of their careers, a number of writers whose formative years were more or less contemporaneous with the process of decolonization expanded their horizons to embrace elements drawn from other cultural spaces, notably those of the Anglophone world. The last major work of the Algerian author Mohammed Dib, published in 2003, was inspired by visits to the United States in the 1970s.[8] Similarly, the works of now canonical Caribbean writers such as Maryse Condé are marked increasingly by processes which have become broadly known as globalization, in which American and other Anglophone influences are prominent.[9]

These trends are stronger still among younger writers originating in former French colonies, especially those born and/or raised by immigrant parents in France. These new generations are distanced both in time and space from the colonial horizons of their parents and grandparents: their formative years came after the end of empire and they were spent in France, rather than in former colonial territories. While they are at one level both Francophone and postcolonial—they are the children or grandchildren of migrants from former colonies and express themselves in French—such labels may be misleading if they are taken to mean that the works of these newer artists are shaped entirely or evenly primarily around the bipolar dynamic which informed the initial waves of Francophone postcolonial writing.

Whereas, among the earliest postcolonial writers of French expression, Anglophone influences were generally a relatively late addition, such influences have been present from the earliest stages of works produced by second-generation members of postcolonial immigrant minorities in France. Azouz Begag and Farida Belghoul, who were among the earliest second-generation Maghrebis ("Beurs") to publish literary narratives, were both influenced by American writers. According to Begag, the first book that moved him to tears was Harriet Beecher Stowe's Uncle Tom's Cabin. The poverty and generosity of the eponymous African American protagonist reminded Begag of his father. And in reading Uncle Tom's Cabin Begag also came to see himself as a person of color, though he already knew that he was both Arab and French.[10] Belghoul's novel Georgette! was inspired by a reading of Invisible Man, by the African American novelist Ralph Ellison.[11] African Americans are by no means the only ethnic group in the United States to interest or influence minority ethnic artists in France. Georgette! contains many references to Native Americans, with whom the narrator-protagonist and her family identify when watching westerns on French TV. Ferudja Kessas's Beur's Story alludes in its title to two American movies, West Side Story and Love Story, the first of which features a love story between a white American male and a young Hispanic woman, while the second features a white American couple whose romance is troubled by class differences.[12] Recent novels by Rachid Djaïdani and Faïza Guène borrow uninhibitedly from virtually every ethnic group in North America, ranging from a white sex-goddess in the center fold of Playboy[13] to African American boxer Carl Lewis,[14] Wonder Woman,[15] and the Hispanic Robin-Hood-style Zorro.[16]

Young Maghrebi writers are by no means alone in borrowing from the Anglophone world in this way. In the late 1970s, one of the first rock bands formed in France by second-generation members of minority ethnic groups performed under the English-language label "Rock Against Police," which was adapted from "Rock Against Racism," a name used at that time in England for antiracist shows given by minority ethnic musicians. In the 1980s, rap music imported from the United States quickly spawned imitations and increasingly distinctive variants produced by groups of mainly minority ethnic youths who, while singing mainly in French, littered their lyrics and stage names with numerous anglicisms. Today they and their successors, combined with burgeoning crossover audiences extending deep into the majority ethnic youth market, have helped to make France the largest producer and consumer of rap outside the United States. American references are equally present in "Beur" cinema. Rachid Bouchareb, one of the first and most successful filmmakers of Maghrebi immigrant origin, has demonstrated a fascination with the United States ever since his first feature-length movie, *Bâton rouge* (1985), in which three young men from the *banlieues* seek a better life in America. Bouchareb would later direct *Poussières de vie* (1995), about abandoned Eurasian children fathered by American soldiers during the Vietnam War, and *Little Senegal* (2001), exploring the experiences of French-speaking Africans living in New York City.

Bearing in mind the fact that most North Africans in France have no ancestral connections with the English-speaking world, their fascination with America is striking. This fascination has two main variants. The first arises from an identification with the Black Atlantic.[17] The other lies in the attractions of what may be broadly called the American Dream. The Black Atlantic symbolizes in part resistance to white domination and stigmatization. The American Dream is more usually associated with majority ethnic, "white" norms. It represents success—most obviously economic—and some would argue that it comes at the price of selling out to a new imperial power, the United States. The temptations of passing for white are openly avowed by the narrator-protagonist in Begag's second novel, *Béni ou le paradis privé*, who endeavors to use an Anglophone-sounding nickname (Béni) to conceal the Maghrebi origins which, when recognized, mark him as ethnically suspect in France.[18] Where an identification with the Black Atlantic may often stand for subversive, oppositional thinking among young North Africans in France, the American Dream represents a kind of escape hatch from the stigmatized status of postcolonial minorities in France to a land of individual opportunity on the other side of the Atlantic. Yet the distinction between these two dimensions of the American experience is less watertight than it may appear at first sight. In their reappropriation of Anglophone cultural spaces, the "Beurs" adapt them to the specificities of their own situation in France. If they identify with African Americans this is not simply because of a shared stigmatized status but above all because African Americans are seen as models of success in countering racism and successfully pressing for inclusion in mainstream society. It should not be forgotten that one of the most eloquent statements of the American Dream was made by an African American, Martin Luther King, in his 1963 speech on the steps of the Lincoln Memorial in Washington.[19] That dream was of the inclusion of previously stigmatized minorities within mainstream society on an equal footing with the majority ethnic population. While some Beur activists have identified with the separatist spirit incarnated in the 1960s by the Black Panthers or more recently by the Nation of Islam, most second-generation North Africans aspire to inclusion within French society rather than separation from it. An American route to incorporation within French society may seem a paradoxical notion. Yet while U.S. global power has engendered deep distrust and resentment among French elites, at a popular level America has long been regarded by many French men and women as the global trendsetter in cultural fashions and the pinnacle of socioeconomic success. In identifying with American models, young North Africans in France have in many ways been sharing in the kinds of aspirations felt by many members of the majority ethnic population. More than anything else, Anglophone popular culture represents for postcolonial minorities in France today the hope of an end to the stigmatization inherited from the colonial period.

Conclusion

A recent novel by Begag, *Le Marteau pique-coeur*, opens with the narrator-protagonist on a lecture tour of the United States, where he finds enthusiastic audiences for his work as a writer and sociologist but has difficulty in reassuring his elderly Algerian parents back in France that they need not fear for him in the land of Uncle Sam:

> je ne savais comment leur expliquer l'Amérique, ni même le sens du mot 'écrivain'. Comment leur parler de géographie alors qu'ils imaginaient le monde comme un segment bordé par Sétif et Lyon?[20]

Begag's remarks typify the ways in which the bipolar world of his immigrant parents—stretched between their native village near the Algerian city of Sétif and their adopted home in the French city of Lyon—has been expanded and reworked by second-generation Maghrebis in ways which were almost literally unimaginable to the older generation. They show that while memories of empires lost remain pertinent to the new generation of writers typified by Begag, they see their future in a more complex, evolving dynamic in which Anglophone dimensions frequently displace and transcend the familiar bipolar frameworks of postcolonialism or *Francophonie*.

Notes

1. Alec G. Hargreaves, "French, Francophone or Maghrebian? Maghrebian Writers in France," in Nicki Hitchcott and Laïla Ibnlfassi (eds.), *African Francophone Writing: A Critical Introduction* (Oxford/Washington, D.C.: Berg, 1996), pp. 33–43.

2. Arnold J. Toynbee, "The Dwarfing of Europe," in *Civilization on Trial* (Oxford University Press: 1948), pp. 97–125.

3. Jacques Chirac, "Eriger la diversité en principe du droit international," in *Le Monde*, 4 February 2003.

4. Luc Bronner, "Moins de 3 percent des élèves pratiqueraient, selon l'éducation nationale," in *Le Monde*, 21 July 1999.

5. Parliamentary statement in *Journal officiel*, Assemblée Nationale, no. 56876, January 2001, p. 1528.

6. Gaye Petek, "Les Elco, entre reconnaissance et marginalisation," in *Hommes et migrations*, no. 1252, November–December 2004, pp. 45–55.

7. Michèle Tribalat, *De l'immigration à l'assimilation: enquête sur les populations d'origine étrangère en France* (Paris: La Découverte, 1996), pp. 188–213.

8. Mohammed Dib, *L.A. Trip: A Novel in Verse*, translated from the French by Paul Vangelisti (Copenhagen and New York: Green Integer, 2003).

9. Nicole J. Simek, "The Past Is Passé: Time and Memory in Maryse Condé's *La Belle Créole*," in Alec G. Hargreaves (ed.), *Memory, Empire and Postcolonialism: Legacies of French Colonialism* (Lanham, MD: Lexington, 2005).

10. Azouz Begag, *Ethnicity and Equality: France in the Balance*, edited and translated by Alec G. Hargreaves (Lincoln: University of Nebraska Press, 2007).

11. Alec G. Hargreaves, *Immigration and Identity in Beur Fiction*, 2nd edition (Oxford/New York: Berg, 1997), pp. 115–17.

12. Ferudja Kessas, *Beur's Story* (Paris: L'Harmattan, 1990).

13. Rachid Djaïdani, *Boumkoeur* (Paris: Seuil, 1999), pp. 52–55.

14. Djaïdani, *Boumkoeur*, p. 57.

15. Faïza Guène, *Kiffe kiffe demain* (Paris: Hachette, 2004), p. 35.

16. Guène, *Kiffe kiffe demain*, p. 37.

17. Paul Gilroy, *The Black Atlantic: Modernity and Double Consciousness* (London: Verso, 1993).

18. Azouz Begag, *Béni ou le paradis privé* (Paris: Seuil, 1989).

19. Describing his dream, King stated: "It is a dream deeply rooted in the American dream." Martin Luther King, Jr: "I have a dream": <http://www.americanrhetoric.com/speeches/mlkihaveadream.htm>.

20. Azouz Begag, *Le Marteau pique-coeur* (Paris: Seuil, 2004), p. 11.

~

CHAPTER FOUR

We, the Virtual Francophone Multitudes?

Neobarbarisms and Microencounters

Mireille Rosello, University of Amsterdam

My point of departure is an observation that I consider as a felicitous problem: the problem is, in itself, a solution. It is, I suggest, becoming more difficult to recognize a clear border between the old "Francophonie" and the new
one(s). Clearly, old patterns survive even their own historical relevance, and
the well-known opposition that Jean-Marc Moura makes between "Francophonie" and Francophonism is far from obsolete. Refining the distinction
between what we perceive as the "French" and the "American" definitions of
"Francophon(i)e," Moura suggests that "Francophonie" is a linguistic community, whereas Francophonism defends the "intérêts économiques et/ou
politiques masqués par la communauté linguistique" (economic or political
interests masked by the linguistic community [Moura 1999, 2]).[1] "Francophonie" and "Francophisme" have always overlapped, but my point today is
that Francophone energies and expressions are evolving and morphing into
new patterns. One of the first and crucial consequences of this change is that
it is even (more) difficult today to draw a clear boundary around the different "disciplines" of Francophonie, by which I mean its political, economic,
or cultural (including literary and cinematographic) manifestations. Consequently, it is increasingly more problematic to distinguish between what
would be a supposedly progressive "Francophonie" that we will wish to support and the more conservative or neoimperial aspects of a "Francophonie"
that we seek to repudiate or at least critique. The blurring of any border area,

however, is not in itself desirable or undesirable and it is not a phenomenon that I intend to celebrate here. Instead, I am suggesting that it is perhaps more and more crucial to be aware of the porosity of our own ethical membranes.

I therefore propose to scrutinize the ways in which we envisage the relationship between the adjective "Francophone" and the noun "un(e) Francophone" (i.e.. a "Francophone" subject, an entity that I here suppose unknown rather than known). I wish to think about the relationship between a given community and a language or between an individual and a language. I do not even want, at this point, to give examples and say that I wish to reassess what we mean when we say "The French" [the people] and French [the language] or even whether phrases such as "The French" or "The Francophones" prescribe communities rather than describe them. I take for granted that the link between the entities that I call here a community and a language is never stable in time and space, although it takes constant efforts to remember that it is not (our amnesia creates a "the French speak French" syndrome). Instead of asking myself "which language do I speak?" (answer: French), I could wonder "*when* do I speak French?" "*with whom* and to what purpose?" "what *type* of French do I speak when and with whom?" Such questions create nodes in a network rather than straightforward links between individuals and an abstract language that has forgotten its connection to politics and history. Multitudes may be replacing communities.[2]

Francophone multitudes are not peoples, nations, or communities. I propose to assume that they *co*-exist even before being capable of demonstrating that they exist. The traces of French left by those multitudes register on new scales that monitor and interpret the chaotic activities of interdisciplinary networks whose nodes and communication protocols are to be explored rather than supposed known. In this article, I propose to look at two specific manifestations of the Francophone multitudes and to describe two of those innumerable nodes and protocols. In the first example, French appears, is heard or read in the vicinity of Internet cafés or of a satellite dish in a country previously colonized by France. In the second example, a different type of French is spoken by subjects whose relationship to France and the Maghreb is complicated by their presence in a third space that exacerbates rather than neutralizes, the potential difficulties of Francophone transactions.

Some of the models or nodes that define the protocols thus created are called "Francophone" but they are not constantly so, they are not systematically so, and they are not always institutional or even institutionizable. And yet, they keep reminding us of old models that are almost impossible to discard although they are very easy to critique, as I propose to demonstrate in the next section of this article.

The Inexistence of a Francophone Federation

Today Francophonie is neither an empire nor a federation. Yet, when I am asked to explain again, for the first time, what the word means, I often find myself falling back on the principle of the world Francophone map. Professors of culture and literature are not the only ones to use maps. During the 2006 "Francofffonies" festival in France, a series of "letters" circulated on the Internet to inform the public about the events were organized in different contexts. In March, a special issue covered the "Salon du livre," focusing on Francophone authors, publishers, and editorial policies. A section was also devoted to L'Organisation Internationale de la Francophonie and the text was accompanied by a familiar map. On this map we see the "états membres (50) et observateurs (13) de l'organisation de la Francophonie." We see large areas of color that stop on the borders of political states.

Whether it is a deliberate message or not, this type of picture invites us to think of the linguistic community as something that can be visualized as a nation. The color code gives us the impression that entire territories share a homogeneous linguistic and cultural practice. But this type of map only represents one form of "Francophonie." In fact, those colored spaces cover (and cover up) extremely fragmented and disjointed usages of what we call "French."

The borders thus drawn lack nuances; they seem to correspond to an imperialistic logic of conquest. Besides, the colors hide the enormous differences that exist within the spaces thus encoded. Sometimes, only a tiny minority of individuals speak "French" in those countries called "Francophone" and where other languages dominate quite clearly. And not only are these territories not homogeneously Francophone spaces but what has happened to "Francophonie" in this postglobalized world and especially in the midst of a European union whose democracies are "in construction" (to adopt Étienne Balibar's phrase [2002]) is radically different from what could have been "Francophonie" when the link was a direct replica or reflection of the colony-métropole axis. Even when current structures of cooperation between countries on the North-South axis are a legacy of the colonial project, even if international relationships remain infected by neocolonial practices, I am willing to claim that we have moved from a postcolonial phase to a postglobalized mentality. Long gone is the time when the only model to be proposed as positive resistance to colonization was for the so-called "évolués" colonized students to congregate in Paris, to share their grievances and hopes in French, and to then disperse again to form, quasi literally, a political and cultural Francophone Diaspora.

Figure 4.1a. L'Organisation International de la Francophonie. Reproduced with permission from Francoffonies/Festival Francophone en France of CULTURESFRANCE.

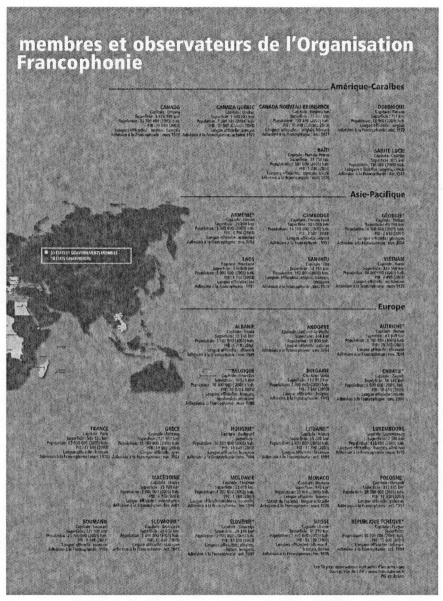

Figure 4.1b. Le Festival Francophone en France. Reproduced with permission from Francoffonies/Festival Francophone en France of CULTURESFRANCE.

In the first half of the twentieth century, this dispersing is perceived as a "return to the native land" not only for Martinican Aimé Césaire who becomes mayor of Fort-de-France and deputy at the French National Assembly, but also for a Senegalese poet who became president of a new independent state. That model is more or less extinct; it no longer functions as a blueprint or mythical model—as it did for Guadeloupean authors such as Maryse Condé, for example. The to-the-metropole-and-back-again narrative coincides with the birth of one very special type of Francophonie: it is often equated with the exalted defense of some transcendental Francophone values that Senghor formulated and promoted. This almost mythical phase has ended and is being replaced by different models.

A recent essay entitled *Demain la Francophonie* symbolizes what I view as the difference between a postcolonial Francophonie and post-globalized Francophone practices. Dominique Wolton, a scholar known for his work on *L'Autre mondialisation* [*The Other Globalization*] claims that it is urgent to reinvent a form of "Francophonie" that correspond to a third stage of globalization (according to him the first wave of globalization is mostly economic and the second one is political). He suggests, for example, that a very specific type of "Francophonie" exists in Europe today, not as a consequence of the colonial past but as a result of the more recent process of Europeanization. He does not deny the significance of colonial ghosts but wishes to take other dimensions into account. For example, he notes that French can no longer be reduced to or exclusively claimed by countries where it happens to be the (or one of the) national languages (France, Belgium, or Switzerland). French, he writes "retrouve les racines en Europe de l'Est et orientale et s'ouvre à la francosphère qui est d'ailleurs une donnée réelle insoupçonnée en France" [rediscovers its East-European and oriental roots and opens itself up to the francosphere which remains a real but unsuspected factor in France] (Wolton 2006, 164). The Francosphere incorporates postcolonial issues of marginality, hybridity, and cultural métissage but also adds to the crucible migrations and practices that will be better described as strange attractors or chaotic rhizomes.

Francophone literatures can no longer be assumed to come "from" countries that constituted the former colonial empire. For example, within the Hexagon, Francophone practices can be Parisian without being French (Parisian Francophones) or Francophone—in the U.S. sense of the term—without ceasing to be Parisian or Hexagonal (Francophone Parisians). In the spring of 2006, during the "salon du livre," books were displayed under labels that proclaimed that something "Francophone" was going on, but flâneurs et flâneuses would have been hard put to formulate in one sentence what all the books shared.

Eloïse Brezault, reflecting the dominant mood, insists on the need to "décloisonner les frontières littéraires" [dismantle literary borders] (Brezault 2006, 8). She speaks highly of the publishing company called "Aube," and more specifically of Marion Hennebert, acquisition editor of the collection "Regards croisés," whose mission is to "héberger des écrivains d'Asie, du Maghreb ou d'Australie, *toutes langues confondues,* comme la Chinoise Francophone Wei-Wei ou le Malgache Jaomanoro, le Marocain Binebine etc." [host writers from Asia, from the Maghreb and Australia, regardless of their language] (Brezault 2006, 8).³ The "confusion" mentioned here evokes a paradoxical Francophone Babel whose hospitality is not even limited to what is written in French.⁴ The image moves away from our usual metaphors of integration or melting pot and it has the advantage of keeping alive the fear of uncontrollable opacity and chaos. It is therefore compatible with, rather than the opposite of, other types of linguistic blending within texts or within languages. Some writings are not only or always Francophone and benefit from the proximity of and encounter with other languages. As Glissant puts it in an article published in *Le Monde des livres* at the time of the "Salon du livre 2006":

Je suis partisan du multilinguisme en écriture, la langue qu'on écrit fréquente toutes les autres. C'est-à-dire que j'écris en présence de toutes les langues du monde. Quand j'écris, j'entends toutes ces langues, y compris celles que je ne comprends pas, simplement par affinité. (Glissant 2006)

I favor multilingualism in writing. The language I write meets all the others. I mean that I write in the presence of all the world languages. When I write, I hear all these languages, included those that I do not understand, simply out of affinity.

Other Francophone trajectories are just as lateral and eccentric vis-à-vis the postcolonial axis. Fouad Laroui lives and works in the Netherlands. As a professor of economy at the Vrij Universiteit in Amsterdam, he neither resides nor works in an officially Francophone country—he does not live in Belgium nor in France for example, but his "Francophone" dimension has to do with the fact that he writes mostly in French (and sometimes in Dutch) and publishes mostly in Paris (but also in Casablanca). Yvonne Philippa, a journalist who writes about his work, declares: "Hij is bijna Franser dan de Fransen" (he is almost more French than the French), an immediately understandable yet problematic reference to the unformulated link between Francophone cultures and Frenchness.⁵

Eduardo Manet, born in Cuba and a resident of France since 1968, would probably be described in a similar way, the double-edged compliment obscuring the differences between the two writers' Francophone practices.[6] On the other hand, it is difficult to pinpoint what type of Francophone Europeanness is inaugurated by authors such Eva Almassy who, after leaving her native Hungary, chose French to write *Tous les jours* (1999) or her recent *Comme deux cerises* (Almassy 2001). A temporary and chaotic Francophone nonterritory is created as these books are displayed on the same Parisian tables or reviewed in the same article in *Le Monde*[7] or discussed on television. The "un livre un jour" FR3 program[8] recently selected the novel *Chercher le vent*, written by a Quebecois author Guillaume Vigneault when the book was republished by Edition Seuil (24 March 2006)[9] and also featured *La Pièce d'or* by Ken Bugul (21 March 2006). Beyond the Hexagon, such programs reach viewers who subscribe to TV5, but also the chaotic community of Internet viewers.

How are these books received or perceived? Few readers will have had the opportunity to become familiar with all the historical frictions and tensions symbolized by some of the writers' migrations. Some will recognize their own heritage in one specific book, others will ignore differences and history altogether. The next generation of Francophone students will inherit a "Francophone culture" that will probably make it impossible to describe them as "Franser dan de Fransen." It is hard to predict what is being taught, to whom, and how and when such events take place, but no matter how we describe the relationship between Manet, Almassy, and French, the old map will not help. Rather than homogeneous and circumscribed territories symbolized by blocks or solid colors, global and local Francophone practices form a multitude of dots with various levels of concentration in several continents or cities.

In other words, just as it is tempting to suggest that Francophone literary and cultural productions (as opposed to strictly French) are in a period of "expansion," the type of expansion I am talking about makes it necessary to withdraw the word, to suggest that the notions of territory and expansion are precisely not so useful anymore. The phenomenon that I am describing desires new paradigms and rejects old ones: for example, the notion of linguistic "community" is not so useful here.[10] What the dots share is that they constitute dynamic moments of Francophone encounters.

Beyond Francophone "Communities"

Renouncing the image of solid patches of color and the assumed cohesion it implies does not force us to abandon the hope that some connections do exist between and within the sixty-three territories, but also opens up the possibility of dreaming up other links even beyond this map (with certain states or regions or cities that do not belong to the official organization) or other dynamic configurations in its midst. There perhaps never was a Francophone "community" that imagined itself as the sum of all the color-coded territories on the map, but it is safe to suggest that even if its existence is conceptualizable in the abstract, it has very little political or cultural significance today because it is in competition with other ways of thinking about the relationship with individuals and the languages they use. If the map now reveals itself as one of the possible metaphorical descriptions of linguistics communities, other images will emerge as alternatives.

For example, the incongruous tree on the poster of the "francoffonies" festival is certainly not more accurate than the map. It is after all easy to critique its ideological implications. Doesn't it place unnecessary emphasis on the importance of a strong and unique Francophone root? If so, doesn't it strangely ignore the importance of Deleuze and Guattari's *Mille Plateaux*, whose denunciation of the values circulated by the myth of the unique root had found a powerful relay in Glissant's reading of their work through his tendency to praise the baroque charms of the rhizome? (Deleuze & Guattari 1980–1987, Glissant 1990–1997a). Or should we, on the other hand, appreciate the performative effect of what could be called an insularization of all these lands? Could this be an example of "archipelic" thinking, a way of imag(in)ing a creolization of the world that would bring us closer to what authors such as Condé and Glissant celebrate (Glissant 1997a&b; Condé 1989a&b). I could ask myself how to interpret the "trunk" of this tree and wonder if any geographical or historical logic is at work here. Must we interpret the colors and the place of each territory within the general picture of the tree? Nothing seems self-evident, and that lack of certainty is probably what is most precious about this representation.

The picture presents itself as a fiction, not as a map that will guide us or a visualization of statistics that will teach us something about history, populations, or demographics. It knows that it is temporary (it will last as long as the francofffonies festival, although this article and the power of the Internet makes even that timing chaotic). It is imaginary, symbolic, and open to criticism or commentary. It is a "pays rêvé," like one of Glissant's poems (Glissant 1985) rather than a Deleuzian tracing faithful to previously drawn maps.[11]

For literary and cultural Francophone analysts, it may even represent that moment where the opposition between the tracing and the map gives way to a new, third logic. Politically, it is hard to instrumentalize except as a critique of the first map (which is what the brochure does by placing them next to each other). The national maps that used to be the only meaningful units are more or less reimported into the tree, so that the legacy of previous references are not discarded but they are also arbitrarily reinserted into an image that

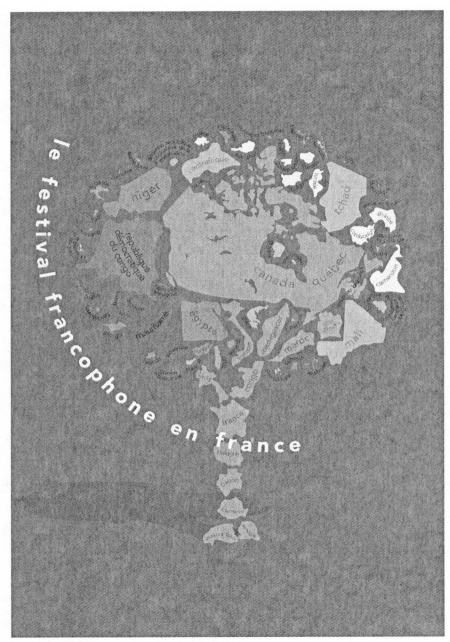

Figure 4.2.

remains both clear and opaque, whose meaningfulness must be invented. The tree fragments the hypothetical community, creates unexpected proximities (France is "north" of Poland, and French Polynesian islands are next to Canada). A new color code replaces the symbolic allusion to nation-states, but the artist has chosen semirealistic hues that are difficult to explain if we do not give up on the national logic. No obvious hierarchy is either inherited or created by this new representation. It makes us imagine the possibility of freeing ourselves from the norm that subordinates the margin to the center, the periphery to Paris. Once the hierarchy is questioned, however, we need not accept the arbitrariness of the new representation as a new discourse of truth: just as Deleuze insists that the rhizome is not to be idealized, the tree is neither here nor there, politically.[12]

One of the advantages of such a potentially disturbing vision is to make us reconsider our assumptions about what a linguistic community is. When we presuppose the existence of a Francophone community, we naturalize the link between a group of speaking subjects and the language that they all share. Pushed to its extreme, this type of thinking leads to the assumption that each nation has a national language and that the "others" speak another tongue that we do not speak or completely understand. This exclusionary logic is what leads Amin Maalouf to oppose the whole notion of "Francophone" authors because it changes a "nous" (the community of people who share the literary use of French) into a "they" (the strangers):

> Car, après tout, qu'est-ce qu'un auteur Francophone? Une personne qui écrit en français. L'évidence . . . du moins en théorie. Car le sens s'est aussitôt per-verti. Il s'est même carrément inversé. "Francophones," en France, aurait dû signifier "nous"; il a fini par signifier "eux," "les autres," "les étrangers," "ceux des anciennes colonies" . . . En ces temps d'égarement où les identités se raidis-sent et où l'universalisme est en perpétuelle régression, les vieux réflexes sont revenus. (Maalouf 2006)

> After all, what is a Francophone writer? A person who writes in French. This seems obvious, at least in theory. For the meaning of the word was immediately distorted and even turned around. "Francophone" should mean "us" and it now means "them," others," "strangers," "those who come from the colonises" . . . In our troubled times when identities rigidify and when universalism regresses, old reflexes reappear.

Maalouf's point is that, within France, it may be strategically desirable not to remember which (national or ethnic) identity hides, so to speak, under the use of French as a literary language. But why would remembering where

Cioran or Apollinaire come from be a discriminatory gesture as long as they continue to be taught?

And doesn't the picture change radically if we do not imagine ourselves based in France? Maalouf writes:

> Réservons les vocables de "Francophonie" et de "Francophone" à la sphère diplomatique et géopolitique, et prenons l'habitude de dire "écrivains de langue française," en évitant de fouiller leurs papiers, leurs bagages, leurs prénoms ou leur peau!

> Let us reserve "Francophone" and "Francophonie" for the diplomatic and geopolitical spheres and let us refer to "writers of French expression" in order to avoid searching through their identification papers, their suitcases, their first names or their skin color. (Maalouf 2006)

But to the extent that the border between a "diplomatic" use and a "literary" recognition of "Francophonie" has always been porous, isn't the legitimate desire to leave "murderous identities" (Maalouf 1998) aside an invitation to reuniversalize a unique French language and to naturalize the definition of a linguistic community?

I propose to move away from a literary and integrated Francophone community, even if it tries to be hospitable and nondiscriminatory. The francoff-fonie tree makes me imagine a series of networks where connections are switched on and off, moments of imbrications that are not constant or always collective. The notion of a linguistic community itself, a concept that the notion of a "Francophonie" needs in order to be understandable, might be in the process of losing its immediate relevance. New paradigms about non-communities are emerging, and it is no coincidence that theorists who explore such patterns are present at this conference. The two case studies of noncommunity-based Francophone encounters, those chaotic Francophone imbrications that I would like to observe in the final sections of this article, are indebted to the models explored in Jocelyne Dakhlia's *Islamicités* (Dakhlia 2005) and in Jean-Loup Amselle's *Branchements* (Amselle 2001).

Francophone Internet and Satellite Connections

The first example recognizes the existence of a virtual and electronic Francophone flow that does not and will not add up as to form a "people." There are no "people of the dish," as least politically or culturally. The people of the dish do not say "we"; it has no collective rights and no duties other than those dictated by individual ethical rules. But this Francophone nonpeople manifests itself: it is a fragmented noncommunity, that shares neither space nor time but connects via Francophone dishes and Internet nodes. The issues raised by such connections affect Francophonie both at the transnational and microlocal levels. In the article published in the recent *Columbia History of Twentieth-Century French Thought*, Christopher Miller suggests, for example, that satellite television may be one of the most recent avatars of the type of Francophonie that Senghor dreamed about: a "spiritual community, a noosphere (sphere of the spirit) around the earth" (Miller 2005, 237). Noticing that Senghor's dream never came true, Miller adds: "the practical (or vulgar) realization of Senghor's noosphere would have to be TV5, which beams a new Francophone culture around the world; but that it is certainly not what he had in mind" (237).

As Miller would be the first to acknowledge, the unexpected realization of an Internet noosphere does not simply replace Senghor's idealized linguistic supranation with a more "vulgar" community. The way in which Francophone networks are organized on the Internet or via satellite media has a radical effect on the definition of Francophonie. So-called Francophone audiences are radically different if they watch TF1 or TV5 in a village in Algeria or in an American campus whose language lab uses the programs as a language acquisition tool. The same "French" news, songs, or films circulate on the Internet thanks to sites that anyone can visit, but the possibility of universal connections does not create a homogeneous network: each node, each "branchement," depends on local and global mediations, equipment, or cultural rules. It is not enough to "have" a dish or a computer since the principles of "owning" and of "access" sometimes depend on local narratives and linguistic usage.

I am thinking here about the research carried out by Ratiba Hadj-Moussa in the Maghreb and specifically in Algeria: the sociologist analyzed how the presence of a satellite dish reorganizes the traditional opposition between inside and outside; men and women (Hadj-Moussa 2003, 457). New temporary communities were created by the way in which cultural norms appropriate satellite television and locally regulates its use.

In that context, a distinction emerges between Francophone and Arab-speaking channels. We may assume that Francophone viewers will watch Francophone channels and that Arabophones will opt for Arab-speaking channels, but in this case, a "Francophone" choice does not depend exclusively on issues of linguistic ability: that category intersects with gender and timing instead. Depending on whether men or women are watching television separately or together (i.e., according to a temporal sequencing that does not necessarily reflect the grid imagined by professionals), viewers will either watch or avoid Francophone channels, regardless of what is on. Here, "Francophone" is a short cut for "possibly disturbing images": a Francophone channel exposes the spectator to pictures that might cause shame and guilt if they are watched in public. Without generalizing (and therefore stereotyping) such practices, we may at least recognize that Francophone channels fragment communities along lines completely unpredicted by the industry. A viewer will choose to avoid being perceived as part of the Francophone linguistic community when the connection risks offending a culturally encoded sense of propriety. Here, Francophone means Western rather than French. On the other hand, Hadj-Moussa notes that news programs are watched according to interpretive grids that are much close to postcolonial logics: Algerians hope to be represented in favorable ways and their expectation is constantly frustrated (Hadj-Moussa, 459).

Francophone Microencounters: Barbaric Narratives

My final example has to do with what I call here "barbaric French": barbaric French is a site or a node rather than a language. It usually is a quasi-microscopic and ignored moment of encounter. It is a set of uncharted, unmapped, both local and global micronarratives that proliferate, replacing the grand narratives whose collapse was, at least according to Jean-François Lyotard, the mark of our postmodern condition (Lyotard 1979). These often-microscopic Francophone connections do not add up to form communities but remain Francophone moments. They are neither necessarily literary, nor even scripted, which means that they will not find their way into books, anthologies, or even maps. They have probably always existed, and we can only take them into account if we direct our attention to what goes on under the Francophone diplomatic or even cultural radar. Strangely enough, the fact that English is used in impoverished and simplified ways throughout the planet is often seen as evidence of the language global dominance. But just as we could identify Anglophone moments whenever an exchange in "globish" or "binglish" occurs in a train, an airport, or a meeting room, similar Francophone moments regularly take place in the street of European cities. The fact that they are not recorded does not stop them from being successful connections, even if they are often ephemeral and imperfect. They plug in [branchent] individuals in ways that are as unpredictable as the results of creolization processes. Sometimes, subjects who have learned French on each side of the colonial borders find themselves in a third space, in the midst of a chaotically enlarging Europe, and new bizarre connections occur between them.

When I first arrived in Amsterdam, I once lost my way and tried to ask for directions. Two connections with friendly strangers aborted prematurely.

They were obviously eager to help, but the few Dutch words that I had carefully lined up were met, the first time, by a sentence in Russian, the second time, by a language that I did not identify. The third attempt, however, led to what I am calling here a Francophone moment and also a barbaric encounter. Identifying through the few words that I had hopelessly mispronounced, an accent whose exact nature remains a mystery to me, the woman I had approached switched to French: "Ti parles français ma fille? J'y parle un peu, dis-moi qu'est-ce que ji peux faire pour toi?"

To claim that I felt "at home" for the first time in weeks would be an insult to the hospitality of the country and to all the Dutch friends and colleagues who went out of their way to welcome me. But the sense of at-home-ness that was created by this unexpected connection, this special use of a type of French I am so intimately familiar with, had nothing to do with professional or personal relationships. It was not created by a tracing or "calque" (Holland is not on the first map we looked at, and the presence of French was not due to the fact that I had, somehow, "gone back" to my native land). The Francophone moment had to do, but in indirect and chaotic ways, both with former colonial axes but also with recent trans-European and transcontinental migrations. Later, once I reached the house of the colleague who had invited us, I found out that I had lost my way in the housing project where the murderer of filmmaker Theo Van Gogh used to live. I was not sure how to connect this piece of information to the messy network of knowns and unknowns that the world had become but it certainly made me appreciate the fact that the "at homeness" that I had just identified was precisely not to be imagined as a safe haven protected by impenetrable barriers. Home is not surrounded by borders capable of keeping violence at bay; home does not isolate us from unresolved conflicts by pushing them far away in a territorial other where people are strangers who speak other languages. It has never been, but it is now harder to forget.

Conclusion

If I wish, or dare, to call this most pleasant, almost tender encounter "barbaric," it is both to accept whatever stigma others will chose to attach to barbarians, Berbers, and others but also to claim and reappropriate barbarianness as a theoretical tool. Barbarianness is the name here given, not to the barbarian's assumed nature but to the act of interpretation chosen, by default by the powerful who only hears noise instead of a language.[13] Incapable of appreciating his or her ignorance, the barbarian subject who ignores him or herself as such declares the other barbaric. In French, a "barbarisme" is not only a display of barbarity but also a word that does not exist, that someone invents, supposedly without being aware of inventing. This making do, which compensates the absence of proper words is also an imaginative production that remains unrecognized as such. It is treated as an error, the signature of the ignorant barbarian. The dominant's "barbarism" has a different name: it is called a "neologism," a verbal invention acknowledged as a (hu)man-made creation, the emergence of a new logos and perhaps logic (also needed to supplement the absence of a proper word but this time, a language rather than a subject, is deemed lacking). I wonder if the subjects who choose to identify a "barbarism" are not imposing a border between neologism and barbarism that is due to their own barbarianness. When I do not recognize or understand the other's language, all I hear is a string of barbarisms (Rancière 1995, 79). Yet, the opposition between a neologism and a barbarism is likely to be troubled by any Bourdieusian approach, any analysis capable of pointing out that the status of barbarism is a question of distinction, that it also depends on the habitus and socioeconomic parameters (Bourdieu 2002). As Glissant suggests, as if in response to Kristeva's allusion to the "barbarophone's" lack of language:

> Mais ce que vous appelez la barbarie est le mouvement inépuisable des scintillations de langues qui charroient scories et inventions, dominations et accords, silences mortels et explosions irrépressibles. Ces langues s'allient, varient, s'opposent tellement vite que les longs apprentissages d'antan n'y valent plus. (Glissant 115)

> But what you would call barbarism is the inexhaustible motion of the scintillations of languages, heaving dross and inventions, dominations and accords, deathly silences and irrepressible explosions, along with them. These languages combine, vary, clash, so rapidly that the lengthy training of earlier times is no longer worth much. (Glissant 115)

Incongruous Francophone trees are also barbaric if we read them as an invitation to create new chaotic connections and nodes. They help us describe the new forms of contemporary Francophone practices by focusing on moments of encounters rather than on preestablished canons and anthologies. It is no longer in the name of universalism (a model where the subject-citizen is expected to conform to a unique model of Sameness) that researchers now insist on the impossibility to surround cultures with borders. When Dakhlia refutes the idea of an exchange between French and Arabic cultures, it is not a regressive move toward some sort of essentialism or relegation but an attempt to think in terms of imbrications and connections rather than in terms of maps and tracing.

Barbaric encounters redefine what it means to "belong" to a linguistic so-called community; it questions the definition of proper usage and the way in which we acquire language proficiency. Even the distinction between poetry and theory breaks down in Glissant's text whose lyrical barbarism rewrites what it means to be a barbarian. When Chouaki writes: "Photos fieilles roussies sépia par tant temps que oh saveur heureuse de déjà rienque" (Chouaki 1988, 9) his French is as barbaric as the encounter with the woman in Amsterdam. A barbaric encounter occurs when the subjects who come to-gether all know that they are the other's barbarians. In other words, there is not just one dominant language and one barbaric or substandard language. This is not to claim that all barbarisms are poetry and all substandard use of any language is to be promoted and naively idealized. Not all barbaric en-counters produce literature, or freedom of expression. A Francophone bar-baric encounter is the name of a node in a network, the moment when mi-croconnections are attempted and result in unpredictable productions: sometimes felicitous poetic texts, sometimes poor translations and fruitful or disastrous misunderstandings. A tentative Francophone logos expresses its desire to reach out not so much in spite of, but as bad grammar, bad register, bad word choice.

Notes

1. The opposition is that it does not overlap with a more familiar binary pair that also reflects the ambivalence of the word "Francophone." In the States, the distinc-tion between Francophone studies and "Francophonie" (the French word) privileges the former. Francophone studies go beyond the narrow national conception of "French" cultures and implicitly criticize linguistic and cultural policies that flirt with neocolonialism. Moura clearly favors a noncolonial Francophone approach, but his argument makes it clear that both Francophonie and Francophone literatures and cultures (to adopt the MLA label) have overt political implications, and that some are more conservative than others.

2. I am borrowing the vocabulary of Antonio Negri and Michael Hardt (2004), al-though the "new barbarian" that appears in *Empire* (Hardt and Negri 2001) is not the model "barbarianness" I explore in the rest of this article.

3. Sur Wei-Wei, voir le texte de Claire Devarrieux, "Comment Wei-Wei déplaça des mantages" dans *Libération*, 3 mars 2006, <http://www.liberation.fr/page.php? Article=363746>

4. What Assia Djebar would call "Francographie" rather than "Francophonie" (Djebar 1999, 29).

5. See <http://www.philippa.nl/Boeken/boek7.htm> (4 August 2006). Laroui's first novel, *Les Dents du Topographe*, was published both in Paris and in Casablanca

in 1997. *Les Chroniques des temps déraisonnables* also appears in Morocco in 2003 as well as a book for children, *La Meilleure façon d'attraper les choses* (2001).

6. Manet's revolutionary past is comparable to Laroui's critique of his native Morocco but "comparable" here means precisely that the differences between the two trajectories should be highlighted rather than forgotten. For a bio-bibliography of Manet see <http://www.evene.fr/celebre/biographie/eduardo-manet-6145.php> (24 March 2006). See also an article published in *Le Monde* (17 March 2006): Manet's answer to the question "Why do you write in French?" is "always the same": "une histoire d'amour ne s'explique pas. Ce n'est pas une boutade. C'est parce que j'aime cette langue que j'essaie de m'exprimer du mieux possible en français" [You can't explain a love story. This is not a joke. I love this language which is why I try to express myself the best I can in French].

7. *Le Monde*, Friday, 17 March 2006 (Special issue on "salon du livre 2006"). Nine authors answer the question "Quel français écrivez-vous?" ["What type of French do you write"] (p. 2).

8. The program runs from Monday through Friday at 6 p.m. See: <http://unliv reunjour.france3.fr/?fichesEmissions=/france3.fr/programmes/unlivreunjour/archives/ 19236881-fr.php> (7 August 2006).

9. See Perrine Parageau's book review (published in *Lire* in March 2006): <http://www.lire.fr/critique.asp?idC=49706/idR=218/idG=3> (6 August 2006).

10. Unless we adopt Lingis's paradoxical vision of communities that have nothing in common (Lingis 2004).

11. If we follow the Deleuzian distinction between the tracing and the map, the Francophone federation is a tracing that simply follows previously cartographied national borders at the very moment when globalization and Europeanization are redrawing those boundaries. In *Demain la Francophonie*, Dominique Wolton suggest that somes types of Francophonie are "ringardes" [obsolete] (15) because they reduce the Francophone community to a "petit bunker linguistique" [tiny linguistic bunker] (15) or a "ligne Maginot" (15). His images evoke wars but also the pathetic ineffectiveness of those barriers that both define and protect an illusory inside.

12. "The rhizome includes the best and the worst: potato and couch grass, or the weed." (Deleuze & Guattari 1987, 6–7).

13. See Kristeva's *Etrangers à nous-mêmes* ("Homère appliquait le mot de 'barbarophone' aux indigènes d'Asie Mineure combattant avec les Grecs, et semble avoir forgé le terme à partir d'onomatopées imitatives: bla-bla, bara-bara, bredouillis inarticulés ou incompréhensibles" [Kristeva 1988, 75]).

Works Cited

"Un livre un jour," France 3/ directed by Olivier Barrot, Michel Bastian, François Chayé, Fabrice Ferrari, Michaël Midoun. Editor in chief: Sandrine Treiner. See: <http://unlivreunjour.france3.fr/?fichesEmissions=/france3.fr/programmes/unliv reunjour/archives/19236881-fr.php> (6 August 2006).

Almassy, Eva. *Tous les jours*. Paris: Gallimard, 1999.

———. *Comme deux cerises*. Paris: Stock, 2001.

Amselle, Jean-Loup. *Branchements: Anthropologie de l'universalité des cultures*. Paris: Flammarion, 2001.

Balibar, Étienne. *Nous, Citoyens d'Europe? Les Frontières, l'État, le peuple*. Paris: La Découverte, 2001.

———. *We, the People of Europe? Reflections on Transnational Citizenship*. Trans. James Swenson. Princeton University Press, 2004.

Bourdieu, Pierre. *Distinction: A Social Critique of the Judgment of Taste*. Trans. Richard Nice. Cambridge: Harvard University Press, 2002.

Brezault, Eloïse. "Visages Francophones dans l'édition française," *Lettre du Bureau International de l'édition française*, 8 March 2006, 7–8.

Chouaki, Aziz. *Baya*. Alger: Laphomic, 1988.

Condé, Maryse. *La Traversée de la Mangrove*. Paris: Mercure de France, 1989a.

———. "Habiter ce pays, la Guadeloupe." *Chemins critiques* 1.3 (1989b): 5–13.

Dakhlia, Jocelyne. *Islamicités*. Paris: PUF, 2005.

Deleuze, Gilles and Felix Guattari. *A Thousand Plateaus*. Trans. Brian Massumi. Minneapolis: University of Minnesota Press, 1987 (originally published as *Mille Plateaux*. Paris: Minuit, 1980).

Djebar, Assia. *Ces voix qui m'assiègent en marge de ma Francophonie*. Paris: Albin Michel, 1999.

Glissant, Edouard. *Poetics of Relation*. Trans Betsy Wing. Ann Arbor: University of Michigan Press, 1997a (originally published *Poétique de la Relation*. Paris: Gallimard, 1990).

———. *Traité du Tout-Monde*. Paris: Gallimard, 1997b.

———. "La langue qu'on écrit fréquente toutes les autres," *Le Monde des livres*, 16 March 2006, 16.03.06 <http://www.lemonde.fr/web/article/0,1-0@2-3260, 36-751247,0.html > (4 August 2006).

Hadj-Moussa, Ratiba. "New Media, Community and Politics in Algeria," *Media Culture and Society*. 25.4 (2003): 451–68.

———. *Multitude, War and Democracy in the Time of Empire*. London: Penguin 2004.

Kristeva, Julia. *Etrangers à nous-mêmes*. Paris: Fayard, 1988.

Laroui, Fouad. *Les Dents du topographe*. Paris: Julliard, 1996, Casablanca: Eddif, 1997.

———. *De quel amour blessé*. Paris: Julliard, 1998.

———. *Méfiez-vous des parachutistes*. Paris: Julliard, 1999.

———. *La Meilleure façon d'attraper les choses*. Rabat: Yomad, 2001.

———. *Le Maboul*. Nouvelles. Paris: Julliard, 2001.

———. *Chroniques des temps déraisonnables*. Casablanca: Tarik éditions-Paris: Emina Soleil, 2003a.

———. *La Fin tragique de Philomène Tralala*. Paris: Julliard, 2003b.

———. *Tu n'as rien compris à Hassan II*. Nouvelles, Paris: Julliard, 2004.

Lingis, Alphonso. *The Community of Those who Have Nothing in Common*. Bloomington: Indiana University Press, 1994.

Lyotard, Jean-François. *La Condition postmoderne*. Paris: Minuit, 1979.

Maalouf, Amin. *Les Identités meutrières*. Paris: Grasset, 1998.

———. "Contre la littérature Francophone," *Monde des livres*, 10 March 2006 <http: www.lemonde.fr> (4 August 2006).

Manet, Eduardo. *La Sagesse du singe*. Paris: Grasset, 2001.

———. *Mes années Cuba*. Paris: Grasset, 2004.

Miller, Christopher. "Francophonie," *Columbia History of Twentieth-Century French Thought*. Ed. Lawrence Kritzman. New York: Columbia University Press, 2005, 235–238.

Moura, Jean-Marc. *Littératures francophones et théorie postcoloniale*. Paris: PUF, 1999.

Negri, Antonio and Michael Hardt. *Empire*. Cambridge: Harvard University Press, 2001.

Rancière, Jacques. *La Mésentente: politique et philosophie*. Paris: Galilée, 1995.

Vigneault, Guillaume. *Chercher le vent*. Paris: Seuil, 2006. (originally published by Boréal in 2001, 2nd edition Balland, 2002).

Wei-Wei. *Fleurs de Chine*. Paris: Aube, 2001.

———. *Une fille Zhuang*. Paris: Aube, 2006.

Wolton, Dominique. *Demain la Francophonie*. Paris: Flammarion, 2006.

CHAPTER FIVE

~

"No Green Pastures"

The African Americanization of France[1]

Tyler Stovall, University of California at Berkeley

In 1951 the African American journalist Roi Ottley published a book, *No Green Pastures*, which stands as a landmark text in the history and historiography of the African Diaspora. In this book Ottley explored the lives of blacks and other minorities in a wide variety of countries. He concluded from this survey that no country he had visited was free of racism, that, in contrast to the perspective of many African American intellectuals upon life abroad, exile abroad offered "no green pastures," no escape from the vicissitudes of bigotry so familiar to blacks in the United States.[2]

For those interested in the state of modern France, Ottley's book seems particularly relevant after the widespread uprisings that struck French suburbia in the fall of 2005. French people have long cherished an image of themselves as a nation free from racial prejudice, a color-blind society *par excellence*. A crucial part of France's republican heritage from the great Revolution, the idea that all citizens were equal both juridically and socially has constituted a key aspect of what it means to be French in the modern era. Racial identities and conflicts might trouble other, less happy, lands, but they had no place in French life.[3] The riots of November 2005 frontally challenged this cozy consensus. The specter of thousands of young people of color burning cars, attacking schools, and in general giving violent expression to their fundamental alienation from French society made it a lot more difficult to claim that race had no place in France. By forcing the nation to confront the conditions of its marginalized postcolonial suburban belt, the uprisings of the fall of 2005 underscored a new vision of France, one in which colonial legacies and racial difference constituted the heart of national identity.[4]

November 2005 had a particular significance for the place of black Americans in French life and culture. During the course of the last century, blacks from the United States have played a complex series of roles in France's racial imaginary. African American expatriates in Paris in particular have often been held up as proof of French tolerance and rejection of racism, especially in comparison to American bigotry. At the same time, postcolonial communities and cultures in contemporary France have borrowed freely from black American cultural models, most notably hip-hop music but also including cinema, dance, and language (for example, the widespread use of the English-language term "black").[5] When the youth of the *banlieues* rose up in revolt during the fall of 2005 commentators on both sides of the Atlantic compared these events to race riots in America, especially those that struck Los Angeles in 1992. An eminently plastic symbol, the African American could represent both color-blind France and the agonies of the postcolonial republic at the same time.[6]

Given this contrast, what do French views of black Americans reveal about their own racial history and contemporary condition? How do the glamorous tales of famous expatriates like Josephine Baker and Richard Wright speak to the gritty realities of crumbling *HLMs*, police harassment, and job discrimination on the outskirts of Paris and other French cities?[7] Could it be that African Americans who come to Paris today in search of the legendary color-blind paradise might only find a world very similar to the one they left behind? Such questions, which concern the global nature of both race in general and black American culture in particular, prompted me to attempt a comparative overview of the black histories of both the United States and France. In doing so, I will pursue two primary themes. The first is that since the mid-twentieth century there has been a certain convergence between the black lives of the two nations. Another way of considering this is the idea that the communities of blacks in France have moved from resembling the life of African American expatriates to a greater similarity to black life back at home in the United States. This convergence has not been one-dimensional, since aspects of African American life have also come to resemble more closely the condition of blacks in France. Finally, I will briefly compare black America and France as a whole. Comparisons between France and America, the two great modern republics, are legion. My specific purpose here is to consider the ways in which contemporary France in general, not just its peoples of color, has manifested traits reminiscent of the black American experience.

This contrast between upscale and ghetto-centric French images of black American life has existed for over a generation, yet the events of November 2005 underscored it graphically. They not only suggested the truth of Roi Ottley's conclusion half a century earlier but also at the same time emphasized the staying power of the African American as an iconic figure in French life. In both regards, they indicate new dimensions of the relationship between blackness and French identity at the dawn of the twenty-first century.

Intersecting Histories

Comparing the black histories of France and the United States is a bit like trying to ally a mouse with an elephant. Not only has metropolitan France historically had a much smaller population of African descent than the United States but also African Americans have generally received much more popular and scholarly attention than their counterparts across the Atlantic.[8] In spite of this major difference of scale, however, the two diasporas do share many traits in common, as well as some important differences.

At the heart of the histories of both black France and black America stands the trans-Atlantic slave trade and the slave societies it produced. Both France and the United States not only practiced slavery but also share conflicted histories that placed into dialogue slavery and republicanism. Since both nations have frequently viewed themselves as beacons of liberty to the world as a whole, this contrast between freedom and slavery goes to the heart of what is has meant to be French and American in the modern era. For France, the political form of the republic has constituted the historical demarcation between absolutist slavery and modern freedom. The nation's two abolitions of slavery, in 1794 and 1848, were both carried out by insurgent republics, and the rebel slaves of Saint-Domingue fought for the republic and liberty against the forces of Napoleon, whose imperial regime had restored slavery in the French Caribbean.[9] Unlike France, the United States has a history as a slave republic, creating a strangely hybrid polity in the antebellum era whose contradictions were only resolved by the Civil War.[10]

The slave heritage of both nations also included the division of the national territory into slave and free zones, a division enshrined in legal theory yet ultimately malleable in practice. Both metropolitan France and the American North increasingly defined themselves as lands of liberty, but the same flag that flew over them also flew over slave territories. This has often been interpreted as a major distinction between the two nations' black histories: whereas the United States had a large population of African descent on its national soil, in France slavery was reserved for the colonies in the modern era.[11] Yet if we think of France and its colonies as one integral unit, or alternately view the antebellum U.S. South as a kind of semicolonial periphery, this difference largely disappears. Or to put it another way, slave and free territories were divided by the Mason-Dixon line in America, by the Atlantic Ocean in France.

A much more salient contrast between the black histories of France and of America is the role of nonslave African migrants. Until very recently, virtually all blacks in the United States descended from slaves brought to the New World as a part of the Middle Passage, either those brought directly to America or migrants from the Caribbean with their own heritage of slavery. The United States never had any African colonies or significant involvement in the affairs of that continent. Africa and African migrants have played a much more prominent role in black life in France. Thanks in part to its belated efforts to stamp out the slave trade, France established a huge formal empire in sub-Saharan Africa in the late nineteenth century. Even after the rapid decolonization of the 1960s, France retains a significant political, cultural, and military influence in Francophone Africa. One consequence of this has been a sizeable African migration to France, starting with the *tirailleurs sénégalais* of the First World War and becoming a mass phenomenon after 1945. Whereas the American black population has been almost entirely a product of the Atlantic diaspora, that of France is divided between descendents of Caribbean slaves and African immigrants. Among other things, this distinction has made it much harder to speak of a single black "community" in France than in America, and even to a certain extent called into question the idea of blackness itself as a social identity.[12]

If the heritage of slavery both unites and differentiates the history of black America and black France, so does the postslave period. Emancipation was an incomplete affair in both the French Caribbean and the American South. In both cases the former slave-holding elites managed to retain decisive political and economic power and to preserve the plantation system of agricultural production. Crucially, in both cases postemancipation regimes refused to break up the plantations and distribute the land to the former slaves, ensuring the continuation of poverty and powerlessness whose legacy remains with both nations to this day. Although both black Americans and blacks in the French Caribbean became citizens after emancipation, their citizenship was in many ways in name only.[13]

The late nineteenth century also witnessed the rise of racialized versions of democracy and imperial expansion in both France and the United States.

American scholars of whiteness have demonstrated how increasingly in the 1800s democracy and liberty were racially coded so that white racial status became an essential requirement for full citizenship. The massive waves of immigration from Europe that peopled nineteenth-century America gradually forced an expansion of the nation's democratic polity, but only to the extent that the new immigrants could claim to be white, and their claims rested above all on establishing distinctions between themselves and peoples of color in general, blacks in particular.[14] In France the achievement of universal manhood suffrage under the Third Republic went hand in hand with the creation of a new republican empire based upon the principles of assimilation and universalism.

Both the United States and France, and essentially those two countries alone, became imperial republics by 1900. Empires without an empress or emperor, this strange and contradictory political formation rested upon racial distinctions. In both countries a nation of citizens ruled over an empire of subjects, and in both the citizens were mostly white, the subjects mostly black and brown.[15] The black citizens of America and France occupied a paradoxical position in these racial empires: largely deprived of democratic rights at home, they were often used as soldiers of empire abroad. France made widespread use of Caribbean soldiers and administrators in Africa, and America used blacks both in the conquest of the Indians in the West and in imperial campaigns in Cuba and the Philippines.[16]

Perhaps the most salient difference between black America and black France in the postemancipation era concerned the level of violence directed against the former slaves. Whereas the brutality of France's slave colonies in the Caribbean was unparalleled, after 1848 the French Caribbean did not know the level of violence experienced by the blacks of the American South. The post-Reconstruction governments of the South were established by and survived thanks to a veritable reign of racial terror, symbolized by the Ku Klux Klan and other white vigilante organizations.[17] Since in the French Caribbean blacks represented the overwhelming majority of the population, whites could not successfully undertake the kinds of lynching, beatings, and wholesale assaults on entire black communities that became a regular feature of life in the American South after the Civil War. The minority status of African Americans was reinforced by a greater level of social isolation than in France. The successful imposition of rigid racial categorizations, notably the famous "one-drop" rule, which made anyone with any discernable African ancestry at all officially black, emphasized the harsh, immutable distinction between whites and blacks in American society, rendering theoretically impossible the kind of *métissage* which created a much more creolized black population in France and its empire.[18]

One potent reaction of blacks to the perils and disappointments of post-emancipation society in both America and France was migration. In both cases, however, this took the form primarily not of exile from their country of origin altogether, but rather a move within the nation from formerly slave to traditionally free territories. In the United States the first great black migration brought hundreds of thousands of African Americans from the South to the North, establishing large new black communities in cities like New York and Chicago. These migrants produced a vibrant black urban culture, one that reached its apogee with the Harlem Renaissance and shaped seminal musical forms like jazz and blues.[19] French blacks also migrated to the metropolis in the early twentieth century, if not in such large numbers. For many Caribbean blacks in particular, the metropolis represented the "good" France of republicanism and emancipation, as opposed to the "bad" France of the white plantation owners and colonial administration.[20]

World War I played a central role in both types of migration. The needs of the American war economy and the temporary cessation of immigration from Europe opened up jobs in the North for American blacks.[21] In France the desperate need for both military and industrial manpower led the government to enlist African and Caribbean soldiers to fight in the European war, bringing to the metropolis the first mass population of color in French history.[22] The *tirailleurs sénégalais* in particular had a major impact on French views of blacks and of Africa, as the history of the famous Banania ads showed. Modern warfare required the social and economic mobilization of all sectors of the national population, and the ideology of the war portrayed it as a struggle for liberty and popular sovereignty. In promoting black migration from black colonies and former slave states to the heart of national territory, the Great War undermined the distinction between these different regions. Although not fully realized until after 1945, the roots of the postcolonial era in France, and of the civil rights movement in America, go back to the First World War.

World War I also brought the first significant African American migration to France, a movement that embodied different aspects of the histories of both black France and black America, and put the two black cultures into dialogue. Although blacks had traveled from the United States to France since the eighteenth century, World War I marked the first time that a critical mass of African Americans settled there, establishing a permanent black community. The war itself brought 200,000 black soldiers and laborers to France from America, and also powerfully reinforced the perception of the

French as a people without color prejudice, in stark contrast to white Americans. The interwar taste for exoticism and black culture, plus the popularity of jazz, made Paris in particular a center for hundreds of African American performers, artists, and writers. Josephine Baker's triumphal Parisian debut with the *Revue nègre* in 1925 cemented the idea of France as a land open to black talent.[23]

This rosy portrait of African American life in Paris contrasted sharply, of course, with the experiences of most French blacks. Like African Americans, many French Caribbean and African soldiers returned home after the war demanding full citizenship, only to be disappointed by the durability of the colonial order of racial inequality. In Francophone Africa, the new emphasis on the economic development of the colonies led to a massive increase in forced labor, often under brutally exploitative conditions. While blacks in the French Caribbean and Africa did not suffer the kind of violence that afflicted American blacks during the race riots of the 1919 "Red Summer," neither did they achieve full acceptance as French citizens during the years after World War I.[24]

The experience of French blacks in the metropolis, like that of African Americans in Paris, constituted a partial exception to this rule. Although many of these blacks were unskilled laborers, a solid core of students and intellectuals also came to France in the 1920s and 1930s. As a counterpart to the world of black American jazz in Montmartre, musicians from the Caribbean established a lively performative culture in Montparnasse, centering on nightclubs like the Bal nègre. The rise of *négritude* in the 1930s brought together young students like Léon Damas, Leopold Senghor, and Aimé Césaire together in Paris to explore the global nature of black culture. This dialogue between Francophone blacks from the Caribbean and Africa constituted a seminal moment in the creation of a black French culture. Moreover, its many interactions with African American intellectuals underscored the parallels between the two black experiences. Langston Hughes, Countee Cullen, and other Americans frequented the weekly *salon* of the Nardal sisters in the Paris suburbs, and Claude McKay's novel *Banjo* became must reading for black students in France. Both *négritude* and the Harlem Renaissance thus exemplified a new black consciousness, emphasizing the African roots of black cultures and their signal contributions to the human experience as a whole.[25]

Toward Full Citizenship?

If the history of African American expatriates in France reflected a certain confluence of the conditions of blacks on both sides of the Atlantic in the interwar years, the aftermath of the Second World War saw it become more a symbol of the difference between these two national experiences. At the same time, the condition of French blacks came to resemble that of American blacks as a whole more than ever before. One example of this is the parallel histories of civil rights in America and decolonization in France. In both cases blacks asserted, more powerfully than ever before, demands for full inclusion into the national community. The parallel is strongest between black America and the French Caribbean: both black communities overwhelmingly rejected the idea of separation from the national community, instead of achieving recognition of their rights as citizens. The end of *de jure* segregation and the granting of voting rights to blacks in the United States strongly resembled the granting of departmental status to Martinique, Guadeloupe, and Guyana in 1946. In contrast, France's sub-Saharan African colonies chose formal independence, but usually in a way that ensured continued close ties to France. In both America and France, therefore, the twenty years after the end of World War II brought at least the promise of full equality for these nations' black populations.[26]

These years also brought unprecedented levels of black migration to national heartlands. This happened most dramatically in France: during the 1960s in particular France brought hundreds of thousands of Caribbean laborers to the metropolis, placing them in both public and private sector employment. Mass migration from black Africa took longer to develop, but by the end of the 1960s one could frequently encounter Africans in the streets of Paris and other French cities. In the United States, the Second World War initiated what has been called the Second Great Migration, even larger than the first, of blacks from the South to the North.[27] The great urban uprisings that shook America during the 1960s illustrated the fact that, for the first time in the nation's history, a majority of its black population lived outside the South. In both cases, large new black populations helped reshape urban structures and society in general. Both France and the United States invested heavily in urban public housing after the war, building the (usually horrendously ugly) high-rise towers known as "housing projects" and "*habitations à loyer modéré.*" Over time these would become centers of black settlement and culture as well as symbols of the limits of migration as a strategy for racial liberation and the failures of societies to integrate fully their black citizens into the life of the nation.[28]

This of course brings us to one of the greatest contrasts of all between black America and black France. African Americans confronted the limits of civil rights with a widespread series of urban uprisings and the development of new ideological forms (i.e., Black Power, black nationalism) that harshly criticized American society and championed black culture and black unity.[29]

At the same time blacks were able to use their numerical weight and political mobilization to push successfully for a number of state practices, ranging from voting rights and antidiscrimination legislation to affirmative action, that brought the dream of full equality much closer to reality, in particular creating a sizeable black middle class. In contrast, the much smaller black communities of France, lacking the dense institutional networks and political power of African Americans, remained much more quiescent. In the Francophone worlds of Africa and the Caribbean black protest was similarly muted. Political movements for independence developed in the French West Indies, but for the most part it lacked mass support or political impact.[30] Francophone Africa became a classic case of neocolonialism, with the French military intervening in the political affairs of the continent more than thirty times from 1960 to the end of the twentieth century.[31] Paradoxically, while black France and black America resembled each other more than ever, these growing similarities also underscored the very real differences between the two nations' black cultures.

The last quarter of the twentieth century brought further shifts that in some ways pointed to a possible convergence of communities of African descent on both sides of the Atlantic. From the late 1970s on black Americans faced a growing wave of racist activism that sought to undo the social and political achievements of the civil rights and Black Power eras. The election of Ronald Reagan as president ushered in a series of attacks on all programs, notably school integration and affirmative action that intended to improve the black condition in America and reaffirmed the intention of the Republican Party to use white racism for political gains. The dawn of the new century witnessed repeated attempts to disenfranchise blacks, not only the electoral chicanery that ensured the election and reelection of George W. Bush as president in 2000 and 2004 but also the imprisonment of huge numbers of black men that has deprived them of, among other things, the right to vote. This climate of racist backlash has threatened to silence African Americans and reverse some of the key gains of the civil rights revolution.[32]

Whereas the full integration of blacks into American society has begun to seem more and more like a dream deferred, during the same period blacks in France began to enjoy more of a presence in national life. The nation's black population has continued to grow, spurred on largely by illegal immigration from sub-Saharan Africa. The rise of the National Front during the 1980s certainly threatened this population, but it also prompted an unprecedented level of antiracist organizing and public activism by black and other minority communities. The most prominent antiracist organization, SOS-Racisme, chose as its head a young black man named Harlem Désir. Blacks also became much more prominent culturally in France. The rise of hip-hop culture from its African American roots to global prominence during the 1980s and 1990s had a particular impact upon France, which soon became the second largest producer of rap music in the world after the United States. French blacks were intimately involved with hip-hop both as musicians, integrating into it musical traditions from Africa and the Caribbean, and as producers. The first TV show in France ever hosted by a black man, Sydney Duteil, was a dance show entitled *Hip-Hop*. The trendy use of the English language term "black" in France also reflected a new awareness of blackness as a social and cultural fact.[33]

If African and Caribbean life in France moved gingerly toward a greater sense of blackness, African American life began also to exhibit some of the traits of French communities. By the end of the century the United States was experiencing a small but noticeable immigration from the African continent. Many leading Senegalese musicians divided their time between Dakar, Paris, and New York, and one could buy the exact same trinkets from African street merchants in American and French cities.[34] Increasingly like France, black life in America was no longer exclusively the product of the trans-Atlantic slave trade.

Another similarity was what one might call the growing "creolization" of African American society. Although privilege and light skin had often gone together, racial traditions like the "one drop" rule and powerful currents within the black community emphasizing social and political unity largely rendered the idea of a separate Creole elite unworkable in the United States. Moreover, interracial sexual relationships had traditionally been far less acceptable than in France, as African American soldiers discovered during World War I. Over the last few decades, however, the number of marriages and other sexual liaisons between blacks and whites in America has risen sharply and has become much more accepted in American culture. One consequence has been a newly assertive mixed-race population, many of whose members have insisted on claiming both black and white identity and distinguishing themselves from African Americans as a social and racial group.[35] The fact that this has been primarily a middle-class phenomenon further underscores the similarity with racial patterns in France and the French West Indies.[36]

These patterns of convergence between black France and black America have changed the significance of African American expatriates in France. The dual impact of decolonization in France and the civil rights movement in the United States cast into question the traditional opposition between a tolerant France and a racist America. As the French population became increasingly multicultural, often with its own patterns of racial segmentation and discrimination, France began to seem more like the country many expatriates sought to escape. Moreover, the makeup of the expatriate population itself shifted. The rise of a large black middle class in the United States meant that increasingly the African Americans who came to France were less likely to be artists, musicians, and writers and more likely to be students, tourists, and people in international business, just like Americans as a whole. Many of these visitors had a strong cosmopolitan interest in black cultures overseas and were as likely to visit Dakar, Jamaica, or Bahia as Paris. Finally, the rise of mass trans-Atlantic air travel in the 1960s meant that settling abroad no longer represented the definitive rupture that it did in the 1920s. As one expatriate commented, when one could breakfast in Paris, take a jet across the ocean, and then dine in New York the same day, the very idea of exile no longer had the same meaning. By the end of the twentieth century, therefore, the black expatriate colony in Paris had become less a separate community and more an extension of the educated African American middle class overseas.

By the beginning of the new millennium, therefore, black France and black America had come to resemble each other more closely, in ways that rendered the trans-Atlantic link historically constituted by African American expatriates less important in effecting a connection between the two. The French suburban uprisings during the fall of 2005 made this clear. One could indeed discern strong parallels (as well as some important differences) between them and the urban riots that shook America in the wake of the 1992 beating of Rodney King. Both arose out of feelings of the exclusion of minority citizens in general and of police harassment and brutality in particular. Both highlighted the particularly difficult conditions of poor young men of color. Both illustrated strong sentiments of frustrated consumerism, as Americans looted stores for goods they could not buy and French people burned cars they could not afford.[37]

But the events of November 2005 also showed the strong differences between black France and the United States. Blacks were not nearly as central to the uprisings as were African Americans in Los Angeles and other U.S. cities. There was much less violence against people in France than in America, and many fewer deaths. Finally, the events in France had a much greater political impact than the Rodney King protests in America: the latter occurred in the middle of a presidential campaign and were completely ignored by all the major candidates, whereas the suburban riots in France dominated that nation's political discourse for weeks if not months. Paradoxically, given the prevalent contrast between a multicultural America and a color-blind France, the November 2005 disturbances showed that the French people were beginning to grapple with fundamental questions of race, power, and citizenship, whereas the 1992 events (and subsequent racial conflicts as well) have underscored the near-impossibility of straight talk about race in mainstream American political discourse.

The events of the fall of 2005 also underscored a rising sense of black consciousness that had been developing in France since the 1990s. In 1998 France formally celebrated the 150th anniversary of the final abolition of slavery in its empire. This became an opportunity for West Indians in both the metropolis and the Caribbean to mobilize around the question of the memory of slavery, and to press their perspectives as a black community within France.[38] They forced their country to confront its history as a slave nation, a process that culminated in the government's formal apology for its historic involvement in the slave trade and the slave system in general.[39] The 1990s also brought a new wave of activism on the part of Africans in France, in particular illegal immigrants. In 1992, for example, hundreds of Malians camped out in front of the Chateau de Vincennes outside Paris to dramatize the plight of African immigrants, and in 1996 police expelled 300 Africans seeking sanctuary in the city's Saint-Bernard church.[40] By the beginning of the twenty-first century black French men and women began creating a series of black communal associations, culminating in November 2005 with the foundation of CRAN (the Representative Council of Black Associations) representing some sixty African and Caribbean groups in France.[41]

Race riots and rising black consciousness: in a France shaped by such concerns, what is the significance of the African American expatriates, or more broadly, how do black Americans outside the United States illustrate and shape the politics of blackness? Have Richard Wright and even Afrika Bambaata been displaced by Colin Powell and Condoleezza Rice as prototypical black Americans in the eyes of the world? Whereas most African Americans in Paris reacted with concern to the suburban disturbances of 2005, they demonstrated no special relationship to them or to the world they inhabited. Most black expatriates live in Paris, not the suburban housing projects. When I talked to one friend, a leading member of that community, last November, he said that he knew little about what was going on "out there." Thanks to the Internet, which allowed people around the world to read the French press and a wide variety of relevant blogs online, I could learn as much about the events in the *banlieues* from my home in California as could many residents of Paris.

Nor, I would argue, did the specter of race riots in France lead many black Americans there to reconsider their reasons for staying, since few today believe in the old notion of color-blind France. The November riots in France suggest a view of African American expatriates as people attracted to life overseas for a number of reasons ranging from personal and family ties to a feeling that a black American can receive more respect and encounter less racism directed toward him or her by leaving the United States. To accuse black American expatriates in Paris of indulging in privileged status is both to ignore the very real differences in racial oppression on different sides of the Atlantic and to deny people the option of achieving liberation through flight that has been a primary means of agency for blacks in both France and the United States over the years.[42] As many Caribbean and African immigrants to the United States have also found, blackness somehow becomes more acceptable when it speaks with a foreign accent. Theorists and celebrants of diaspora should thus also consider the ways in which migration can bring both greater freedom and greater privilege, and the relationship between the two.

Finally, the uprisings of the fall of 2005 also crystallized a new image of France that bears more than a little similarity to traditional views of black America. The most obvious symbol is the huge popularity of hip-hop among young French people of all colors. However, if this alone symbolizes a similarity with American blackness then the whole world is African American (including much of the United States). More significant in the case of France are the difficulties in social, economic, and political life that the riots highlighted. For decades now France has been portrayed as a land in crisis, economically stagnant and unwilling to abandon the welfare state of the late twentieth century in favor of neoliberal orthodoxies.[43] The idea of France as overdependent on the welfare state resembles the classic idea of black Americans as dependent on welfare and lacking entrepreneurial drive. Both the suburban upheavals of the fall of 2005, and the disturbances provoked by the government's attempts to change youth employment laws in early 2006, played into this idea of France as socially troubled and economically retrograde.

Foreign policy, surprisingly enough, constitutes another area of similarity. Ever since the start of the second Iraq war the Bush administration and its allies, notably Tony Blair's Britain, have tended to regard France as politically out of step with the "war on terror" and its assertion of neoimperialist global hegemony.[44] Only in the summer of 2006 did the congressional cafeteria in Washington drop the name "freedom fries" in favor of the traditional "French fries."[45] Just as American blacks have continued to resist neoliberal politics domestically, voting overwhelmingly for the political opposition, so has France come to symbolize a rejection of those policies internationally. The fact that two leading proponents of the Bush administration's foreign policy, Colin Powell and Condoleezza Rice, are black underscores this similarity, since their opposition to the French replicates their isolation from the political views of the vast majority of African Americans. The November 2005 uprisings were widely interpreted in the American media and elsewhere as ominous manifestations of the new Muslim Europe, a kind of European intifada, and were often blamed erroneously on Islamic fundamentalism.[46] The idea of France as a land of social and political danger in the heart of the Western world resonates with the view of black American ghettos as the haunts of the underclass at the center of the imperial United States.

A final similarity between France and black America arises from this view of France as a center of opposition to neoimperialist hegemony. A key theme of the African American experience has been the contrast between blacks as socially and politically excluded from American life in general and their central role in American culture. From food to music to political ideology, the black experience has been so central to what it means to be American that one simply cannot imagine the United States without it. Yet blacks have also remained marginal to the opportunities offered by American society and to America's view of itself: witness the difficulty of integrating an analysis of slavery into the dominant image of the United States as a beacon of freedom. Strikingly, American views of France seem to be replicating this paradox. For all the condemnations of French society and politics, the elite role of French culture in American life remains unquestioned. The best restaurants in any American city invariably serve French cuisine (in fact, traditional peasant foods like "cassoulet" often benefit from a trans-Atlantic status upgrade), and those who turn up their noses at French fries happily indulge in bistro fare or French-inspired nouvelle cuisine. The same is true of cultural production in the arts and humanities. Even those American conservatives who snub French culture do so by portraying it as a symbol of cultural elitism, in contrast to their own jingoist populism. In short, on a global scale the French seem to be experiencing what African Americans have long known: people can love what you do while ultimately hating who you are.[47]

The crisis of the fall of 2005 in France did not constitute the first time that African American expatriates had to confront the limits of French tolerance; the Algerian war and the rise of a multicultural population in France during the second half of the twentieth century had already done so. It did, however, highlight important similarities and convergences between black France and black America and underscore the importance of a dialogue between the two. On the one hand, these convergences and increased opportunities for dialogue undercut the historically seminal role of African American expatriates in bridging the two experiences: African American culture is everywhere today, and television and the Internet render it immediately accessible to people around the world. On the other hand, this process of convergence suggests a new role for black Americans in France, one that show-cases the possibilities of a diasporic black community, exploring its advan-tages and limitations. Since French blacks also travel and live abroad, to the United States and elsewhere, such a role speaks to another kind of trans-At-lantic convergence. The triangular diaspora of Senegalese musicians between Dakar, Paris, and New York is a case in point. One may say, in conclusion therefore, that the history of black American expatriates in France may be entering a new phase; one marked less by American exceptionalism and more by integration into the tradition of black diasporas as a whole. In this spirit, Paris may no longer constitute a refuge from racism but rather the front lines of diasporic and global debates about what it means to be black.

Notes

1. Earlier versions of this paper were presented at the Museum of the African Di-aspora in San Francisco, Stanford University, and Northwestern University. I would like to thank Waldo Martin, Trica Keaton, Elisabeth Mudimbe-Boyi, and Louis Chude-Sokei for their kind and helpful comments.

2. Roi Ottley, *No Green Pastures*, New York: Scribner, 1951.

3. On questions of race and republicanism in France, see among many works Sue Peabody and Tyler Stovall, eds., *The Color of Liberty: Histories of Race in France*, Durham: Duke University Press, 2003; Herrick Chapman and Laura Frader, *Race in France: An Interdisciplinary Approach to the Politics of Difference*, New York: Berghahn Books, 2004; Maxim Silverman, *Deconstructing the Nation: Immigration, Racism and Citizenship in Modern France*, London and New York: Routledge, 1992; Michel Wiev-iorka, *Une société fragmentée? Le multiculturalisme en débat*, Paris: La Découverte, 1996.

4. As yet there is little scholarly literature on the suburban uprisings of 2005. The press, of course, covered the issue in detail. See "An Underclass Rebellion—France's Riots," *The Economist*, November 12, 2005; Adam Sage, "A National Idea Goes up in Flames. Observations on France," *The New Statesman*, November 14, 2005; "Paris Is Burning," *Maclean's*, November 14, 2005.

5. Alec Hargreaves and Mark McKinney, eds., *Post-Colonial Cultures in France*, New York: Routledge, 1997; Paul Silverstein, "'Why Are We Waiting to Start the Fire?' French Gangsta Rap and the Critique of State Capitalism," in Alain-Philippe Durand, *Black, Blanc, Beur: Rap Music and Hip-Hop Culture in the Francophone World*, Lanham, MD: Scarecrow Press, 2002; "Black: Africains, Antillais . . . Cultures noires en France," special issue of *Autrement*, #49, April 1983.

6. Colin Nickerson, "Youths' Poverty, Despair fuel Violent Unrest in France," *Boston Globe*, November 6, 2005.

7. Trica Keaton, "The Interpellation of 'Black American Paris': Migration Narratives of Inclusion and Social Race in the Other France," unpublished paper

presented to the conference "Paris Is Burning," Museum of the African Diaspora, San Francisco, April 2006. On contemporary African American tourism in Paris see Tyler Stovall, "Paris Soul"; Bennetta Jules-Rosette, "Black Paris: Touristic Simulations," *Annals of Tourism Research* 21, no. 4, 1994; Ervin Dyer, "Passage to Paris: A New Wave of Black Americans Is Calling The French Capital Home," *The Crisis*, January/February 2006; Christiann Anderson and Monique Y. Wells, *Paris Reflections: Walks through African American Paris*, Blacksburg, VA: McDonald and Woodward, 2002.

8. This is of course reflected in the historiographies of the two subjects. A comprehensive listing of major texts on African American history would take up far more space than that available for this entire article, whereas the number of studies of black France is relatively limited. For the former, some key texts are: John Hope Franklin, *From Slavery to Freedom: A History of African Americans*, New York: McGraw Hill, 1994; Manning Marable, *Living Black History: How Reimagining the African American Past Can Remake America's Racial Future*, New York: Basic Civitas, 2006; Evelyn Brooks Higginbotham, gen. Ed., *The Harvard Guide to African American History*, Cambridge, MA: Harvard University Press, 2001; see also the brief but stimulating essay by Thomas Holt, "*From Slavery to Freedom* and the Conceptualization of African American History," *Journal of Negro History*, vol. 77/#2, Spring 1992. On the history of black France, see Shelby McCloy, *The Negro in France*, Louisville: The University of Kentucky Press, 1961; Pascal Blanchard et al., *Paris Noir*, Paris: Hazan, 2001; Pap Ndiaye, "Pour une histoire des populations noires en France: préalables théoriques," *Mouvement social*, Fall 2005; Mar Fall, *Les Africains noirs en France: des tirailleurs sénégalais aux . . . blacks*, Paris: Harmattan, 1986; Philippe Dewitte, *Les mouvements nègres en France, 1919–1939*, Paris: Harmattan, 1985.

9. Louis Sala-Molins, *Dark Side of Light: Slavery and the French Enlightenment*, Minneapolis: University of Minnesota Press, 2006; C. L. R. James, *Black Jacobins: Toussaint L'Ouverture and the San Domingo Revolution*, New York: Random House, 1963; Carolyn Fick, *The Making of Haiti: The Saint Domingue Revolution from Below*, Knoxville: University of Tennessee Press, 1990; Laurent Dubois, *Avengers of the New World: The story of the Haitian Revolution*, Cambridge, MA: Harvard University Press, 2004; Lawrence Jennings, *French Anti-Slavery: The Movement for the Abolition of Slavery in France*, Cambridge: Cambridge University Press, 2000.

10. David Brion-Davis, *Inhuman Bondage: The Rise and Fall of Slavery in the New World*, New York: Oxford University Press, 2006; George M. Frederickson, *The Arrogance of Race: Historical Perspectives on Slavery, Racism, and Social Inequality*, Middletown, CT: Wesleyan University Press, 1988.

11. Sue Peabody, *"There Are No Slaves in France": The Political Culture of Race and Slavery under the Ancient Régime*, New York: Oxford University Press, 1996.

12. Félix German, "Dangerous Liaisons: The Lives and Labor of Antilleans and Sub-Saharan Africans in 1960s Paris," PhD dissertation, University of California, Berkeley, forthcoming.

13. Frederick Cooper, Thomas C. Holt, and Rebecca Scott, *Beyond Emancipation: Explorations of Race, Labor, and Citizenship in Postemancipation Societies*, Chapel Hill: University of North Carolina Press, 2000; Leon Litwack, *Been in the Storm So Long: The Aftermath of Slavery*, New York: Knopf, 1979; Auguste Cochin, *L'abolition de l'esclavage*, Paris: Désormeaux, 1979; Mickaëlla L. Périna, "Construire une identité politique à partir des vestiges de l'esclavage? Les departments français d'Amérique entre heritage et choix," in Patrick Weil and Stéphane Dufoix, *L'esclavage, la colonization, et après* . . . Paris: Presses Universitaires de France, 2005; Kim D. Butler, "Abolition and the Politics of Identity in the Afro-Atlantic Diaspora: Toward a Comparative Approach," in Darlene Clark Hine and Jacqueline McLeod, eds. *Crossing Boundaries: Comparative History of Black People in Diaspora*, Bloomington and Indianapolis: Indiana University Press, 1999.

14. On whiteness theory see David C. Roediger, *The Wages of Whiteness: Race and the Making of the American Working Class*, London: Verso, 1991; Roediger, *Colored White: Transcending the Racial Past*, Berkeley and Los Angeles: University of California Press, 2002.

15. Alice Conklin, *Mission to Civilize: The Republican Idea of Empire in France and West Africa*, Stanford: Stanford University Press, 1997; Ann L. Stoler, ed., *Haunted by Empire: Geographies of Intimacy in North American History*, Durham: Duke University Press, 2006.

16. Willard B. Gatewood, *Black Americans and the White Man's Burden, 1898–1903*, Urbana: University of Illinois Press, 1975; Véronique Hélénon, "Les administrateurs coloniaux originaires de Guadeloupe, Martinique et Guyane dans les colonies françaises d'Afrique, 1880–1939," PhD thesis, École des Hautes Études en Sciences Sociales, Paris, 1997.

17. C. Vann Woodward, *The Strange Career of Jim Crow*, New York: Oxford University Press, 1965; Leon Litwack, *Trouble in Mind: Black Southerners in the Age of Jim Crow*, New York: Vintage, 1999.

18. F. James Davis, *Who Is Black? One Nation's Definition*, University Park, PA: Pennsylvania State University Press, 1991; David A. Hollinger, *Cosmopolitanism and Solidarity: Studies in Ethnoracial, Religious, and Professional Affiliation in the United States*, Madison: University of Wisconsin Press, 2006; Owen White, *Children of the French Empire: Miscegenation and Colonial Society in French West Africa, 1895-1960*, Oxford: Oxford University Press, 1999; Emmanuelle Saada, *Les enfants de la colonie. Les métis de l'empire français entre sujétion et citoyenneté*, Paris: La Découverte, 2004.

19. Alain Locke, *The New Negro*, 1925, reprint New York: Atheneum, 1989; George Hutchinson, *The Harlem Renaissance in Black and White*, Cambridge, MA: Harvard University Press, 1989; David Levering Lewis, *When Harlem Was in Vogue*, New York: Oxford University Press, 1989; James R. Grossman, *Land of Hope: Chicago, Black Southerners, and the Great Migration*, Chicago: University of Chicago Press, 1989.

20. Michel Giraud, "Les enjeux presents de la mémoire de l'esclavage" in Weil and Dufoix, op. cit.

21. William Trotter, Jr., *Black Milwaukee: The Making of an Industrial Proletariat, 1915-1945*, Urbana: University of Illinois Press, 1985; Trotter, ed., *The Great Migration in Historical Perspective: New Dimensions of Race, Class, and Gender*, Bloomington: University of Indiana Press, 1991.

22. Joe Lunn, *Memoirs of the Maelstrom: A Senegalese Oral History of the First World War*, Oxford: James Currey, 1999; Gregory Mann, *Native Sons: West African Veterans and France in the Twentieth Century*, Durham: Duke University Press, 2006; Marc Michel, *L'Appel à l'Afrique: Contributions et Réactions à l'Effort de Guerre en A.O.F. (1914-1919)*, Paris: Publications de la Sorbonne, 1982.

23. Tyler Stovall, *Paris Noir: African Americans in the City of Light*, Boston: Houghton-Mifflin, 1996; Jody Blake, *Le Tumulte Noir: Modernist Art and Popular Entertainment in Jazz-Age Paris*, University Park, PA: Pennsylvania State University Press, 1999; Petrine Archer-Shaw, *Negrophilia: Avant-Garde Paris and Black Culture in the 1920s*, New York: Thames & Hudson, 2000; Brett Berliner, *Ambivalent Desire: The Exotic Black Other in Jazz-Age France*, Amherst: University of Massachusetts Press, 2002; Phyllis Rose, *Jazz Cleopatra: Josephine Baker in Her Time*, New York: Doubleday, 1989; Elizabeth Ezra, *The Colonial Unconscious: Race and Culture in Interwar France*, Ithaca: Cornell University Press, 2000.

24. Conklin, op. cit.; Gary Wilder, *The French Imperial Nation-State: Negritude and Colonial Humanism between the Wars*, Chicago: University of Chicago Press, 2006; Tony Chafer and Amanda Sackur, eds., *French Colonial Empire and the Popular Front: Hope and Disillusion*, New York: Palgrave, 1999; Martin Thomas, *The French Empire between the Wars: Imperialism, Politics and Society*, Manchester: Manchester University Press, 2005.

25. Lilyan Kesteloot, *Black Writers in French: A Literary History of Negritude*, Washington, D.C.: Howard University Press, 1991; Brent Hayes Edwards, *The Practice of Diaspora: Literature, Translation, and the Rise of Black Internationalism*, Cambridge, MA: Harvard University Press, 2003; T. Denean Sharpley-Whiting, *Negritude Women*, Minneapolis: University of Minnesota Press, 2002; Claude McKay, *Banjo: A Story without a Plot*, 1929, reprint New York: Harcourt, Brace, and Jovanovich, 1957.

26. On the American civil rights movement see Taylor Branch, *Parting the Waters*, New York: Simon and Schuster, 1988; David Garrow, *Bearing the Cross: Martin Luther King, Jr., and the Southern Christian Leadership Conference*, New York: Vintage, 1986. On departmentalization in the French West Indies see Richard D. E. Burton, *La Famille coloniale: la Martinique et la mère patrie, 1789-1992*, Paris: Harmattan, 1994; Armand Nicolas, *Histoire de la Martinique*, vol. 3, Paris: Harmattan, 1998.

27. Nicholas Lemann, *The Promised Land: The Great Black Migration and How It Changed America*, New York: A.A. Knopf, 1991.

28. Elizabeth Huttman, et al., *Urban Housing Segregation of Minorities in Western Europe and the United States*, Durham: Duke University Press, 1991; Thomas Sugrue, *The Origins of the Urban Crisis: Race and Inequality in Postwar Detroit*, Princeton: Princeton University Press, 1996; Mehdi Lallaoui, *Du bidonville aux HLM*, Paris: Diffusion Syros, 1993.

29. Stokeley Carmichael and Charles V. Hamilton, *Black Power: The Politics of Liberation in America*, New York: Vintage, 1967; Joseph E. Peniel, ed., *The Black Power Movement: Rethinking the Civil Rights-Black Power Era*, New York: Routledge, 2006; Jeffrey Ogbonna and Ogbar Green, *Black Power: Radical Politics and African American Identity*, Baltimore: Johns Hopkins University Press, 2005.

30. Richard D. E. Burton, *Assimilation or Independence? Prospects for Martinique*, Montreal: McGill University, 1978; Alain Blérald, *La question nationale en Guadeloupe et en Martinique: essai sur l'histoire politique*, Paris: Harmattan, 1998.

31. Patrick Manning, *Francophone Sub-Saharan Africa, 1880–1995*, New York: Cambridge University Press, 1998; Tony Chafer, *The End of Empire in French West Africa: France's Successful Decolonization?*, New York: Berg, 2003.

32. Thomas Byrne Edsall and Mary D. Edsall, *Chain Reaction: The Impact of Race, Rights, and Taxes on American Politics*, New York: Norton, 1992.

33. Harlem Désir, *Touche pas à mon pote*, Paris: B. Grasset, 1985; Fred Constant, "Talking Race in Colorblind France: Equality Denied, 'Blackness' Reclaimed," unpublished paper presented at the conference, "Black Europe and the African Diaspora," Northwestern University, April 2006; Andre Prevos, "Postcolonial Popular Music in France: Rap Music and Hip-Hop Culture in the 1980s," in Tony Mitchell, ed., *Rap and Hip-Hop Outside the USA*, Middletown, CT: Wesleyan University Press, 2001.

34. James Winders, *Paris Africain: Rhythms of the African Diaspora*, New York: Palgrave Macmillan, forthcoming.

35. Naomi Zack, ed., *American Mixed Race: The Culture of Micro-Diversity*, Lanham, MD: Rowman and Littlefield, 1995; Jon Michael Spencer, *The New Colored People: The Mixed-Race Movement in America*, New York: New York University Press, 1987; David A. Hollinger, *Postethnic America: Beyond Multiculturalism*, New York: Basic Books, 2000.

36. Michel Giraud, *Races et classes à la Martinique*, Paris: Editions Anthropos, 1979.

37. Jewelle Taylor Gibbs, *Race and Justice: Rodney King and O. J. Simpson in a House Divided*, San Francisco: Jossey-Bass, 1996; Min Hyoung Song, *Strange Future: Pessimism and the 1992 Los Angeles Riots*, Durham: Duke University Press, 2005.

38. Constant, op. cit. Catherine Reinhardt, "Slavery and Commemoration: Remembering the French Abolitionary Decree 150 Years Later," in Alec Hargreaves, ed., *Memory, Empire, and Postcolonialism: The Legacies of French Colonialism*, Lanham, MD: Lexington Books, 2005.

39. "France Pays Homage to Victims of African Slave Trade," *San Francisco Chronicle*, May 11, 2006.

40. Winders, op. cit., chapter 4.

41. Constant, op. cit.

42. Here I disagree with Ch. Didier Gondola; see his "'But I Ain't African, I'm American!': Black American Exiles and the Construction of Racial Identities in Twentieth-Century France," in Heike Raphael-Hernandez, *Blackening Europe: The African American Presence*, New York: Routledge, 2004.

43. Timothy Smith, *France in Crisis: Welfare, Inequality, and Globalization since 1980*, New York and Cambridge: Cambridge University Press, 2004.

44. Daniel Levy, et al., *Old Europe, New Europe, Core Europe: Transatlantic Relations after the Iraq War*, London: Verso, 2006.

45. "Au Revoir, Freedom Fries!," *The New York Times*, August 4, 2006.

46. See, for example, "War on Terror—Battleground France," *National Review*, December 5, 2005; "Falluja-sur Seine," *Daily Standard*, November 8, 2005.

47. Greg Tate, ed., *Everything But the Burden: What White People are Taking from Black Culture*, New York: Broadway Books, 2003.

PART TWO

CROSS-TEXTUAL ENCOUNTERS

~

CHAPTER SIX

A Poetics of Relationality

Victor Segalen's Stèles

Yvonne Hsieh, University of Victoria, Canada

In an article ambiguously entitled "Glissant est-il égal à Segalen?" ("Does Glissant equal Segalen?"), Jean-Louis Cornille stresses Edouard Glissant's indebtedness to Victor Segalen. For him, most of the Martiniquan writer's theoretical concepts derive from the reflections of his French predecessor:

> Dans son fondamental inachèvement, l'*Essai sur l'exotisme* [de Victor Segalen] ne demandait qu'à être continué [. . .]. [Segalen ne parvient] qu'à donner une définition négative de l'exotisme: ce qu'il n'est pas, les vieux usages du mot dont il faut se débarrasser avant de pouvoir s'en servir à nouveau [. . .] . En privilégiant le terme positif de "Divers," Glissant entend redéfinir, en la repositivant, la tâche que s'était donnée Segalen: il avance les mots qui manquaient à ce dernier.

> In its essentially unfinished state, [Victor Segalen's] *Essay on Exoticism* simply begs for a continuation. . . . [Segalen only manages] to provide a negative definition of exoticism: what it is not, outdated usages of the word which need to be jettisoned before it can be used again. . . . By favoring the positive term "Diversity," Glissant attempts to redefine in a positive light the task Segalen had taken on: he proposes words which the former could not find.[1]

Indeed, Segalen's *Essay on Exoticism: An Aesthetics of Diversity*, consists simply of notes accumulated between 1904 and 1918. Thirty-six years after the author's death in 1919, extracts of this unfinished work were published in the review *Le Mercure de France*.[2] That same year (1955), Segalen's collection of poetry, *Stèles*, was republished by the Club du Meilleur Livre. In all likelihood, it was in 1955 that Edouard Glissant first discovered Victor Segalen, who would become a lifelong inspiration.

In his study, Cornille points out that "Glissant n'a jamais admis sa dette envers Segalen que sur le seul plan conceptuel." ("Glissant has never admitted his debt toward Segalen, other than on a conceptual level.")[3] For him, however, Glissant's epic poem *Les Indes*, composed between April and June 1955, bears a striking resemblance to *Stèles* in its form. Both texts are divided into six parts, in addition to a narrative or descriptive prose section printed in italics. In *Stèles*, this prose section, composed of six distinct paragraphs each separated by an asterisk, takes the place of the preface, whereas in *Les Indes*, it precedes each of the six *chants* ("songs"). *Stèles* contains sixty-four poems; *Les Indes*, sixty-four fragments plus one (the final song, separated from the rest of the text).[4] For Cornille, the formal organization of *Les Indes* was clearly influenced by Glissant's recent reading of *Stèles*.

Rather than analyzing Glissant's indebtedness to Segalen, this study aims to show how these two writers, both reputed to be difficult, can shed light on each other when read in conjunction. Glissant's theories can be used to explain the poetics practiced by Segalen in *Stèles*; conversely, *Stèles* can serve to illustrate key Glissantian notions. It is necessary, however, to begin with a brief summary of Glissant's appraisal of Segalen and the definition of a few principal concepts in his poetics of Relationality.

"C'est par la Différence, et dans le Divers, que s'exalte l'existence," ("It is through Difference and in Diversity that existence is made glorious,")[5] Segalen contends in his *Essay on Exoticism*. This powerful statement, written in 1917, seems to have landed Segalen squarely in the camp of postcolonial writers, even though he should have joined the ranks of colonial writers by dint of his era (1878–1919), his adherence to the colonial machine as an officer and physician in the French navy, and his reactionary attitude in politics.[6] But his condemnation of the disastrous consequences suffered by the colonized Polynesians in his very first novel, *Les Immémoriaux* (1907; translated as *A Lapse of Memory* and published in English in 1995), his contempt for exotic literature in the style of Pierre Loti, and his denunciation of the progressive impoverishment of the world as a result of diminishing diversity suffice, in the eyes of certain critics,[7] to count him among the postcolonial writers. And none has contributed as much as Glissant to the consecration of Segalen as a precursor of postcolonial thinking.

In his book *L'Intention poétique* (1969), Glissant affirms that "Segalen est exemplaire: d'avoir pleinement essayé d'être l'Autre; d'avoir accompli le Même [. . .]. [I]l a voulu réaliser totalement l'Autre dans le Même (et c'était là une démarche originale).” (“Segalen is exemplary in having tried fully to be the Other, and in having accomplished the Same . . . He wanted to fulfill completely the Other in the Same [and this was original].”)[8] Glissant again refers to Segalen several times in his *Poétique de la Relation* (1990). According to him, it was Segalen who wrote “le premier édit d’une véritable poétique de la Relation,” (“the first edict of a true poetics of Relationality,”) by transforming recognition of the Other into an aesthetic constituent.[9] The title of another work by Glissant, *Introduction à une poétique du Divers* (1996), alludes to the subtitle of Segalen’s *Essay on Exoticism*: “An Aesthetics of Diversity.” While paying homage to his predecessor, Glissant nonetheless acknowledges the contradiction inherent in the latter. But this only seems to make the French writer more admirable in the eyes of Glissant:

> Un poète comme Victor Segalen, qui était un médecin militaire, qui travaillait sur un aviso militaire, produit, invente, imagine et construit un système de pensée de l’exotisme tel qu’il combat à la fois tout exotisme et toute colonisation [. . . .] Pour moi Segalen est un poète révolutionnaire. Honneur et respect à Segalen. C’est le premier qui a posé la question de la diversité du monde, qui a combattu l’exotisme comme forme complaisante de la colonisation.

> A poet like Victor Segalen, who was a military physician working on a military dispatch boat, produces, invents, imagines and construes a system of thought on exoticism in such a way as to combat both exoticism and colonization. . . . For me, Segalen is a revolutionary poet. Honor and respect to Segalen. He was the first to raise the question of diversity in this world, and to oppose exoticism as a complacent form of colonization.[10]

After this brief summary of Glissant’s appraisal of Segalen, let us now review a few Glissantian concepts which are especially relevant for this study. The first is the notion of “creolization” (*la créolisation*), defined by Glissant as follows: “La créolisation exige que les éléments hétérogènes mis en relation ‘s’intervalorisent’, c’est-à-dire qu’il n’y ait pas de dégradation ou de diminution de l’être, soit de l’intérieur, soit de l’extérieur, dans ce contact et dans ce mélange.” (“Creolization requires that heterogeneous elements placed in a relationship valorize each other, that there be no degradation or diminution of being, either from within or from without, in this contact or mixture.”)[11] Glissant then affirms that “la créolisation est imprévisible alors que l’on pourrait calculer les effets d’un métissage.” (“Creolization is unpredictable, whereas the effects of *métissage* [the mixing of two races or cultures] can be calculated.”)[12] Moreover, creolization is not creolism (*le créolisme*), which Glissant defines as the introduction of Creole words into the French language, or the creation of new French words out of

Creole words. An example of creolization would be "engendrer un langage qui tisse les poétiques, peut-être opposées, des langues créoles et des langues françaises." ("the production of a language which weaves together different, perhaps opposing poetics, of Creole and French tongues.")[13] Creolism, which can be spotted at a glance, appears amusing or exotic to a French reader, while "la poétique, la structure du langage, la refonte de la structure des langages lui paraîtront purement et simplement obscures." ("The poetics, the structure of the language, the overhaul of the structure of languages would simply appear obscure to him.")[14]

In second place, we note Glissant's idea that the human imagination is in need of all the languages in this world: "avec toute langue qui disparaît, disparaît une part de l'imaginaire humain, avec toute langue qui est traduite s'enrichit cet imaginaire." ("With the disappearance of every language disappears a part of the human imagination; the translation of each language enriches this imagination.")[15] This line of thinking is similar to Segalen's firm belief in the enrichment occasioned by every sensation of exoticism: "La sensation d'Exotisme augmente la personnalité, l'enrichit, bien loin de l'étouffer." ("Far from stifling it, the sensation of Exoticism enhances and enriches one's personality.")[16]

The third key Glissantian notion particularly useful for our study is "multilingualism" (multilinguisme): "la présence des langues du monde dans la pratique de la sienne." ("The presence of the world's languages in the practice of one's own.")[17] It is not a question of knowing, but of imagining languages. It is not about juxtaposing languages, but about interweaving them ("leur mise en réseau.")[18] Glissant points out that up till the nineteenth century, writers wrote in a monolingual fashion. Voltaire, who knew English, found Shakespeare to be a barbarian (un sauvage); English writers of the same period considered Racine a sissy (une femmelette).[19]

Victor Segalen's Stèles presents a unique case in French Literature of an encounter between French and classical Chinese, between the thoughts of a French poet/sinologist and "archaic Chinese dress" ("habits archaïques chinois"—a term Segalen used in a letter addressed to Claude Debussy),[20] between two imaginations and two literary traditions. It is a work that illustrates perfectly Glissant's concepts of "creolization" and "multilingualism."

Inspiration for this collection of prose poems came from real stelae Segalen saw in China, which bore inscriptions of the most insipid official texts. For this reason, he merely borrowed the "form" of the stela, choosing to write on entirely different subjects. The first edition of forty-eight Stèles was published in Beijing in 1912; a second edition consisting of sixty-four poems appeared in 1914. Each poem is printed within a rectangle (or two rectangles at most) in order to create the impression of a text inscribed upon a stone tablet. The first word of each "paragraph" (or "verse") extends into the left margin. According to Segalen, this is an adaptation of the Chinese practice of beginning a vertical line one or two characters above the top margin, every time a person deserving of special respect is evoked.

The presence of a Chinese epigraph makes each *stèle* a bilingual poem. In addition to having an obvious visual function, the epigraph has a semantic one as well: it reflects the Chinese predilection of summing up an anecdote by a brief formula, most often consisting of just four characters. The French text is composed in a highly literary, sometimes even archaic, style. In his foreword, Segalen explains that "le style en doit être ceci qu'on ne peut pas dire un langage car ceci n'a point d'échos parmi les autres langages et ne saurait pas servir aux échanges quotidiens: Le Wên." ("The style [of these texts] must be such that it cannot be mistaken for ordinary language, for it has no echo among other languages and cannot be used for daily exchanges: it is Wen.")[21] *Wen* is the Chinese word for "literature": when Segalen was writing in the 1910s, the formal written language in China was still classical Chinese, completely distinct from vernacular Chinese in its many dialectic variations. Using as his springboard a Chinese historical anecdote, rite, custom, or concept, Segalen would move quickly into the allegorical realm, frequently ending the poem on a personal note. The sixty-four stèles are divided by theme into six categories: 1. *Stèles* facing South, 2. *Stèles* facing North, 3. *Stèles* facing East, 4. *Stèles* facing West, 5. *Stèles* by the Wayside, 6. *Stèles* of the Middle. To illustrate Glissant's notions of creolization and multilingualism, I have chosen two short poems in the collection: "Les cinq relations," the first of the "*Stèles* facing East," poems on the topic of love; and "Trahison fidèle," classified among the "*Stèles* facing North," devoted to the theme of friendship.[22]

The "five relationships" refer to a Confucian concept according to which "les cinq sortes d'obligations communes aux hommes de tous les temps et de tous les lieux sont les devoirs mutuels du prince et du sujet, du père et du fils, du mari et de la femme, du frère aîné et du frère puîné, des collègues ou des amis." ("The five kinds of obligations common to men of all times and all lands are the mutual duties between prince and subject, between father and son, between husband and wife, between older brother and younger brother, and between colleagues or friends.")[23] Segalen took as his starting point this common Chinese notion of interpersonal relationships, only to express a totally personal and Western vision of love at the end.

The first part of the poem plunges the reader into the Chinese world. The elliptical language takes on the density of classical Chinese, in which all unnecessary words may be omitted. Here, all the verbs have disappeared. The Chinese epigraph demonstrates this characteristic density. Although it comprises merely four characters,[24] the French translation provided by Segalen himself contains nine words: "Du mari à la femme doit régner la Différence." ("Between husband and wife, Difference must reign.") In order to avoid monotony, Segalen varies the order within each relationship. In the first two sentences, the superior is mentioned before the subordinate ("father" before "son," "Prince" before "subject"); in the third sentence, it is the reverse ("younger brother" before "elder"). In the fourth sentence, where the relationship is between equals, three qualities are given ("confidence," "unconstraint," "similarity") rather than a single one, as in the previous sentences. Absent from this verse is the husband-wife relationship, which forms the subject of the second part of the poem.

The tone and style change dramatically in the second verse, as we pass from the impersonal Chinese world into the personal world of the speaker. The collective or communal voice of the first verse gives way to a lyrical voice. The expansive style here is closer to the spoken language, an impression reinforced by the punctuation: the hyphens, exclamation mark, and semicolons separating the three relative clauses. In this verse, the four relations indicated previously are repeated, but in reverse order. Moreover, three out of the four terms are feminized. "Father" at the beginning of the first verse thus becomes "mother" at the end of the second; "Prince" is repeated in "Princess"; "delightful elder sister" in the second verse echoes "elder" in the first. Only "friend" remains "friend" (ami) in the masculine. The contrast between two styles—an elliptical style reminiscent of classical Chinese in the first verse, a more lyrical French style in the second—reflects the confrontation of two cultures. We see the disproportionate importance given to the man-woman relationship in Western culture, where the beloved is expected to play the roles traditionally reserved for mother, sovereign, sister, and friend. By contrast, the husband-wife relationship is but one among five in the Chinese culture. The poem's conclusion recalls Segalen's personal philosophy, his "aesthetics of diversity": the woman is loved precisely for her difference.

On a stylistic level, a synthesis of the first two verses is implemented in the third, which is less elliptical than the first, yet less expansive than the second. The last three terms in this verse ("distance," "extremity," "diversity") echo the last three terms of the first verse ("confidence," "unconstraint," "similarity"), while "diversity" contrasts with "similarity." This third verse has retained a certain density—reminiscent of the first verse—by dint of its irregular syntax (e.g., "by nature and destiny"). Unlike "Les cinq relations," "Trahison fidèle" does not appear at first glance to interweave linguistics characteristics of French and classical Chinese. Except for the slightly elliptical "Je sais ton âme tendue . . ." (one would have expected "Je sais *que* ton âme *est* tendue . . ."), there is nothing strikingly unusual in the syntax of the four verses. The poem begins with a much condensed quotation from a letter written to Segalen by his friend Henry Manceron. Manceron had written:

> Et ta lettre, comme l'appel entendu d'une voix familière et proche, secoue en sursaut la torpeur qui paralysait ma plume. Il faut que je te réponde de suite: je suis là, fidèle à l'écho de ta voix, attentif aux suggestions de ta pensée, ardemment fraternel à toutes les émotions et les fluctuations de ta vie.
> "Des lointains, des si lointains j'accours, ami, vers toi le plus cher. Mes pas ont dépecé l'horrible espace entre nous." Ai-je passé de longs mois sans t'écrire? Stupide paralysie de ma plume. Tu me connais, taciturne, inexprimé, mais fidèle et inchangé.

> And your letter, like the heeded call of a familiar and intimate voice, shakes off with a start the torpor which was paralyzing my pen. I must answer you right away: here I am, faithful to the echo of your voice, attentive to all the suggestions of your thoughts, sharing in all the emotions and changes in your life like a brother.
> "From distances, from such great distances, I run to you, my friend, to you, dearest one. My steps have carved up the horrible space separating us." Have I spent so many long months without writing to you? Stupid paralysis of my pen. You know me, silent, unexpressed, but loyal and unchanged.[25]

Born in the same year, Segalen and Manceron had been friends since the age of ten. Their lifelong friendship, as well as Manceron's letter dated 17 January 1913, clearly inspired this poem.

The epigraph, however, already reveals Segalen's habitual practice of writing in the presence of another language. The three Chinese characters, *qiu you sheng*—which can be translated as "in search of a friend's voice" or "voice in search of a friend" ("voice" and "friend" can also be rendered in the plural)—is both a condensed reference to Manceron's letter ("Et ta lettre, comme l'appel entendu d'une voix familière et proche [. . .] je suis là, fidèle à l'écho de ta voix [. . .]"), *and* an abbreviated quotation from an ode entitled "*Famu*" (literally meaning "Hewing Trees") in the *Shi Jing*:

> *Ding, ding* goes the woodman's axe;
> *Ying, ying* cry the birds,
> Leave the dark valley,
> Mount to the high tree.
> "Ying" they cry,

Each searching its mate's voice [*qiu you sheng*].
Seeing then that even a bird
Searches for its mate's voice [*qiu you sheng*],
How much the more must man
Needs search out friends and kin.[26]

An analysis of the two principal images in the poem further confirms the presence of classical Chinese within Segalen's French. The depiction of a person listening for the sound of the sea in a seashell suggests the geographical separation of two friends and their longing for each other. It is a Western, perhaps universal, image. The evocation of the lute player, however, is purely Chinese. It alludes to a famous story of friendship between two men from antiquity: Yu Boya and Zhong Ziqi. Yu Boya was a scholar and an accomplished lute player; Zhong Ziqi was an uneducated logger. Despite their dissimilar backgrounds, the two men became best friends through their common love of music. Zhong could guess Yu's thoughts simply by listening to the music he was playing at the moment. When the logger died, the scholar destroyed his lute and gave up playing altogether, since never again would he find anyone capable of understanding his music so well as his late friend. The story of this celebrated friendship generated the expression *zhiyin* (literally: "one who understands music"), which designates a kindred spirit or an *âme sœur*. A related, but opposing, expression would be *dui niu tanqin* ("playing the zither to a cow"), used to express one's frustration at not being understood. Without knowledge of this historical reference, a reader of this stèle would not fully appreciate the appropriateness of the lute-playing image, nor the poignancy of the refrain "C'est pour toi seul que je joue." ("It is for you alone that I play.") The speaker is offering a variation of the Chinese story: although he does not break his lute when friendship dies, as Yu did at Zhong's death, he continues to play only for his lost friend. There is perhaps no "mise en réseau" of two poetics in "Trahison fidèle," as in "Les cinq relations"; nevertheless, Segalen has again provided a clear example of what Glissant calls "the presence of the world's languages in the practice of one's own."

V. P. Bol, in his meticulous study of the language in *Stèles*, draws our attention to this surprising fact: despite the impression of foreignness we experience while reading these sixty-four poems, only one common noun in the entire collection is a foreign word.[27] Everywhere else, Segalen has taken the trouble to translate a Chinese reality into Western terms: for instance, a Chinese string instrument is a lute, and Chinese aristocrats are referred to as dukes or lords.[28] In other words, there are no "creolisms" in *Stèles*. It is evident that in "Les cinq relations" and "Trahison fidèle," all the words are

French words. Exoticism is not generated through the poem's vocabulary but via the syntax or the poetics of the language or by allusions to the Chinese culture.

Francis de Miomandre, one of the earliest critics to realize that Segalen's work does not belong to the category of "exotic literature," describes his experience of reading *Stèles* as follows:

> Tous les ponts sont coupés, toutes les transitions supprimées . . . Le caractère de l'étrangeté qu'il présente ne vient pas du tout de l'extérieur. Encore une fois, nul exotisme. Mais une pensée infiniment secrète et lointaine est là, vivante, dans une sorte de confidence mystérieuse et terrible [. . .] il s'agit de confronter notre âme à l'âme éternelle de la Chine.

> All bridges are burned, all transitions suppressed . . . The impression of foreignness does not come from without. Once again, there is no exoticism. But an infinitely secret and distant way of thinking is there, alive, revealed to us in a mysterious and terrifying manner. . . . Our very soul is confronted with the eternal soul of China.[29]

Segalen himself claims that his exploration of the Chinese world led invariably to self-discovery: "On fit, comme toujours, un voyage au loin de ce qui n'était qu'un voyage au fond de soi." ("As always, we journeyed afar while journeying only within ourselves.")[30] The idea that exposure to alterity invariably enriches our identity coincides with Glissant's belief that with every language that disappears, a part of the human imagination is lost. The sixty-four *stèles* illustrate clearly Glissant's concepts of "multilingualism," "creolization," the "interweaving" (*mise en réseau*) of languages, and the extension of the Western imagination through knowledge of another language and culture.

In his *Introduction à une poétique du Divers*, Glissant expresses the following wish: "[J]'essaie d'écrire en vue de ce moment où le lecteur ou l'auditeur [. . .] sera ouvert à toutes sortes de poétiques et pas seulement aux poétiques de sa langue à lui." ("I attempt to write in view of the moment when the reader or listener . . . will be open to all kinds of poetics and not only to the poetics of his own language.")[31] This implies that the longed-for moment has not yet arrived; it also leads us to one further Glissantian notion, that of opacity. Glissant states in *Poétique de la Relation*: "L'opaque n'est pas l'obscur, mais il peut l'être et être accepté comme tel. Il est le non-réductible." ("The opaque is not always obscure, but it can be obscure and accepted as such. It is that which cannot be reduced.")[32] He then goes on to claim for all the right to opacity.[33] Segalen defined exoticism as "la perception aiguë et immédiate d'une incompréhensibilité éternelle," ("the keen and immediate perception of an eternal incomprehensibility,") and advised us to rejoice in our inability ever to assimilate the customs, races, nations, and others who differ from us, as this preserves for us the enduring pleasure of savoring diversity.[34] The opacity of a work like *Stèles*, a result of its essential bilingualism and creolization, is no doubt discouraging for its reader. But Segalen's opacity is no longer obscure. Thanks to the proliferation of critical studies and the existence of two annotated editions (one by Henry Bouillier, the other by Christian Doumet), the opacity of this text has been greatly reduced. Still, Segalen had to wait a very long time to find his public, which remains as yet limited, while Claudel and Saint-John Perse—writers to whom he has often been compared, and who exhibit similar traits of *créolisation* in their writings, albeit to a lesser degree than Segalen—were both canonized in their lifetime. It is to be hoped that the admiration and endorsement of an important writer and cultural theoretician such as Edouard Glissant will encourage more readers to conquer their fears before this opacity and to fully appreciate Victor Segalen's "aesthetics of Difference" and "poetics of Relationality."

Notes

1. Cornille, Jean-Louis, "Glissant est-il égal à Segalen?", *French Studies in Southern Africa* 32 (2003). Unless otherwise indicated, all English translations from the French are my own.

2. The entire *Essai sur l'exotisme* was published by Fata Morgana Press only in 1978. The English translation appeared in 2002.

3. Cornille, 11.

4. Cornille, 6–7.

5. Segalen, Victor, *Essai sur l'exotisme* (Paris: Livre de poche, 1986), 77. *Essay on Exoticism: An Aesthetics of Diversity* (Durham, NC: Duke University Press, 2002), 61. Trans. Yaël Rachel Schlick. I would be more inclined to translate "l'existence s'exalte" by "existence *elevates itself*."

6. For instance, Segalen lamented the fall of the monarchy in China and vehemently opposed Chinese attempts at democratization and modernization.

7. The Martiniquan authors of *Eloge de la Créolité* (1989), a seminal text in postcolonial theory, quote Segalen in the first two epigraphs of their book. The first quotation is precisely "C'est par la différence et dans le divers que s'exalte l'Existence." The Moroccan writer, Abdelkebir Khatibi, begins his *Figures de l'étranger dans la littérature française* (Paris: Denoël, 1987) with a discussion of Segalen. His appreciation of the French writer is, however, not without reserve. Despite lauding him as one of the founders of "literary internationalism" (14–15), Khatibi nonetheless condemns Segalen's ethnocentrism and aristocratic snobbishness, manifest in his stereotypical depiction of Chinese women and his contempt for the Chinese proletariat (51–52).

8. Glissant, Edouard, *L'Intention poétique* (Paris: Seuil, 1969), 96. Hereafter referred to as *IP*.

9. Glissant, Edouard, *Poétique de la Relation* (Paris: Gallimard, 1990), 42. Hereafter referred to as *PR*.

10. Glissant, Edouard, *Introduction à une poétique du Divers* (Paris: Gallimard, 1996), 76–77. Hereafter referred to as *IPD*.

11. Glissant, *IPD*, 18.

12. Glissant, *IPD*, 19.

13. Glissant, *IPD*, 121.

14. Glissant, *IPD*, 121.

15. Glissant, *IPD*, 46.

16. Segalen, *Essai*, 57; *Essay*, 40.

17. Glissant, *IPD*, 42.

18. Glissant, *IPD*, 122–23.

19. Glissant, *IPD*, 48.

20. "J'y dirais toutes sortes de pensées miennes, vêtues de notions et d'habits archaïques, chinois, mais dépouillés de toute chinoiserie." ("I'll express in it many different thoughts of mine, clothed in Chinese notions and Chinese archaic dress, but stripped of all *chinoiserie*.") Segalen, *Stèles, Peintures, Equipée* (Paris: Club du Meilleur Livre, 1955), 591.

21. Segalen, *Stèles* (Paris: Le Livre de poche classique, 1999), 45. Ed. Christian Doumet. Henceforth, all quotations from *Stèles* will refer to this edition. For my English translations, I have consulted Michael Taylor's *Stèles* (Santa Monica, CA: The Lapis Press, 1987).

22. See Appendix for the two poems in the original and in their English translation.

23. *Li Ki*, II, 451. Trans. Séraphin Couvreur. Quoted by Christian Doumet in *Stèles*, 142.

24. The four characters (*fu fu you bie*), read from top to bottom, signify literally: "husband, wife, have, difference." Qin Hai ying has identified the source of this epigraph in its exact wording as a quotation from Mencius on the five relationships, translated by Séraphin Couvreur (*Les Quatre Livres, Meng-tzeu*, Livre III, chap. 1, 424–25) (Qin, 16–17).

25. Segalen, Victor, and Henry Manceron, *Trahison fidèle: Correspondance 1907–1918* (Paris: Seuil, 1985), 126. "Des lointains, des si lointains [. . .] l'horrible espace entre nous" ("From far away, from so far away [. . .] the horrible space between us") is a quotation from the *stèle* "Des lointains," also classified among the "Stèles facing North" (poems on friendship).

26. The *Shi Jing*, translated variously as *The Book of Songs*, *The Book of Odes*, or *The Book of Poetry*, is an anthology of 305 poems dating mostly from the eleventh to the seventh century BCE (Zhou dynasty). Edition of this collection was traditionally attributed to Confucius (although there is little ground for this claim), and the *Shi Jing* is counted among the great Confucian Classics. This English translation is by Arthur Waley (*The Book of Songs*, 137, ode 165, "The Woodsman's Axe").

27. The word is *koumys*, a Mongolian drink. There are of course many proper nouns taken from the Chinese civilization, mainly names of dynasties and historical personages.

28. V. P. Bol, *Lecture de* Stèles *de Victor Segalen* (Paris: Lettres Modernes Minard, 1972), 107–8.

29. Francis de Miomandre, *Le Pavillon du Mandarin* (Paris: Emile-Paul Frères, 1921), 99–100.

30. Victor Segalen, *Les Origines de la statuaire de Chine* (Paris: Editions de la dif-férence, 1976), 42–43.

31. Glissant, *IPD*, 122.

32. Glissant, *PR*, 205.

33. Glissant, *PR*, 209.

34. Segalen, *Essai*, 38; *Essay*, 21.

Works Cited

Bernabé, Jean, Patrick Chamoiseau, and Raphaël Confiant. *Eloge de la créolité*. Paris: Gallimard/Presses Universitaires Créoles, 1989.

Bol, V. P. *Lecture de* Stèles *de Victor Segalen*. Paris: Lettres Modernes Minard, 1972.

The Book of Songs (*Shi Jing*). Trans. Arthur Waley. New York: Grove Press, 1996.

Cornille, Jean-Louis. "Glissant est-il égal à Segalen?" *French Studies in Southern Africa* 32 (2003): 1–13.

Glissant, Edouard. *Les Indes*. Paris: Seuil, 1956.

——. *L'Intention poétique*. Paris: Seuil, 1969.

——. *Introduction à une poétique du Divers*. Paris: Gallimard, 1996.

——. *Poétique de la Relation*. Paris: Gallimard, 1990.

Khatibi, Abdelkebir. *Figures de l'étranger dans la littérature française*. Paris: Denoël, 1987.

Miomandre, Francis de. *Le Pavillon du Mandarin*. Paris: Emile-Paul Frères, 1921, 89–111.

Qin Hai ying. "*Stèles*: épigraphes chinoises et stratégie d'une écriture transculturelle." *Lectures de Segalen:* Stèles *et* Equipée. Ed. Marie Dollé. Rennes: Presses Universitaires de Rennes, 1999, 113–123.

Segalen, Victor. *Essai sur l'exotisme*. Paris: Livre de poche, 1986.

——. *Essay on Exoticism: An Aestheics of Diversity*. Durham, NC: Duke University Press, 2002. Trans. Yaël Rachel Schlick.

——. *Les Immémoriaux*. Paris: Seuil, 1985.

——. *A Lapse of Memory*. Brisbane: Boombana Publications, 1995. Trans. Rosemary Arnoux.

——. *Les Origines de la statuaire de Chine*. Paris: Editions de la Différence, 1976.

——. *Stèles*. Edition critique d'Henry Bouillier. Paris: Mercure de France, 1982.

——. *Stèles*. Présentation et notes de Christian Doumet. Paris: Le Livre de poche classique, 1999.

———. *Steles.* Santa Monica, CA: The Lapis Press, 1987. Trans. Michael Taylor.
———. *Stèles, Peintures, Equipée.* Paris: Club du Meilleur Livre, 1955.
Segalen, Victor, and Henry Manceron. *Trahison fidèle: Correspondance 1907–1918.* Paris: Seuil, 1985.

Appendix

夫婦有別

LES CINQ RELATIONS

Du Père à son fils, l'affection. Du Prince au sujet, la justice. Du frère cadet à l'aîné, la subordination. D'un ami à son ami, toute la confiance, l'abandon, la similitude.

○

Mais pour elle, — de moi vers elle, — oserai-je dire et observer ! Elle, qui retentit plus que tout ami en moi ; que j'appelle sœur aînée délicieuse ; que je sers comme Princesse, — ô mère de tous les élans de mon âme,

Je lui dois par nature et destinée la stricte relation de distance, d'extrême et de diversité.

Figure A.1. ***Les Cinq Relations.***

Source: Excerpted from "Segalen and the Postcolonial," ***Glasgow Introductory Guide to French Literature*** ©2007. University of Glasgow French and German Publications. Reprinted with permission.

The Five Relationships

From father to son: affection. From Prince to
subject: justice. From younger brother to
elder: deference. From friend to friend:
confidence, unconstraint, similarity
O
But for her,—from me unto her,—dare I say
And observe this! She who echoes within
Me more deeply than any friend; whom I
Call delightful elder sister; whom I serve as
My Princess,—O mother of all my soul's impulses.
By nature and destiny I owe her a strict relation
of distance, extremity, and diversity.

Figure A.2.   The Five Relationships

TRAHISON FIDÈLE

求
友
聲

Tu as écrit : « Me voici, fidèle à
l'écho de ta voix, taciturne, inexprimé. »
Je sais ton âme tendue juste au gré des
soies chantantes de mon luth :
C'est pour toi seul que je joue.

Écoute en abandon et le son et l'ombre du son
dans la conque de la mer où tout plonge.
Ne dis pas qu'il se pourrait qu'un jour tu
entendisses moins délicatement !

Ne le dis pas. Car j'affirme alors, détourné de
toi, chercher ailleurs qu'en toi-même le
répons révélé par toi. Et j'irai, criant aux
quatre espaces :

Tu m'as entendu, tu m'as connu, je ne puis pas
vivre dans le silence. Même auprès de cet
autre que voici, c'est encore,
C'est pour toi seul que je joue.

Figure A.3.   Trahison Fidele.

Source: Excerpted from "Segalen and the Postcolonial," **Glasgow Introductory Guide to French Literature** ©2007. University of Glasgow French and German Publications. Reprinted with permission.

Loyal Betrayal

You have written: "Here I am, loyal to the
  echo of your voice, silent, unspoken." I
  know your soul to be perfectly attuned to
  the singing silk of my lute:
    It is for you alone that I play.

Listen with abandon to the sound and the
  shadow of the sound in the conch shell of
  the sea where everything is plunged. Do not
  say that one day, you may hear it less delicately!

Do not say this. For turned away from you, I
  will then claim to seek elsewhere than in
  you the response revealed by you. And I
  will wander, crying to the four spaces:

You have heard me, you have known me, I
  cannot live in silence. Even in the company
  of this other, it is still
  For you alone that I play.

Figure A.4.   Loyal Betrayal

CHAPTER SEVEN

~

Whose Other?

The Centrality of Language to Identity and Representation in Roumain's Gouverneurs de la rosée

Kathy Richman, University of the Pacific, Stockton, California

The framework of this collection of essays, France and its other worlds, implies a difference—as well as a relationship—between France and other countries in the Francophone world. Rather than consider differences between France and its other worlds, though, I would like to examine how difference within a single country plays out in literature. I take as my primary example the Haitian Jacques Roumain's *Gouverneurs de la rosée*, published in 1946, a novel that calls attention to questions of identity and difference in its themes and use of language as well as in the distance between the author and his subject. What can we learn from a work in which a highly educated member of the urban elite in Port-au-Prince, an ethnologist, politician, and diplomat, writes about illiterate subsistence farmers suffering from crushing poverty, drought, political repression, and a deadly family feud? Part of the answer lies in recognizing Roumain as an author who calls on his multiculturalism and multilingualism to represent a people with whom he shares a nationality but not a social position, a people whose social and political situation he portrays at least in part to make them known outside of their community. This positioning and approach recall works found in the literary tradition of nineteenth-century France, when that country was working through political, economic, and social upheavals that are now more frequently associated with what are referred to as "developing countries." As for Roumain in Haiti, the Other for the majority of French novelists and intellectuals of the nineteenth century could be and often was "local," that is, poor urban dwellers or rural inhabitants who shared part of the authors' identity but belonged to a different world.

Reading *Gouverneurs* in the company of two such unlikely companions as George Sand's *François le Champi* (1848) and Eugène Sue's *Mystères de Paris* (1842) brings to the fore the potential of Roumain's novel for political and social impact. The power of *Gouverneurs* results from the author's straddling two worlds, not in spite of it. All three works engage seriously and sincerely with an Other, an identity that is not their own nor that of their intended readers, an Other that is marginalized in society as well as in literature. These novels take on urgent social and political issues of their times and present the suffering Other with an eye to raising awareness, if not inspiring activism, in their intended reader. For Eugène Sue in *Les Mystères de Paris*, it is the poor and suffering of Paris. For George Sand in *François le Champi*, it is the rural orphan as disenfranchised member of society. And for Jacques Roumain in *Gouverneurs de la rosée*, it is Haitian farmers who, because of the hardships of subsistence farming, suffer from drought worsened by deforestation as well as from political oppression and corruption, conditions that still afflict this population sixty years later. What is telling is not just the difference in identity between Sue, Sand, and Roumain and the Others they represent in their works, but rather the ways in which they mediate between the universe of the Other and that of the implied reader to make identification and empathy with the Other possible.

Gouverneurs de la rosée is the story of the people of Fonds-Rouge, a community in rural Haiti that, at the opening of the novel, is suffering from a terrible drought. Manuel, a young man and native of Fonds-Rouge, returns after cutting cane in Cuba for fifteen years. He finds a community on the very last of its food supply, which is prompting despair in all, resignation in some, and the decision to emigrate in others. In his absence two important events have occurred: the deforestation of the hills and a deadly split in the extended family which has resulted in two warring sides in the community. The day of his return he also meets a beautiful young woman from the village who is serious, stately, and marriageable, but unfortunately a member of the other side of the family. Manuel uses logic and perseverance to find a source of water, then tries to reconcile the enemy sides so that they will work together to bring the water to the village for irrigation. He wants to revive one of the old ways of the community, the *coumbite*,[1] or collective work group, to tap the water source and build the necessary canal. Bienaimé, Manuel's father, recalls the power and camaraderie experienced by members of the *coumbite*, describing it with a nostalgia that implies the practice is lost forever: "A l'époque, on vivait tous en bonne harmonie, unis comme les doigts de la main et la coumbite réunissait le voisinage pour la récolte ou le défrichage . . . Ah ces coumbites, songe Bienaimé."[2] Manuel builds on the traditional solidarity of the *coumbite* with his recent experience of a successful cane cutters' strike in Cuba. Before he can finish his work of rebuilding the community, Manuel is killed by a jealous rival and opponent of reconciliation. His legacy lives on in an irrigation system built by the *coumbite* and in the child his pregnant fiancée will bear.

What interests me in *Gouverneurs de la rosée, François le Champi,* and *Les Mystères de Paris*—and in the novelists themselves—is the intersection of identity and representation. As readers and scholars, we usually think of representation in terms of mimesis, but representation can also take the form of advocacy. Two definitions of the word "represent" are at work at the same time: to depict or portray, *and* to act as a spokesperson for. The novels bring to light contemporary social conditions in two ways. First, they portray members of society who are otherwise underrepresented in literature, and often in political debate as well. Second, they advocate for the underrepresented, or as the root *vocare* suggests, calls out to others. In Aristotle's *Poetics*, mimesis is meant to elicit pity, or empathy, in the audience.[3] This emotion depends a great deal on identity and identification: the separate identities of self and Other, and at the same time a link between them, an identification of the self in the Other. That identification is what enables compassion to take place, and it is why the various identities at play within and without these three novels are so important.

Jean-Paul Sartre signals the role of the author as go-between and the question of the author's identity, or as he puts it, "condition," in his discussion of "la littérature engagée" in "Pour qui écrit-on?," part of *Qu'est-ce que la littérature?,* published more or less contemporaneously with *Gouverneurs de la rosée:* "L'écrivain est médiateur par excellence et son engagement c'est la médiation. Seulement s'il est vrai qu'il faut demander des comptes à son oeuvre à partir de sa condition, il faut se rappeler aussi que sa condition n'est pas seulement celle d'un homme en général mais précisément aussi d'un écrivain."[4] Sartre identifies an identity that is multiple in the writer. First, there is the multiplicity involved in whatever his or her "condition" is (social class, nationality, gender, etc.). In addition to this there is his or her "condition" as writer. The "comptes" demanded of the work (not explicitly of the author him- or herself) by engagement includes taking a stand and mediating between differences, both of which are contingent on the author's multiple position in society. The author's "prise de position" involves not only taking a stand on a subject but also taking a stand *as* a subject.

Advocacy in *Gouverneurs de la rosée*, *François le Champi*, and *Les Mystères de Paris* grows out of this double "prise de position" by the authors.

The evolution of Eugène Sue's identity could be neatly summed up as dandy turned socialist, "passant du Jockey Club aux bouges."[5] Born into a family of very successful physicians and a newcomer to high society, he takes up writing as a profession when he spends his considerable inheritance to establish his social status. Given the assignment to write a serial novel destined "à l'usage du beau monde,"[6] and piggybacking on the success of a novel about the insalubrious side of London, Sue researches his subject by dressing as a worker, visiting taverns and poor neighborhoods, and learning "argot."[7] As the serial progresses from its beginning in 1842 to its end in 1845, so, too, does Sue's experience with poor people and criminals and their struggles in parts of Paris previously unknown to him. What begins as research that would lend verisimilitude to his representation leads Sue personally to empathy with and advocacy for the poor, changes that make their way into *Les Mystères*. One can see the evolution of Sue's position vis-à-vis his subject in the difference between the introduction and later chapters.

On the first page the omniscient narrator offers a sensational representation of an Other who is completely different from the implied reader, the inhabitants of the "bas-fonds" of Paris, criminals and prostitutes who congregate around the then-poor neighborhood of Notre-Dame Cathedral: "Ce début annonce au lecteur qu'il doit assister à de sinistres scènes; s'il y consent, il pénétrera dans des régions horribles, inconnues; des types hideux, effrayants, fourmilleront dans ces cloaques impurs comme les reptiles dans le marais."[8] As the novel progresses, though, Sue characterizes some of these characters in a more positive way. He depicts the hero, a prince, telling a former murderer, le Chourineur, that he has "du coeur et de l'honneur" (*MDP* 62). When the prince reaches out to shake the man's hand, the narrator notes the "abîme" (*MDP* 63) that separates the two but which is bridged nonetheless by the prince's recognition of worth in le Chourineur. The example set by the prince lessens the gap between the Other and the implied reader by making identification and empathy with the characters easier. The novel begins to advocate for the disenfranchised of Paris by setting an example, depicting fictional solutions like model farms, no-interest pawnshops, and "la Banque des Pauvres." The reader encounters an even less subtle advocacy in long passages by the narrator and in footnotes that opine on unhealthy working conditions, the plight of old, pensionless workers, and the harmful conditions of prisons and asylums, among other social problems of 1840s Paris.

The amalgam of binary oppositions lived by George Sand constitute a "condition" that is kaleidoscopally multifaceted. Raised primarily as the daughter of nobility on an estate in Berry, but painfully aware of her mother as "une fille du peuple," she is at the same time Parisian and *berrichonne*, mother and cross-dressing dandy, prolific writer and, thanks to her good works, "Bonne Dame de Nohant." In the two prefaces to *François le Champi* Sand writes from a position encompassing several of these aspects of her identity, and she makes plain that her concerns in the novel are both aesthetic and social. In the *Notice* she recommends *François le Champi* "[p]our ceux des lecteurs qui, artistes de profession ou d'instinct, s'intéressent aux procédés de fabrication des oeuvres d'art,"[9] which include a discussion of the legitimacy of "le langage figuré du pays" and her encounter with a *champi* (rural orphan) that serves as inspiration for the book. It also discusses the problem of *champis* (social prejudice, inadequate government support) and her own successful charitable experiences in providing for them. In the *Avant-propos* the (male) author Sand and another *berrichon*, R***, discuss the relative merits of peasant and intellectual life, "la vie primitive" and "la vie factice." (*FLC*, 42) As a writer with a foot in both worlds or, as R*** puts it, with "nos oreilles du terroir," (*FLC* 55) Sand is eager to translate the lyricism and beauty, as well as the moral, of a *berrichon* story s/he has heard at a "veillée" so that Parisians can understand and appreciate it. The novel functions as an exemplum, showing how the efforts of individuals can transform a boy with no place in society into an adult so well integrated into that society that he can improve it. The juxtaposition of prefaces suggests that the political and the aesthetic in *François le Champi* are intertwined and inextricable.

Jacques Roumain "belonged," to quote the African American poet Langston Hughes, one of the translators of *Gouverneurs de la rosée*, "to one of the first families of Haiti," and, as he further notes, "Money and position were part of Roumain's heritage."[10] Ethnographer, author, and organizer of the Communist Party in Haiti, Roumain was imprisoned several times in Haiti and sent into exile as a diplomat to Mexico. Like Sand, then, his position is one of intermediary, a person of social privilege in his country who has an engagement with the rural people he writes about. There are no overt commentaries by Roumain to that effect in or around the novel, as there are for Sue and Sand, but the following thought of the hero of *Gouverneurs*, Manuel, may be indicative of Roumain's conception of his relation to Haiti and its people:

> Si l'on est d'un pays, si l'on y est né comme qui dirait: natif-natal, eh bien, on l'a dans les yeux, la peau, les mains, avec la chevelure de ses arbres, la chair de sa terre, les os de ses pierres, le sang de ses rivières, son ciel, sa saveur, ses hommes et ses femmes: c'est une présence, dans le coeur, ineffaçable, comme une fille qu'on aime (*GDR* 25–26).

The enumeration of body parts and their attribution to both a person and the native land is like Sand's "oreilles du terroir" multiplied many times over.

Like their authors, the heroes of these three novels are bilingual and bi-cultural. They mediate between one society and another, suggesting that there needs to be outside perspective mixed with local knowledge to be in-novative enough to resolve the problems the author deals with in the plot. In all three texts, it is characters who are at the same time members of the community and outsiders who bring new ideas and solutions to the community represented. In *Les Mystères* it is Prince Rodolphe, a German, who has gained a near-native knowledge of the poor and criminal populations of Paris by taking on the personae of different classes of workers. He speaks "argot comme père et mère"(*MDP* 176), and "les manières et le langage qu'il affec-tait avec une incroyable aisance donnaient à Rodolphe une complète ressem-blance avec les hôtes de l'ogresse"(*MDP* 42). Passing successfully as a worker, he can use his princely power and money to transform the lives of individu-als and create institutions that will help the "deserving" poor. Part of the transformation includes teaching his beneficiaries to imagine a better future and recognize their own value as members of society.

By virtue of his marginal position as a *champi*, Francois has the freedom to develop into a kind of new man, a model husband and a kinder, gentler cap-italist. He is integrated into the community when the miller's wife, Madeleine, adopts him and teaches him her self-sacrificing Christian ways by example. Forced to leave and find work in another village, François acquires the knowledge and language of business and law. He carries out what he calls "un coup de commerce" and states that he "sai[t] bien comment ces-affaires-là se conduisent"(*FLC* 196). These transform him from a boy others find doltish into a man who can outwit speculators who threaten Madeleine and others in the community. François' version of capitalism ensures no harm comes to misguided investors; the marriage he undertakes with Madeleine is one of gender and financial parity and is grounded in mutual love. A boy born outside a direct patriarchal line—Madeleine remarks with astonish-ment, "Tu ne sais pas le nom de ton père?" (*FLC* 58)—he is free to invent idealized incarnations of patriarchal institutions.

Manuel, too, has been away and returned to his community with new knowledge gained abroad. His bridging of the outside world and his village of origin is symbolized by his bilingualism in Creole and Spanish. His first word in the novel is Spanish ("Carajo"), and he sometimes begins a sentence in one language and finishes it in another. Manuel is at home again in Fonds-Rouge; "il est chez lui, avec les siens, ramené à son destin" (*GDR* 36). But in his fifteen years' cutting cane in Cuba he has learned from personal experience with a labor strike and from his "*compañero* à Cuba, celui qui lui parlait politique, au temps de la grève. Il en savait des choses, *el hijo de . . . su madre*, et les situations les plus embrouillées, il te les démêlait que c'était une merveille" (*GDR* 166). His mother recognizes that his new ideas stem from his life outside of Fonds-Rouge and expresses their foreignness to her understanding: "Tu as la langue habile et tu as voyagé dans les pays étrangers. Tu as appris des choses qui dépassent mon entendement" (*GDR* 53). Part of Manuel's role in Fonds-Rouge is to explain what he has learned, instilling it in others so that they, too, can pass on the knowledge. Manuel's understanding extends to the natural world as well. He not only explains solidarity to his neighbors, "Manuel avait traduit en bon créole le langage exigeant de la plaine assoiffée, la plainte des plantes, les promesses de tous les mirages d'eau" (*GDR* 147). Manuel thus "translates" the natural environment they have grown up in, in order for them to be able to imagine a future there.

Language is central to the author's task of mediation described by Sartre. It is by using a combination of standardized French and what are considered minority languages—Haitian Creole, *berrichon*, the regional language of Berry, and criminal and working-class *argot*—that Roumain, Sand, and Sue bridge the society of their implied readers and the underrepresented society for which they advocate. The key role of language appears throughout the plot of *Gouverneurs* as well. It is Manuel's eloquence that enables him to mediate between old and new ideas, as well as between different factions in the community, to bring about the resolution of the problems of drought and feuding.

George Sand articulates the mediating work of the author overtly in the *Avant-propos* to *François le Champi*. There, Sand discusses a dilemma with her interlocutor R***, how to represent the story of a *berrichon* peasant faithfully while making it intelligible to sophisticated Parisian readers. For Sand, bridging two cultures in literature is such a difficult question of poetics that the author accuses R***, "tu m'imposes un travail à perdre l'esprit" (*FLC* 52). Yet what eventually makes writing the novel possible is the author's double positioning as a member of both rural *berrichon* society and the Parisian intelligentsia. Sand can understand and be sensitive to the nuances of the local tale of François le Champi because she can listen with the "oreilles du terroir" as well as write "la langue de l'Académie" (*FLC* 48). R*** proposes solving the problem of mediation by retelling the local story "comme si tu avais à ta droite un Parisien parlant la langue moderne, et à ta gauche un paysan devant lequel tu ne voudrais pas dire une phrase, un mot où il ne pourrait pas pénétrer" (*FLC* 53). The position of the author is thus as interpreter, placed squarely between the metropolitan, or centrally located, implied reader and what is considered the socially marginalized group. According to the prefaces, it is a group whose story merits attention on aesthetic and political grounds and which deserves to be told.

Sand's choice to use *berrichon* in the text and, even more prominently, in the title goes beyond a desire for local color or realist detail. It is a gesture of advocacy, underlining the value of a language—and culture—considered backward or unimportant when compared to the "langue moderne" of the Parisian. Indeed, Sand uses *berrichon* to point out the connection through language between the peasant and the Parisian. When R*** objects that Sand is starting her literary effort badly with the very title because "[c]hampi n'est pas français," Sand defends its legitimacy by pointing out its presence in the dictionary and noting that it was used by Montaigne:

> Je te demande bien pardon, répondis-je. Le dictionnaire le déclare *vieux*, mais Montaigne l'emploie, et je ne prétends pas être plus Français que les grands écrivains qui font la langue. Je n'intitulerai donc pas mon conte François l'Enfant-Trouvé, François le Bâtard, mais François *le Champi*, c'est-à-dire l'enfant abandonné dans les champs, comme on disait autrefois dans le monde, et comme on dit encore aujourd'hui chez nous (*FLC* 55).

"Champi" is not merely regional but an ancestor of the Parisians' "langue moderne," a word found worthy by Montaigne, an author they recognize as a forefather of the French literary canon and the French language itself. In this way Sand underlines language as a key link in mediating between rural and Parisian societies.

In the body of the novel Sand carries out this delicate balancing act of mediation by writing the vast majority of *François le Champi* in "la langue moderne" of the Parisian, interspersing it with moments of "countrified" language. She uses the device of two *berrichon* narrators who take turns telling the tale and who appear infrequently to comment on the plot and their choice of language. The intimations of country flavor appear in the form of less-learned syntax used by the characters ("M'est avis que") and the narrators ("comme je vas vous le faire assavoir") (*FLC* 208). There are also expressions based in rural life, such as "La Sévère ne l'écouta plus que le tondeur le mouton" (*FLC* 116). A song in *berrichon* which François remembers is introduced in the narration as "une chanson bien ancienne . . . dans le parlage du vieux temps de notre pays" (*FLC* 246). These departures from standard French are either explained in the narrative or simple enough to be comprehensible to the implied Parisian reader. Contrary to the advice in the *Avant-propos*, it is *berrichon*, the Other language that is presented so that it is the Parisian, not the peasant, who will not find "une phrase, un mot, où il ne pourrait pas pénétrer."

In *Gouverneurs de la rosée* Roumain shares the same predicament as Sand: How to faithfully represent the experience of Haitian farmers while making their story comprehensible to an audience that is "foreign" to it, whether they dwell in Haitian cities or overseas? Like Sand, Roumain chooses standard French for the vast majority of the narration, even though, as in *François le Champi*, the narrator identifies himself as one of the country people: "Nous avons un mot pour ça, nous autres nègres[11] d'Haiti: *le téléguele* que nous disons" (GDR 145). The French of the narration is made to appear invisible or "natural," as we can see by contrasting it with rare use of the creolized French of the peasants' prayers at Manuel's wake: "Pa'quel excès dé bonté vous vous êtes cha'gé di poids dé nos crimes, vous avez souffè 'ine mô crielle pou' nous sauvé dé la mô" (GDR 190). The elements implying a Creole accent here are the absence of a pronounced "r" and the lack of nasal vowels. In another passage Simidor describes the very particular use of French among people whose first language is Creole:

> De mon temps cette question des filles: c'était un tracas et une difficulté. Il fallait des manoeuvres, des feintes, *des parler-français*, enfin toutes les macaqueries, toutes les simagrées . . . A l'époque, on était plus éclairé que vous autres nègres aujourd'hui, on avait de l'instriction [sic]: je commence donc dans mon français: "Mademoiselle, depuis que jé vous ai vur, sous la galérie di presbytè, j'ai un transpò d'amou pou toi" (GDR 44–45). (Emphasis mine).

Creole, the language of the vast majority of Haitians,[12] is interspersed here and there in dialogue, expressions, and song, especially the songs of the *coumbite*, and is translated into French in footnotes or explained by the narrator.

> Atè
> M'ap mande kimoun
> Ki andedan kay la
> Konpé reponn:
> Se mwen ak kouzin mwen
> Ase-he!

(Translated in the footnote as "A terre—Je demande—Qui est dans la case— Le compère répond:—C'est moi avec ma cousine—Assez, eh!") (GDR 15).

There are also frequent insertions of nonstandard sentence structure that mimics Haitian Creole or translates common Creole sayings, as in this exchange between Manuel and his mother: "Tu m'entends, pitit mwen? Je t'entends, oui. Ce sera pour après-demain, si-dieu-veut" (GDR 65). "Pitit mwen," "mon petit," is appended to a sentence in standard French; "Si-dieu-veut" in Creole is "si dye vle."[13]

The aesthetic choice of Roumain to use Creole and "countrified" language as an accent rather than the main language of the text adds a sense of authenticity in an attempt at realism. It is also, as it is in Sand, a celebration of the language and a signaling of its lyricism and richness. If *Gouverneurs* does not make a historical link between the language of the people and "la langue moderne," as Sand does in the *Avant-propos*, it does make the point that the "bourgeois de la ville" depend on the labor of the peasants (GDR 22). When Laurélien asks, "Alors qu'est-ce que nous sommes, nous autres, les habitants, les nègres-pieds-à-terre, méprisés, maltraités?," Manuel answers:

> Ce que nous sommes? Si c'est une question, je vais te répondre: eh, bien, nous sommes ce pays et il n'est rien sans nous, rien du tout. Qui est-ce qui plante, qui est-ce qui arrose, qui est-ce que récolte? Le café, le coton, le riz, la canne, le cacao, le maïs, les bananes, les vivres, et tous les fruits, si ce n'est pas nous, qui les fera pousser? (GDR 77).

But the overriding explanation is that Roumain, like Sand, is using this combination of languages to mediate between the marginalized population he portrays and an implied metropolitan reader. Though the implied reader is not explicitly identified, as in Sand's prefaces, one can deduce his or her identity from Roumain's choice of language. If the intended reader were the majority of Haitians, whose language is Creole, there would be no need for translation or explanation. In fact, in the 1940s a relatively small percentage of Haitians were literate,[14] as was the case of French peasants in the 1840s, and Creole, a traditionally oral language, did not as yet have an officially recognized standardized spelling.[15] Roumain's representation of the struggles in Fonds-Rouge, then, is meant for readers "other" than the people his protagonists represent.

This mediating role of the novels turns more overtly to advocacy, in the sense of "giving voice to," when characters directly express the effect that knowledge of their situation would have on people whom they imagine have the ability to change it. Through these moments the texts call attention to the work of advocacy they carry out. For example, an impoverished worker's cry from *Les Mystères de Paris*—"Si les riches savaient!" (MDP 430)—points to an important raison d'être of that novel: to make known the situation of the poor in 1840s Paris. The implication is that if the rich were aware of the poor's misery, they would certainly act. In Sand's novel, François asks if being a *champi*, or field foundling, is "bad," since people use the word as an epithet. His stepmother replies:

—Mais non, mon enfant, puisque ce n'est pas ta faute.

—Et à qui est-ce la faute?

—C'est la faute aux riches (to which Francois replies)

—Pourtant il y a de bons riches, puisque vous l'êtes, vous . . . c'est le tout de se trouver au droit: pour les rencontrer (*FLC* 100).

Sand's novel—as well as her account of her own charity in the *Notice*—encourages readers to be "de bons riches" rather than, one must suppose, ordinary "riches" by offering them an example of the difference one individual's actions can make.

Roumain's peasant narrator is far less conciliatory and far more militant in describing the relationship of otherness between the urban bourgeoisie and himself and his fellow peasants:

Mais ces habitants des mornes et des plaines, les bourgeois de la ville ont beau les appeler par dérision nègres pieds-à-terre, nègres va-nu-pieds, nègres orteils (trop pauvres qu'ils étaient pour s'acheter des souliers), tant pis et la merde pour eux, parce que, question de courage au travail, nous sommes sans reproche; et soyez comptés, nos grands pieds de travailleurs de la terre, on vous les foutra un jour dans le cul, salauds (*GDR* 22).

This is not the hopeful sigh of the worker in *Les Mystères* nor the sermonizing good example in *François le Champi*. At first glance the threat of feet in the derrière and the epithet "salauds" imply a total rupture between the peasants and "bourgeois de la ville," one that will only be resolved by an uprising of the former. The narrator places himself unequivocally among the "travailleurs de la terre" with the phrase "nous sommes sans reproche"; he puts himself in opposition to the "bourgeois de la ville" by addressing them as "vous." But the narrator also offers the explanatory parenthesis for the mocking invective "nègres orteils (trop pauvres qu'ils étaient pour s'acheter des souliers)" to an implied reader other than the "travailleurs de la terre," who *already* know they have large, deformed feet because they have no shoes. Despite the threat against the "bourgeois de la ville," this mild, instructive aside *is* in fact aimed, along with the prospective kick in the seat, at what Sand calls "de bons riches" among the urban upper class in Haiti and elsewhere.

So far, I have considered the use of language by Roumain, Sand, and Sue in creating a bridge between a community of readers and the communities represented in their novels. Now I will turn to the representation of language within *Gouverneurs de la rosée* as the principal means to effect change. In *Gouverneurs* it is language that makes it possible to unite the feuding families of Fonds-Rouge, which in turn enables them to work together to bring water to the community and save its very existence. Manuel imagines that "l'eau les unirait à nouveau . . . la communauté fraternelle renaîtrait avec les plantes nouvelles" (*GDR* 83). The connection between the word and water is made very early in the novel and is continued as a sustained metaphor throughout. Bienaimé, Manuel's father, remembers the old days of the *coumbite* in a reverie and uses the conditional tense as an indication of repeated habit in the past:

> Le chant prendrait le chemin des roseaux, le long du canal, il remonterait jusqu'à la source tapie au creux d'aisselle du morne, dans la lourde senteur des fougères et des malanga macérés dans l'ombrage et le suintement secret de l'eau (*GDR* 16).

The "chant" or work song of the *coumbite*, makes its way from the field, along the canal, to reach the source of water, which is "hidden" and "secret" even at the best of times. It is the *word* that finds the water, much as Manuel's use of words makes it possible for his community to bring the water from its source to their fields. The "chant" of the *coumbite*, sung word and drumming, provides a single rhythm to unite the workers in synchronized movement. It is an integral part of the collective work of the *coumbite*, and Antoine, known as Simidor,[16] the musician of Fonds-Rouge, feels useless that he is no longer fulfilling what he considers his natural role, just like the farmers "à leurs bras désoeuvrés" (*GDR* 44):

> Et à quoi bon vivre, si je ne peux plus passer mon tambour en bandoulière et conduire le coumbite en chantant et boire mon compte de clairin après? J'étais né pour ça avec des doigts comme des baguettes et à la place de la cervelle une nichée d'oiseaux musiciens. Alors, je te demande, pourquoi je vis encore? Mon rôle est fini" (*GDR* 113).

The whole village is silent with drought. As the narrator recounts in Délira's thoughts:

> La vie est tarie à Fonds Rouge. On n'avait qu'à écouter le silence pour entendre la mort, se laisser aller à cette torpeur et on se sentait ensevelie. Le heurt

régulier et répété des pilons dans les mortiers s'était tu . . . et ce qu'il était loin le temps des coumbites, du chant viril et joyeux des hommes . . . et les voix insouciantes des jeunes négresses jaillissaient comme une fontaine dans la nuit . . . c'est fini" (*GDR* 124).

Silence here denotes death. Sound, even the nonhuman "pilons," but especially the "chant" and the "voix," denote life. The imagery associates speech with spouting water and the spouting implied by male virility. Perhaps even more telling is the detail that the only existing body of water Bienaimé knows is "la mare Zombi . . . une eau pourrie comme une couleuvre morte, enroulée, une eau épaisse et sans force pour courir" (52). The pond is triply associated with death here ("pourrie" and "morte"), especially since in the *vodun* religion in Haiti, a "zombi" is a person who has died and walks the earth in a supernatural state.

To revive the *coumbite*, to revive Fonds-Rouge, Manuel metaphorically takes the singer Simidor's place in the *coumbite*, using words to unify his neighbors to work for a common cause. Once he explains his plan to some sympathetic listeners, they begin to call him "chef," "maître," etc. To extend the metaphor of words for water, because Manuel is a "gouverneur de la rosée," he is also a "gouverneur de la parole." Like Simidor, Manuel must call on his creativity and rhetorical skills to compose an argument powerful enough to unify and guide. Manuel's eloquence is described with some awe by other characters. His friend and ally Laurélien says, "Je n'ai jamais vu un nègre avoir la langue plus habile que toi" (*GDR* 141). His skill, like his other successes, is due in part to traditions of his community in Haiti and in part to his experience in Cuba. He has grown up with the important oral traditions of the *coumbite* song and his mother's storytelling in the *Cric-Crac* tradition of Haiti.[17] In Cuba he has learned another vocabulary, that of political solidarity and resistance. He recounts the strike, or "huelga," in Cuba to Annaïse, but she does not know the word "grève" either, when he translates it for her:

—Qu'est-ce que c'est ce mot: la huelgue?

—Vous autres, vous dites plutôt la grève.

—Je ne sais pas non plus ce que ça veut dire" (*GDR* 95).

It is the concept of a strike as much as the language that is foreign to Annaïse. Manuel explains it to her with the metaphor of weak individual fingers joining to make a powerful fist, the same one his father thinks of when he remembers the *coumbite*:

> Manuel lui montra sa main ouverte:
>
> —Regarde ce doigt comme c'est maigre, et celui-là tout faible, et cet autre pas plus gaillard, et ce malheureux, pas bien fort non plus, et ce dernier tout seul et pour son compte. Il serra le poing:
>
> —Et maintenant, est-ce que c'est assez solide, assez massif, assez ramassé? On dirait que oui, pas vrai? Eh, bien, la grève, c'est ça: un NON de mille voix qui ne font qu'une et qui s'abat sur la table du patron avec le pesant d'une roche (*GDR* 95–96).

Manuel teaches as much as he convinces. His words, here compared again in a simile to flowing water in the sun, shed light on the mind and a hope that is like "la fraternité," an expression of family and political unity:

> —Tu dis des paroles conséquentes, oui, fit Laurélien . . . Dans le retrait le plus inarticulé de son esprit accoutumé à la lenteur et à la patience, là où les idées de résignation et de soumission s'étaient formées avec une rigidité tradition-nelle et fatale, un rideau de lumière commençait à se lever. Il éclairait un es-poir soudain, obscur encore et lointain, mais rude, certain et véridique comme la fraternité. Il cracha un jet de salive entres les dents.
>
> —Ce que tu dis là est clair comme l'eau courante au soleil . . . Alors adieu, chef' (*GDR* 78).

Through his words Manuel enables others to imagine the future he envi-sions, one of renewed agricultural and social fertility: "Il les avait promené d'avance à travers leurs récoltes: leurs yeux brillaient, rien qu'à l'entendre" (*GDR* 147). With the young woman he loves, Annaïse, he asks whether she can see various crops growing, urging her to close her eyes and imagine:

> —Tu vois la richesse? Elle ouvrit les yeux.
>
> —Tu m'as fait rêver. Je vois la pauvreté.
>
> —C'est pourtant ce qui serait, s'il y avait quoi, Anna? . . . l'arrosage, n'est-ce pas . . . Suppose, Anna, suppose que je découvre l'eau, suppose que je l'amène dans la plaine (*GDR* 94).

This scene very closely resembles a key one in *Les Mystères de Paris* in which Rodolphe describes an ideal farm to Fleur-de-Marie, one of his beneficiaries and, in the way of many *feuilletons*, his unrecognized long-lost daughter. He encourages her to dream along with him, "à faire des châteaux en Espagne" (*MDP* 102), but like Annaïse, Fleur-de-Marie realizes the gap between dreams and reality:

> Un moment abusée par les paroles de Rodolphe, elle avait oublié le présent, et le contraste de ce présent avec le rêve d'une existence douce et riante lui rappelait l'horreur de sa position . . .
> —Ah! monsieur Rodolphe, sans le vouloir, vous m'avez fait bien du chagrin . . . j'ai cru un instant à ce paradis" (*MDP* 105).

But Rodolphe has in fact brought Fleur-de-Marie to a real, model farm he has established, where he intends her to live a new life. While Manuel describes the *possible* future he has imagined for Annaïse and Fonds-Rouge, Rodolphe "peignai[t] d'après nature" (*MDP* 105). It is a sign of the greater emphasis on community effort (and greater realism) in Roumain's work that the water does not appear magically in Fonds-Rouge thanks to the plan of a rich benefactor. But the effect of these lessons in imagination is the same in both novels. Annaïse and Fleur-de-Marie take on the role of their teachers, Manuel and Rodolphe, by spreading the word to others. In a later scene Fleur-de-Marie leads her own beneficiary through the exercise of "châteaux en Espagne" to help the latter reform her life.

Manuel enlists Annaïse in his rhetorical campaign; rehearsing her in the words she should say to other women in the village to convince them of the need for cooperation:

> Tu feras le tour des commères avec ces paroles, mais avec précaution et prudence . . . Si ça prend, les femmes vont rendre leurs hommes sans repos. Les plus récalcitrants vont se fatiguer de les entendre jacasser toute la sainte journée, sans compter la nuit: de l'eau, de l'eau, de l'eau . . . Ça va faire une sonnaille de grelots sans arrêt dans leurs oreilles: de l'eau, de l'eau, de l'eau . . . jusqu'au moment où leurs yeux verront vraiment l'eau courir dans les jardins, les plantes pousser toutes seules, alors ils diront: Bon, oui, femmes, c'est bien, nous consentons (*GDR* 97).

Manuel is a source of words that flow through Annaïse to the women in the community, who will then release a torrent of language—"de l'eau, de l'eau, de l'eau"—on the village men that will eventually wear down the latter's resistance to reconciliation.

The lack of water in Fonds-Rouge has led to a drought of words in its inhabitants, especially the men. "Les femmes étaient les plus enragées . . . Mais les injures des femmes ne tirent pas à conséquence, ce n'est que du bruit fait avec du vent. Ce qui était plus grave, c'était le silence des hommes" (*GDR* 82). The narrator considers the silence among the men dangerous in general, but in two characters in particular, inarticulateness is connected directly to violence. For one man, Nérestan, "Les discours, ça n'avait jamais été son fort. De là, sa violence de taureau sauvage. Ce qu'il ne pouvait expliquer avec les mots, il les mettait sous le nez avec son poing" (*GDR* 149). Gervilen, who directly opposes Manuel's plans for reconciliation in the community and is his rival for Annaïse, lacks Manuel's facility with language entirely and relies on violence as a response: "Il avait crié, mais sa voix était restée dans le fond de sa gorge, rauque et gonflée de fureur" (*GDR* 103). When he proposes taking the water by force, "[s]a voix . . . était âpre et grinçante comme une rape. Les mots passaient avec effort entre ses dents serrés" (*GDR* 151). In the end, Gervilen's physical attack on Manuel is silent and fatal. However, in Roumain's novel violence cannot trump language.

By the time of Manuel's death, his words have grown within the inhabitants of Fonds-Rouge just as his child grows in Annaïse. Laurélien thinks at Manuel's funeral, "'Mais tes paroles, nous ne les oublierons pas'" (*GDR* 203). At the end of the novel, after Manuel's murder, the warring sides of the community do reunite in a *coumbite* to bring the water to Fonds-Rouge. Manuel himself is no longer necessary to this success because he has already planted the idea in the community. He has "confié une mission" to his mother, who finishes his work of convincing the inhabitants. She particularly emphasizes two of his dying wishes: "'Dis-[l]ui la volonté de mon sang qui a coulé: la réconciliation, la réconciliation (il l'a dit deux fois) pour que la vie recommence, pour que le jour se lève sur la rosée'" and "'Chantez mon deuil, qu'il a dit, chantez mon deuil avec un chant de coumbite'" (*GDR* 208–9). Through his words, Manuel's plan to master the water lives on, as does the renewal of the *coumbite* and the very future of the population of Fonds-Rouge.

Manuel's individual role as teacher and inspiration is crucial, but his two last wishes emphasize the greater importance of solidarity. This is consistent with many of his comments earlier in the novel, the most powerful of which speaks broadly to the importance of unity:

> [N]ous sommes misérables, c'est vrai. Mais sais-tu pourquoi, frère? à cause de notre ignorance: nous ne savons pas encore que nous sommes une force, une seule force: tous les habitants, tous les nègres des plaines et des mornes réunis. Un jour, quand nous aurons compris cette vérité, nous nous lèverons d'un point à l'autre du pays et nous ferons l'assemblée générale des gouverneurs de

la rosée, le grand coumbite des travailleurs de la terre pour défricher la misère et planter la vie nouvelle" (GDR 77–78).

In Manuel's vision "le grand coumbite" will put its collective skills to use up-rooting poverty and creating a new society. Since the image transcends the single case of Fonds-Rouge to encompass all of Haiti, it is not difficult to read it as a more universal claim for the power of worker solidarity.

One sentence from *Gouverneurs de la rosée* sums up the overall ethic of sol-idarity in the novel: "L'entr'aide, c'est l'amitié des malheureux, n'est-ce pas"[18] (GDR 13). Roumain cannot actually participate in the equal exchange of mutual aid represented by the *coumbite*, but we can see his novel and its ges-ture of advocacy as a gesture of solidarity with "les malheureux." Like "M'sieur Paulma," le "mulâtre" "au bourg" (GDR 144) whom Manuel hires to write his marriage proposal to Annaïse's family, Roumain the literate city dweller expresses the situation of those who cannot write for themselves. Like George Sand and Eugène Sue before him, Roumain takes it upon him-self to fictionalize a contemporary social problem to make it comprehensible not to the people who are suffering through it, but to those with the politi-cal and social power to effect change. By representing the threat of a "coup de pied dans le derrière" and what the rural police officer calls Manuel's "paroles de rebellion" (GDR 84), Roumain offers a warning to an implied reader who is part of an educated, literate élite, much as Manuel plans to "touch" his recalcitrant neighbors "dans le sensible de leur intérêt" (GDR 141). But Roumain softens the aspects of *Gouverneurs* that are strident po-litical manifesto by embedding them in a romantic paean to nature, a love story, and a moving family reunion. Roumain appeals both to the intellect *and* the sentiments of the implied reader. In much the same way, while Manuel will urge, "Laissez la raison parler" (GDR 139–40), he also recognizes that "il y a des fois, tu sais, le coeur et la raison c'est du pareil au même" (GDR 97). In *Gouverneurs*, passion without reason plays out as resigned reli-gious faith or enraged violence. Reason without passion is embodied by the calculating police chief, Hilarion, who mercilessly hopes for continued drought so he can buy the peasants' land cheaply.

The didactic and sentimental elements of *Gouverneurs de la rosée* may seem out of place in a work from 1946. They also account for many of the similarities between it and *François le Champi* and *Les Mystères de Paris*, nov-els from one hundred years earlier. The somewhat puzzling kinship among these three novels is elucidated by Philip Fisher in *Hard Facts*, his study of the sentimental novel and other popular genres in the nineteenth-century

United States. According to Fisher, novels that are often considered trite by later critics or literary fashions because of their use of sentiment in fact perform crucial cultural work—what he calls "the active transformation of the present"—in the society in which they were written.[19] By introducing ways of thinking—and feeling—about contentious contemporary issues, these novels eventually make new attitudes toward these issues acceptable and even commonplace. Their very success at normalization, in changing the minds—and hearts—of readers and the larger society, later relegates such novels to lesser literary status when compared to more "modern"[20] works that challenge society through their form rather than their theme. Viewed in this light, the "cultural work" that Roumain undertakes in *Gouverneurs de la rosée*—depicting "classes of figures from whom [humanity] has been socially withheld" (Fisher 99) for an implied reader who differs from these Others— is of a kind with the cultural work performed by Sand and Sue in their works, despite the different social and historical contexts presented by nineteenth-century France and twentieth-century Haiti.

Notes

1. A note in the edition of *Gouverneurs de la rosée* defines *coumbite* as "Travail agricole collectif" (*GDR*, 12). The *Haitian-English Dictionary* of the Institute of Haitian Studies, Lawrence, Kansas, defines *konbit*, or *koumbit*, as: "n. cooperative peasant work team for clearing land and harvesting, community agricultural work fest, workbee (c.f. American 'barn-raising')."

2. Jacques Roumain, *Gouverneurs de la rosée*, Coconut Creek, FL: Educa Vision, 1999, 12. References to this novel will hereafter be given as *GDR* and the page number.

3. Aristotle, *Poetics*, trans. Richard Janko, Indianapolis: Hackett Publishing Company, 1987.

4. Jean-Paul Sartre, *Qu'est-ce que la littérature?* Paris: Éditions Gallimard, 1948, 98.

5. Jean-Louis Bory, *Eugène Sue: le roi du roman populaire*, Paris: Hachette, 1962, 12.

6. Armand Lanoux, "Introduction" in Eugène Sue, *Les Mystères de Paris*, Paris: Éditions Robert Laffont, 1989, 4.

7. Defined as "Langage cryptique des malfaiteurs, du milieu" in the *Nouveau Petit Robert*.

8. Eugène Sue, *Les Mystères de Paris*, Paris: Éditions Robert Laffont, 1989, 31. References to this novel will hereafter be given as *MDP* and the page number.

9. George Sand, *François le Champi*, Paris: Éditions Gallimard, 1976, 37. References to this novel will hereafter be given as *FLC* and the page number.

10. Langston Hughes, *Collected Works of Langston Hughes*, vol. 16: *Translations: Federico García Lorca, Nicolas Guillén, and Jacques Roumain*, Columbia, MO: University of Missouri Press, 2002, 131.

11. "Nèg" in Creole is defined as "man, male; Black man; friend, pal, guy, fellow," according to Freeman's *Haitian-English Dictionary*. From usage and context, I believe that Roumain's use of "nègre" in the French narrative of *Gouverneurs* is meant to echo the Creole use of the word rather than any particular racial designation.

12. In his *Learner's Dictionary of Haitian Creole* Valdman states that Creole "is the sole language for approximately 85 percent of the population" (ix).

13. Bryant C. Freeman and Jowel C. Laguerre, *Haitian-English Dictionary*, Lawrence, KS: Institute of Haitian Studies, 1996, 70.

14. UNESCO put the percentage of illiterate Haitians at 89 percent in 1950, according to Mirville's pamphlet on fighting illiteracy in Haiti.

15. Valdman, x–xi.

16. "Simidò" is defined in Freeman as "composer/singer at konbit, popular danses, etc." So, in fact, this character is named according to his profession.

17. Manuel's mother reminds him of his begging her as a child, "maman, raconte-moi ce conte . . . et je commençais: Cric? Crac . . . "(107). "[K]rik! krak!" is defined as an interjection and "introductory formula (folk stories, riddles)" in the *Haitian Creole-English-French Dictionary*.

18. The statement of this belief is strengthened even further by the use in the text of a period rather than the question mark expected after the phrase "n'est-ce pas."

19. Philip Fisher, *Hard Facts: Setting and the Form in the American Novel*, New York: Oxford University Press, 1987, 7.

20. Fisher's examples are works qualified as modernist.

Works Cited

Aristotle. *Poetics*. Trans. Richard Janko. Indianapolis: Hackett Publishing Company, 1987.

Bory, Jean-Louis. *Eugène Sue: le roi du roman populaire*. Paris: Hachette, 1962.

Fisher, Philip. *Hard Facts: Setting and the Form in the American Novel*. New York: Oxford University Press, 1987.

Freeman, Bryant C. and Jowel C. Laguerre. *Haitian-English Dictionary*. Lawrence, KS: Institute of Haitian Studies, 1996.

———. *Haitian Creole-English-French Dictionary*. Bloomington, IN: Indiana University Creole Institute, 1981.

Hughes, Langston. *Collected Works of Langston Hughes*, vol. 16: *Translations: Federico García Lorca, Nicolás Guillén, and Jacques Roumain*. Columbia, MO: University of Missouri Press, 2002, 131, <http://site.ebrary.com/lib/stanford.edu.html> (3 April 2006).

Kaussen, Valerie. "Slaves, *Viejos*, and the *Internationale*: Modernity and Global Contact in Jacques Roumain's *Gouverneurs de la rosée*." *Research in African Literatures* 35, no. 4 (2004): 121–141.

Mirville, Solon. *L'Ecole primaire et la lutte contre l'analphabétisme en Haïti*. Port-au-Prince: La Phalange, 1959.

Roumain, Jacques. *Gouverneurs de la rosée*. Coconut Creek, FL: Educa Vision, 1999.

Sand, George. *François le Champi*. Paris: Éditions Gallimard, 1976.

Sartre, Jean-Paul. *Qu'est-ce que la littérature?* Paris: Éditions Gallimard, 1948.

Sue, Eugène. *Les Mystères de Paris*. Paris: Éditions Robert Laffont, 1989.

Targète, Jean and Raphael G. Urciolo. *Haitian Creole-English-French Dictionary*. Kensington, MD: Dunwoody Press, 1993.

Valdman, Albert. *A Learner's Dictionary of Haitian Creole*. Bloomington, IN: Indiana University Creole Institute, 1996.

CHAPTER EIGHT

~

Shadowing Assia Djebar

André Benhaïm, Princeton University

In and out, over and under, between Orient and Occident, between Algeria and France, between Arabic and French, between women's voices and men's laws, and in so many other ways, Assia Djebar's text is in perpetual motion, made of a writing whence pulsates an incessant and unpredictable rhythm. Moving, Djebar's writing is elusive, difficult to grasp because it is made of ambiguities and paradoxes set to avoid the dead ends of textual authority. Reading Assia Djebar as a weaver convenes all the senses that the French language attributes to *filer*—whether it evokes (literally) the textile work of spinning, or whether it is to be understood (in its figurative sense) as the action of dashing or fleeing. Weaving recalls the physical, corporeal practices which appear to be at the origins of Djebar's poetics: walking and sewing.

Walking, as the author has often said, inspires her writing. It also animates her books peopled with characters strolling, wandering around, and prowling about, all these beings who travel through her texts on foot, running or limping. This said, although physical motion affects both genders, Djebar's walk seems to be resolutely a woman's concern (or ordeal). And the same goes for sewing (and its derivations). From footwork to threadwork, from sewing to walking lies one of the fundamental dynamics of Djebar's writing, between mobility and confinement, a dynamic that it would be tempting to see in different ways, such as the dynamic between France and Algeria, for example, with on one hand the "Occidental" emancipated woman who is free to walk, and on the other hand, the "Oriental" cloistered woman whose main physical creative activity is to sew. Reading Djebar's oeuvre as a weaving text could lead us to think that walking and sewing are in opposition. But, for Djebar, these two actions actually coincide with each other. Reading Djebar's oeuvre as a weaving text means challenging duality. The antagonistic elements that in other texts stand visibly apart (the usual duels: man/woman, colonizer/colonized, French/Arabic . . .) become with Djebar mingled in a pattern made of paradoxes. Step by step, thread by thread, the weaving writer inextricably links all sides (including the shores of the Mediterranean, between France and Algeria), inseparable even as they drift apart, challenging the reader to keep pace with her.

"Watch the Step" *Les Alouettes Naïves,* or a Daughter's Awkward Return

One reads Djebar watching one's step. Like in this odd return of Nfissa, finally coming home, freed by her father from a French military jail during the Algerian War of Independence. An awkward return, indeed, for this daughter who, pausing on the threshold, struggles to recognize the house where she was born and raised, and that she had left only to go fight underground, in the *maquis.* Her father is showing her in, whispering a warning: "'Watch the step,' . . . as he would always do with visitors." (AN, 19) ["Fais attention à la marche," murmurait-il ainsi qu'il le faisait toujours avec les visiteurs."][1] The daughter has returned, but estranged, alienated, watching her step as if she had become a stranger—a stranger to her father, a stranger in her own house. Thus opens the most remarkable (if not the most famous) of Djebar's novels, *Les Alouettes naïves* [*The Innocent Larks*], published in 1967. Overlooked by the critics, this book is nevertheless a primordial, seminal space in the author's entire oeuvre.[2] In fact, this novel not only makes a step but it *is* also a step, like a threshold, as it stands as the fourth and last book of her first period, concluding the first cycle, that of juvenilia, about which the author reveals another unique aspect, that it brought her "to ten years of silence . . . A voluntary silence. A deliberate silence." (CV, 64) *Les Alouettes naïves* engaged the march toward the period when between 1967 and 1980, until *Femmes d'Alger dans leur appartement,* Djebar did not publish a single book. Yet, it made a step toward another *kind* of writing: cinema (with Djebar writing and directing two films during this time), and also toward another *way* of writing, a way revealed by the *Alouettes* which introduced "autobiographical, very intimate elements." (Djebar, "Interview," 1984) More than a transition,

Les Alouettes naïves ties together the two great sides of Djebar's oeuvre: the side of fiction novels set in the Algerian War, and the side of the second period, postcinematographic, more autobiographical narratives. The writer's long editorial silence seems to have been caused by the sudden emergence of her life in her own writing. As Djebar herself confides, writing is an arduous march that becomes perilous as the subject of writing gets too close to the writer:

> I started writing as a wager, almost a dare, to keep as far away from my real self as possible. When it came to my fiction, I would open some sort of parenthesis from my real life. And then came *Les Alouettes naïves* . . . My fiction had suddenly caught up with me . . . *My life as a woman tripped me up* . . . In *Alouettes* . . . I understood that writing always brings one back to oneself . . ." (Zimra 1992: 168–69. Emphasis mine.)

The paradox of this stepping stone (autobiography), which provokes a *misstep*, simultaneously generating and interrupting the progression of writing, spawns the dynamic at the origin of the novel. This *leitmotiv* is announced by the exergue taken from Franz Kafka's *Journal*, where he evokes an impossible, vertical walk that only leads backwards. But, even before the strange walk of this exergue, the author's foreword, published separately in *Jeune Afrique* (October 1967), thus addressed to newly independent readers from former colonies, concludes that *Les Alouettes naïves* embodies "a relentless pitching" ("*un tangage incessant*"):

> Because we are constantly doing the splits between the past paralyzed within the present and the present delivering the future, we, Africans, Arabs, and certainly others from elsewhere, *we walk limping* when we think we are dancing, and vice versa. This is why we sometimes wonder if we are going forward. As for me, I claim I only go forth by writing." (AN, 8–9. Emphasis mine.)

Let us then embark on the rhythmic journey engaged by *Les Alouettes*—be it on ship, as the *tangage* suggests, or on foot, limping—in the wake of the author's footsteps, following her thread, coming and going relentlessly, back and forth.

Les Alouettes, the Horde, and the Harem: *Reprises of Femmes d'Alger*

To begin, let us follow the elusive yet compelling thread that ties the chapter "Yesterday" ["*Hier*"] at the end of the first part of *Les Alouettes naïves* to the novella "Nostalgia of the Horde" in *Femmes d'Alger dans leur appartement*—two texts seemingly separated by a thirteen-year silence.

The thread appears in the story told by the great-grandmother to her young great-granddaughters. Married at their age, when she was twelve, spoiled by her father, she could not do anything: "Neither knead the bread, nor turn the sieve for the couscous . . . And no notion of wool work! But what is a woman who cannot work the wool worth?" (AN, 168) The story she tells the girls recalls the day when she was forced to work "a ton of wool"—to wash it, beat it, clean it, card it, then thread it, and, at last, weave. Eventually, she mastered the loom, threading, as her mother-in-law in awe would exclaim, "a wool as fine as the snake's tongue." (AN, 170) Finally, the matriarch tells about her own grandmother, Mma Rékia, with her five sons, and her sole daughter, the newborn who died in a double cry, one night, the year the French entered her town—like a primordial cry that inspires the voice of the work that thus goes back to 1830, when the French conquerors, and the French language, arrived.

Mise en abyme, a motif in a larger canvas, this text is paradoxical, both unique and doubled, dividing itself into a replica of sorts. After first appearing in *Les Alouettes naïves*, it reappears in *Women of Algiers in Their Apartment* [*Femmes d'Alger dans leur appartement*] under the title "Nostalgia of the Horde" ["Nostalgie de la Horde,"] the last novella of the section "Yesterday," at the end of the collection. In a note in the Acknowledgments, the author reveals its origin: "'Nostalgia of the Horde' is a text that, as do some others, enters as collective feminine murmuring into the composition, third part, of my novel *Les Alouettes naïves*. (Julliard 1967) I chose that story at the end of this collection, for the memory of a chain of grandmothers comes back to the [1830s] in which Delacroix appears in Algiers as the only foreign witness among so many invaders." (WA, 154) An oral tale, verbal memory of a threading girl, this textile text that unites girls/daughters and time unfolds as it repeats itself, from *Les Alouettes* to the *Femmes d'Alger*, thus devising the solidarity and the solidity of Djebar's writing, tying together the two sides of her oeuvre separated by a ten-year void.

In Djebar's new "Nostalgia" (of *Women of Algiers*), I am confused by an "error." This error is all the more compelling because it is discrete, appearing not in the body of the rewritten text but in the paratext, in the note that aims to explain the origins of the "reprint." Thus, contrary to what the author claims, "Nostalgia of the Horde" does not come from the "third part" of *Les Alouettes naïves*, a part entitled "Today" ["*Aujourd'hui*"]. It comes from the end of its first part, called "In the Past" ["*Autrefois*"]. By transforming (and transporting) "The Past" into "Today," this strange error reveals one of the most fundamental movements of Djebar's oeuvre, where the time line (*fil du temps*) becomes entangled, and where, especially after this "Nostalgia of the Horde," the narrative of the country's history and the story of the narrator's life become intertwined. This text is thus a thread between two times, between two sides of the oeuvre. And the rewriting of this text that, as we recall, had introduced the autobiography into the fiction, which also had led the writer to stop writing (or at least *printing*), the *reprise* or the (altered) *reprint* of this text is like *reprendre le fil*, taking up again the thread of the writing that had been lost. In the end, however, the "error" (a "lapse of memory"?) from the author that displaces the origin of the primordial text shows the ambiguities of her writing, of her weaving this thread as both a guide and a lure, a thread to be followed or whose entanglement will get us lost, and even perhaps make us miss a step and trip. This error makes the reader err.

Reading Djebar as a work that weaves entails accepting that writing and reading partake of an odd, ambiguous walk. Walking oddly is also the condition, or the ordeal of most of Djebar's characters, like Nfissa, the female protagonist of *Les Alouettes naïves*, in perpetual motion, but also like its male narrator. Effaced witness of the affair, the *liaison* between Nfissa and her fiancé, he exclaims: "Here I am, I, the author—no, the imitator who, limping slightly, follows the same path." (AN, 183) This works turns its author, her characters, and her readers into vagabonds. But these vagabonds sometimes have their word to say like, precisely, this narrator who speaks up one last time: "And here I am interrupting, I who have followed them step by step up to here and who, now that everything begins for them, am getting ready to cut the thread of their story." (AN, 481) This outcry says that telling the story of others is done by *shadowing* them.[3]

The First Step of the Text (*Fantasia* in the Father's Shadow)

Strangely, the ominous, ambivalent shadow(ing) of the male narrator of *Les Alouettes* recalls another one, raised by the grandmother's story: the shadow of the father. And this presence appears in the very first walk. The walk of the "little Arab girl going to school for the first time, one autumn morning, walking hand in hand with her father." (F, 3) Thus is the overture of *Fantasia. An Algerian Cavalcade* [*L'Amour, la Fantasia*] is the first book of Djebar's autobiographical project, the "Algerian Quartet." And the first scene of the autobiography is that of the walk with the father, an Algerian wearing a traditional fez with a European suit, taking his little girl (the narrator, Djebar's double) to the French primary school where he is a teacher. The first step of the testimonial writing is thus to recall the first walk with the father, he who will give his daughter the gift of an education, will teach her how to speak, read and *write* in French, and will give her the liberty to walk about, to move freely in the outside world. But, in a dramatic instance of the essential Djebarian paradox, this first step of the autobiography is also the place to recall that the same father, both her liberator and her guard(ian), both her tutor and her censor, will not only tear apart the first love letter she will receive at seventeen but will also keep her locked up in her house.

This first step, the primordial walk hand in hand with the father, makes a powerful image, a tableau really, as evoked by the title of this first chapter, "Fillette arabe allant pour la première fois à l'école," literally "Little Arab Girl Going to School for the First Time," which suggests another *reprise* of Delacroix. And this peaceful picture (a little girl walking) is simultaneously opposed to the antiphrastic command uttered by the narrator: "So wrap the nubile girl in veils," as the ironic conclusion of the father's hostile action, to show the contradictions of his dual behavior: on one hand giving the liberating French, and on the other hand forbidding its free usage. From the very beginning, walking is therefore written and proclaimed *against* the veil, against the fabric that conceals and confines a woman's body.

A Strange Pattern (or *Patron*)

In this contradiction we also find a variation of it in the strangeness of the first childhood memory that the *Fantasia*'s narrator recalls. It is the story of the "Three Cloistered Girls," the three sisters whom the narrator would visit during school vacations, and who wore veils. But in spite of this veil that separates them, they were still very close, secretly conniving, even accomplices in subversive acts like their intrusion into the world of letters and men, into the library of the absent brother, where they discovered French literature and erotic photographs of Algerian women.[4] When they emerge from there, they imagine having "trespassed into some forbidden territory," and they feel they "have aged." (F, 11) As well as an accomplice, the narrator is the sister's confident, the recipient of a "strange and weighty, unexpected [*exceptionnel*]" secret:

> These girls, though confined to their house, were writing . . . to men in the four corners of the world; of the Arab World, naturally . . . Letters from pen-pals chosen from adverts appearing in a women's magazine with a wide circulation at the time in the harems. With every number, the subscriber received a pattern for a dress or a housegown that even the illiterate woman could follow. (F, 11)

This odd pattern is a palimpsest that shows that each of Djebar's text is always double, textile and textual, a text(ile) recalling its mixed origin, etymological homonymy: *textus*, in Latin, conveyed both the fabric and the text.

But the pattern, *patron* in French, also recalls, still via Latin, the language of the first conquerors of Algeria, the *pater*, the father at the origin of the word. However, if the *pater* gives a woman the pretext for writing, can a woman write to become her own *patron* (boss, in French)? Paradoxically, it appears that it is not with her pen that Djebar became "le patron." It was with her camera. In *So Vast the Prison*, the third volume of her autobiographical project, "*patron*," (VP, 112/199) or "boss" (SV, 115/204) is indeed what she is called by the men (technicians and actors) she directs on the set of her first feature film, a film by a woman for women, *La Nouba des femmes du mont Chenoua*.[5] Djebar thus recalls that it was during the thirteen-year silence, spawned by *Les Alouettes naïves* and finally interrupted by *Women of Algiers*, that she became "*le patron*"/"the boss," while directing "the first shot [*plan*] of [her] life" (SV, 178), her very first scene: "A man sitting in a wheelchair has stopped at the entrance [*le seuil*] to a room; he is watching his wife sleep inside. He is unable to enter: the two steps up to the room are impassable for his wheelchair." (SV, 178–79) Watch the step, indeed. The step of the women who now, thanks to the female *patron* look and write and move, set in motion by this "action"/"*moteur*," the step of the *Patron* Djebar who turns the veil inside out to transform it into a stirring camera.

This transformation is what Mireille Calle-Gruber calls a "narrative diffraction": "As a process of *trans*——transport, transfigure, transfiguration, transit——the diffracted narrative [*le récit diffracté*] seems to be, within the Djebarian scene, the only possible step [*la seule démarche possible*] to go outside, the only walk able to bring to the light of day the scene of the secret which is par excellence that of Muslim women——kept in solitary confinement [*maintenues au secret*], secreting immemorial legends." (Calle-Gruber, 214) The transformative step engaged by Djebar's scene reveals the two sides of the veil, and her "diffracted narrative" underscores the ambivalence she seems to display about it. There is the veil that oppresses, but which, for example in *Les Alouettes naïves*, allows women to walk in public to observe the others without being identified. For Djebar, French is not the language of love. The language of love is the mother's tongue.

Bearing the Word, Wearing the Text

In our search to find what in Djebar's writing binds walking and text(ile), an element, omnipresent since the beginning, has become paramount: voice.

Speech or song, the ability to speak or sing, sets Djebar's text in motion, and keeps it going. Djebar's work contrasts orality and literacy, the spoken (or sung) and the written word—voice and text. Voice and text, that is, of women. But her major quandary arises with a specific voice. It is at the end of the first movement, the voice of Cherifa, which she had listened to and transcribed, the woman who, at her request and for her purpose, had recalled her life in the *maquis* during the Algerian war of independence. Tragedy shudders as the author evokes Cherifa, whose voice "embraces [*enlace*] the bygone days": "Strange little sister, whom henceforth I leave veiled or whose story I now transcribe in a foreign tongue." (F, 141) ["*Petite sœur étrange qu'en langue étrangère j'inscris désormais, ou que je voile.*"] Here is then the admission of a failure, the helplessness of the woman writer who wanted to be an aural witness, both listener and transmitter of the feminine vocal memory but whose use of French to write this testimony is in itself a catastrophic counterpoint:

> Cherifa! I wanted to re-create your flight [*ta course*] . . . I have captured your voice; disguised it with my French without clothing it. I barely brush the shadow of your footsteps! The words that I thought to put in your mouth are shrouded in the same mourning garb as those of Bosquet or Saint-Arnaud. Actually, [they are written] using my hand [*ils s'écrivent à travers ma main*],[6] since I condone this bastardy [*bâtardise*], the only cross-breeding [*métissage*] that the ancestral beliefs do not condemn: that of language, not that of the blood. (F, 142)

The French language the woman writer uses veils women like a second veil—betraying them. Writing in French brings the woman writer closer to the French oppressors, military commanders responsible for massacres during the conquest of Algeria, than to the women who had to face them, and of whom she imagines herself the sister. The woman writer can only speak the women's revolt and liberation using the foreigner's language. This acknowledgement makes us hear the cross-breeding, the *métissage*, in a more dreadful sound—like a "*mé-tissage,*" or "mis-weaving."

But oddest of all is Djebar's other confession in which she does not claim "to be either a story-teller or a scribe. [*Je ne m'avance ni en diseuse, ni en scripteuse*]. . . I would cast off my childhood memories and advance naked, bearing offerings, but to whom? To the [l]ords of yesterday's war, or to the [roaming] young girls [*les fillettes rôdeuses*] who lay in hiding and who now inhabit the silence that succeeds the battles." (F, 142) Between walking and weaving, what keeps Djebar's writing together is the act(ion) of *bearing* a text.

Bearers of texts populate Djebar's work—messengers, interpreters, mail-men . . . , virtually all of them doomed, whether they are guardians of a for-eign, enemy voice, or the recipients of a secret text. Djebar, for one, declares herself to be less of a spokesperson (a *porte-parole*, literally word-carrier) than bearer of gifts (*porteuse d'offrandes*). But as we heard, she is also the bearer of an equivocal, even fatal present, because of this language that is her sole in-strument to accomplish this act. The paradox, however, lies at the very ori-gin if this gift. In the novel's fifth and final movement, the writer recalls the first image: "[The] father . . . walks down the village street; he pulls me by the hand and I, who for so long was so proud of myself—the first girl in the fam-ily to have French dolls bought for her, the one who had escaped cloistering and never had to stamp and protest at being forced to wear the shroud-veil." (F, 213) It is the same image, only inverted: instead of walking hand in hand, the father now pulls the girl. The march is now forced.

For Djebar, language is foremost a physical, corporeal element. It is a mus-cle, an organ—heart and lungs. It is a limb—a hand or a foot. But her last metaphor also expresses how language expands the body, how the narrator feels she was left empty like a city (recurrence of the analogy woman/city) deserted by its inhabitants, when Arabic disappeared from her—Arabic which she considers, as she specified earlier, the language of love: "I speak of Arabic script; to be separated from it is to be separated from a great love." (F, 181) ["Je parle de l'écriture arabe, dont je m'absente comme d'un grand amour."] Djebar distinguishes between the *oral* Arabic, whose motherly love sounds like songs, and the *written* Arabic whose love was taught at the Quranic school.

The coming of age embodied in the passage from orality to literacy is not only voluptuously erotic; it is also more powerfully athletic: "Just as the pen-tathlon runner of old needed the starter, as, as soon as I learned the foreign script, my body began to move as if by instinct." (F, 181) If love gives wings, writing gave Djebar strong, unstoppable legs. When the writing is in French, that is. Because when it is in Arabic, this love seems to have the opposite ef-fect on the girl's body. At the Quranic school, that she was forbidden to at-tend at ten or eleven, right before puberty, the *taleb* made children sit cross-legged to teach them the holy writing. This writing position was an impediment for the girl whose "legs must have been too long." (F, 183) But the physical hindrance was worsened in her case as she struggled to hide her legs under her skirt: "There is no doubt that it's easier to sit cross-legged when wearing a *seroual*[7]: a young girl's body that is beginning to develop more easily conceals its form under the ample folds of the traditional cos-tume. But my skirts, justified by the attendance at the French school, were ill adapted to such a posture." (F, 183) And this astonishing revelation becomes all the more so as we recall that in French to sit cross-legged is said "*en tailleur*"—literally as a tailor. Between running legs and sewing hands, the Djebarian formula which states that a woman writes a text(ile) *as* she walks *and* (at the same time) weaves.

And weaving, of course, must be heard also as the unpredictable, curving moves a walker or a runner makes to elude any potential follower (or shadow). As the novel reaches its end revelations become more unnerving: "'I write,' declares Michaux, 'to undertake a journey through myself' [*pour me parcourir*]. I journey [*Me parcourir*] at the whim of the former enemy, the enemy whose language I have stolen . . . While I thought I was undertaking a 'journey through myself,' I find I am simply choosing another veil." (F, 216–17) A strange journey, the seemingly liberating act of writing thus only leads to another veil—an uncanny, *circular* move.

> The language of the Others, in which I was enveloped from childhood, the gift my father lovingly bestowed on me, that language has adhered to me ever since like the Tunic of Nessus; that gift from [the] father who, every morning, took me by the hand to accompany me to school. [L]ittle Arab girl, in a village of the Algerian Sahel . . . (F, 217)

In a third movement, like a third variation, the narrator has again come full circle back to the first image. But each time, this return entails yet another transformation. After he was initially recalled as taking his daughter by the hand; after, in a second more portentous return, he was said to have *pulled* her by the hand, the father now becomes, in a third occurrence of the same scene[8] the origin of a terrible, deadly gift. And this last dreadful transformation comes as a contradiction to what Djebar said before of her usage of the French language as a "bastardy, the only cross-breeding [*métissage*] that the ancestral beliefs do not condemn: that of language, not that of the blood." (F, 142) In the end, not only does she negate the bastardy of French by recalling the seminal role of her father in its becoming, but, precisely because of the words she uses in French, she is also effectively saying that this cross-breeding is nothing but of blood. For, as she writes in French, French is "*la langue encore coagulée des Autres*" [AF, 302], a strange, foreign blood "still clotted" over her, enveloping her, an alien coagulated blood given by her father for her to wear like the tunic of Nessus.

In the ancient Greek and Roman, the "original" Mediterranean myths whose voices echo in Djebar's writings, the tunic of Nessus may be one the most terrible text(ile) she could have invoked—and the most dreadful passage. It recalls Hercules killing the Centaur Nessus with a poisoned arrow while he was trying to rape his wife Deianeira, whom the Herohad left alone in the Centaur's boat as they were crossing the impassable Euneus river. Before he died, Nessus planning revenge gave Deianeira his shirt soaked in his blood, "a talisman," he said, "to kindle love," and which Deianeira later gave to her husband to fortify his "failing love," as she feared he was leaving her. "And Hercules receiving the gift and on his shoulders wore, in ignorance, the [poisoned] gore."

In the context of Djebar's account, the mythical text is no longer a mere "image" equating the father's gift of French to that of a poisoned gift. Once its origins are revealed the metaphor of the tunic of Nessus—the story of an abandoned woman,[9] a story of rape, blood, and death, a story of deadly and dying love, a story also of deadly mistakes and missteps—becomes the epitome of Djebar's terrible ambivalence to French, and writing. Like the cloth it tells about, the story of the tunic of Nessus reveals French though a new, dreadful metamorphosis, as a mythical, paternal, and fatal gift of love. But the tunic of Nessus also renders French under surprising dimensions—or revives long-forgotten elements—dimensions of hybridity and wanderings. This story of crossings, the tragic end of a fabulous epic, recalls the mythical disastrous death of two "cross-breeds," a Half-God and a Centaur, an oral Greek myth as written in Latin by Ovid in his *Metamorphoses*.

The tunic of Nessus is thus the ultimate paradoxical text(ile) that Djebar weaves within her own text. "Because he was a teacher of French, he had assumed a first hybridity (*métissage*)" says Djebar of her father, as she acknowledges that "the French language, body and voice, is settling [*s'installe*] in [her] like an arrogant presidio, while the maternal language, all in orality, in tattered rags [*en hardes dépenaillées*], resists and attacks, between two instances of breathlessness." (CV, 46) When Mireille Rosello shows that for Djebar "*métissage* is not presented as a solution to the difficult relationship between France and the Maghreb," that she "seems to resist the comfort of bicultural or binational *métissage*," she does so by exploring narratives where the author "fictionalizes what she calls the original 'couple' (France-Algeria) as an encounter between two characters whose complex trajectories represent [an] unstable protocol of cohabitation." (Rosello 2005, 48–49) Rosello convincingly shows how for Djebar "hybridity" is more of a "performative encounter," such as the dynamic that (in *Oran, langue morte*, for instance) governs the names of the children of a French-Algerian couple: these given double names (one Christian, one Muslim) that seemed at first to symbolize the "felicitous encounter" between the French mother and the Algerian father, eventually generate multiple transformations. Here, the performativity of the encounter goes well beyond the name. "Nessus," himself a hybrid (Centaur), killed by another hybrid (Hercules, half-god), becomes the bearer of the worst kind of encounter. As the tunic of Nessus, French becomes a poisoned gift of the father to his daughter, it appears as the ultimate *mé-tissage*, a "mis-weaving," an evil textile, telling the violence already perceivable in the tattered rags of the mother tongue, in the tear of the Centaur's cloth and in the blood staining it, the violence of the ambivalence at work in her writing.

The Lost Thread

As for the author herself, which text does she bear? Which text will she wear (out)? We shall ask another subtext(ile), the most revealing of Djebar's subtitles:

> *Ces Voix qui m'assiègent*
> . . . en marge de ma Francophonie

The title of this collection of essays—many of them talks delivered over many years—may be translated as "Voices Besieging Me . . . (In the Margins of my *Francophonie*). But in the margins' margin, in the "Foreword" (Avant-propos), the author comments on the subtitle, which oddly enough appears only inside the book, not on the cover but on the title page, as if this "margin" was a secret of sorts:

> "In the margins of my *Francophonie*" my subtitle announces. I would be tempted to complete it: "In the margin" but also "in the march/marching" [*en marche*]. Yes, my French writing is really a march, even imperceptible; isn't language, in its plays and its stakes [*ses jeux et ses enjeux*], the only good, the only property the writer can claim? (CV, 7)[10]

Writing *weaving* can only lead one to walk off the fringes, to write in the margins—to write *besides*, as an outcast, always outside, beyond all limits. And this margin that sets off a march also opens other ways for other wanderings, and other voices.

La Disparition de la langue française may be Djebar's strangest book thus far—the most *misleading*. Misleading, for a start, is its title that sounds like one of an essay. But as specified on the cover, it is really a "novel"—though still paradoxical: before a disappearance, it tells the story of a return. And what is perhaps even stranger than the return that its story tells is the return of the *way* to tell a story, intertwining story and history. *La Disparition* recalls *Les Alouettes*.

Like in *Les Alouettes*, the novel interlaces times, two major periods of Algerian history, two wars. But while *Les Alouettes* bound the French conquest and the War of Independence, *La Disparition* joins the War of Independence to the Civil War that scarred Algeria between 1992 and 2002, after the Islamists won the country's first multiparty elections. Like in Djebar's early novel, with the War of Independence as the passageway between them, the protagonist recalls taking part in the struggle for independence, although much less proactively than Nfissa, as well as experiencing French military prisons and, still unlike Nfissa, torture. And if the *Disparition's* story is that of a return to Algeria and more precisely to Algiers' Casbah after a long exile in France, it is also the story of resisting speaking while being forced to speak. With a narrator who comes home to finally begin writing, *La Disparition* tells the story of the return of a voice. A voice unheard since *Les Alouettes naïves*: the voice of a man.[11] Like in *Les Alouettes naïves*, the narration alternates with Djebar's favorite motion, going back and forth, interlacing two voices, that of the male protagonist and the voice of an omniscient narrator whose gender remains elusive, a voice that sounds like Djebar's.

In *La Disparition*, as Ruhe justly underlined, "Berkane's birth as a writer (*naissance à l'écriture*) is like a shortcut of some of the great themes of Djebar's oeuvre that all pertain to language . . . In some way, Berkane travels the author's path (*refait en quelque sorte le chemin de l'auteur*)." (Ruhe 2005) Like Djebar who wrote again after a long silence, he resumes writing a book long abandoned. As Ruhe again points out with insight, this novel bears striking similarities to Camus's *Le Premier homme*. For Ruhe, who quotes Djebar's *Algerian White* where she refers to Camus's last book, unfinished (as Berkane's), the manuscript of which was found in the wreck of the car where he died, on the side of the road, Djebar, who evokes Camus's last moments, saying that "Camus ran, in a unique movement, in his text and towards his death," seems to be talking about her own work.

But in *La Disparition*, misleading is also the name of the hero. Where does Berkane come from? The return of a man's voice, unheard since *Les Alouettes*, marks also the return of Djebar's tutelary figure. Does Berkane not come from Berkani, the Berkani of the Dahra, the tribe of origins of Bahia Sahraoui, Assia Djebar's mother? In other words, *La Disparition de la langue française* makes the ultimate transformative passage, and the most compelling return: that of the mother, and the mother's ancestors, those who have always been for Djebar the ultimate guardians of the "original" memory, of the time of the

French invasion—the mother returning with the voice and the first name of a man.

The Eternal Return (In the Name of the Father)

In guise of conclusion, let us reflect on this stumbling return. Does it not remind us of another? Another man who, like Berkane, returns to his homeland after a twenty-year exile. Although Berkane claims his was even longer:

> When Odysseus returns, after an absence less long than mine, it is in Ithaca that he lands, in anonymity, even though only the dog who smells him recognizes him underneath his vagabond rags. (DLF, 89)[12]

This explicit reference to *The Odyssey* by Djebar is as rare as it is significant. Ruhe has shown with brilliance how, in *La Femme sans sepulture*, Djebar "depotentializes" Odysseus by metamorphosing him many times, and especially by feminizing him and his companions, by evacuating all men from the story and replacing them with women. Odysseus, that the narrator (Djebar) discovers represented in the mosaics in the museum of her native Caesarea/Cherchell, in the scene of the Sirens, is soon identified with Zoulikha, the woman warrior, heroine of the Algerian War, who vanished after being captured by the French army. But the figures of the Sirens and Odysseus are themselves like empty signs, like masks that women pass from one to the other, as shows the epilogue of her text. Djebar has returned to Caesarea/Cherchell to bear and transmit (*"pour dire"*) Zoulikha's song, the song of she whom the French made disappear. Djebar says she hears her but finds herself "almost in the situation of Odysseus, the traveler who did not plug his ears with wax, without nonetheless risking trespassing the frontier of death for this, but to hear, never again forget the sirens!" (FSS, 236) Paradoxically, then, Djebar transforms Zoulikha into the Sirens and herself into Odysseus. (Ruhe 2003)

As for Berkane, like Homer's hero, he returns to his native land a vagabond, a stranger at home. And in the end, like Odysseus again, he returns home . . . to disappear almost right away—to set off to die. Or at least, to his forecast death. Thus goes the tragic dénouement of Djebar's last novel. After Islamists have won the elections and the country has begun to dive into the darkness of civil war, Berkane, who was on his way to the site of his French prison at the end of the War of Independence, disappears on a road in Kabylia. Only his car is found, in a ditch. Berkane thus disappeared like Camus. But contrary to Camus, his body will never be found. Like Zoulikha.

In the end, Berkane embodies Odysseus's other name as he becomes "No-Body." "Nobody" is indeed the name that Odysseus invents for himself, his *own* pseudonym—his greatest invention, a life-saver, and his gravest error, the origin of his errancy. "Nobody" is the name Odysseus gave to the Cyclops as he and his companions fell victims to his horrific hospitality. And after he had blinded him, the giant could only cry out to his friends that "Nobody" was killing him . . . This is how Odysseus, a much more powerful poet than warrior, proved that before the gravest danger, life would be saved not by the sword but by the word. Yet, Odysseus almost instantaneously stumbled, making the astonishingly foolish error to yell in anger his real name to the Cyclops from his ship that was slowly getting away: "Cyclops—if any man on the face of the earth should ask you who blinded you, shamed you so—say Odysseus, raider of cities, *he* gouged out your eye, Laertes' son who makes his home in Ithaca!" (IX, 558–62) This mistake is Odysseus's demise, identifying him to Poseidon, the Cyclops's father, who would thus banish him from returning home. This story tells of the *tripping* power of language. It tells of the dreadful potential of the name. And it tells of the risks of trespassing the limits of both. But it tells also the story of the *erring* that can be done in (or because of) the name of the father. Odysseus loses what he had gained (his freedom) as he transforms himself from "Nobody" into "the son of Laertes." And from one wronged son to another, he will be punished, banished, "vanished" by the Cyclops's father.

Homer's *Odyssey* is in many ways the journey of *The First Man*, where Camus's alter ego, like Telemachus, sets off to seek the grave of his "disappeared" father—the father he never knew, killed in World War I. And like Odysseus's son, Jacques Cormery crosses the Mediterranean *for* his mother who cannot travel. As for Djebar, when she returns to Algeria after a twenty-year absence, like Odysseus, it is not first to speak for Zoulikha, the woman with no sepulture, but to bury her own father—in her father's name, the name she takes up again after her divorce, the name of her "first identity." (Ruhe 2003)

As for Berkane, we must now recall what he added to his comparison to Odysseus: "[Since] I do not have a faithful wife at home, some may notice that I have engulfed myself in my return after she broke up with me, she, the 'French one' as my mother called her, with melancholy!" Indeed, what of Penelope? Berkane's story, as Ruhe puts it, seems like "an inversion of the ancient epic." (Ruhe 2003) This woman, a theater actor who bears two names, her real name and her stage name, Marise/Marlyse, in many ways the writer's muse, seems a very paradoxical Penelope: although she is the reason the hero came home, she is the woman he left (or rather who left him).[13] Ruhe may be right: she is more like Calypso than Penelope.

Penelope, the woman who wove because she could not leave, she who threaded and unthreaded rhythmically, by day, by night, to not forget, and to pull the thread of the story as long as possible, is she not like Homer himself? Homer is "the greatest of rhapsodes," as Ruhe recalls the origin of the word, the poet who *sews together* chants. Like Djebar herself who claims to "adjust and sew the songs,"[14] who, even as a filmmaker, says she weaves sounds together with the humility of "a poor seamstress," who, at the end of her "transhumance," says she "braids" (*tresse*) this deceptively clear language in the "weft" (*la trame*) of the cries of her illiterate sisters, and writes everything in the Latin alphabet. (CV, 184)

But in the end, in fact at the very beginning of the book, when Berkane-Odysseus returns, when he speaks for the first time, he who circumnavigates between his mother tongue and the colonial language, tells his story neither in French nor Arabic:

> I have thus returned, this very day, to the country . . . "Homeland," the word, strangely in English, sung, or danced in me, I don't remember: what is this day where, facing the sea intense and green, I started to write again."[15]

As if Odysseus, after so many years in exile, after such a long absence, had forgotten his mother tongue. As if the eternal journey had effaced his "own language." And what if this was the reason for his sudden new departure after he had barely returned? As if Odysseus, who comes back after an eternity to say he must leave again, to see his father one last time before he goes off to find, far from the sea, well into hinterland, a place to rest in peace forever, as if Odysseus had found that between exile and home, between war and peace, there was another way.

At last, points the ultimate paradox. Writing the disappearance of the French language, Assia Djebar wrote in an altogether different language. English, the language of her other exile, to America. And in the wake of this text on the disappearance of the French language, signed from "New York," Djebar was elected to the Académie Française,[16] where she will help fulfill the mission "with all the care and diligence possible, to give sure rules to our language, to make it pure, eloquent and capable to treat arts and sciences."[17]

Notes

1. All the translations are mine unless indicated otherwise in the bibliography.
2. Assia Djebar's first cycle is made of four novels: *La Soif*, Paris: Julliard, 1957 (*The Mischief*, trans. F. Frenaye, New York: Simon & Schuster, 1958); *Les Impatients*,

Paris: Julliard, 1958; *Les Enfants du nouveau monde*, Paris: Julliard, 1962 (*Children of the New World: A Novel of the Algerian War*, trans. M. de Jager, New York: The Feminist Press at CUNY, 2005); and *Les Alouettes naïves*, Paris: Julliard, 1967. Here is how Djebar presents her first books: "In my first novel, *La Soif*, I had masked myself. In my second novel, *Les Impatients*, I remembered. In my third novel, *Les Enfants du nouveau monde*, I wanted to take a look at my people. Lila's position, at the same time on the side, inside and witness, it is a little like me. *Les Alouettes naïves*, it is more complete. It is a true point of departure for me." "Interview with Wadi Bouzar, 1984." http://www.assiadjebar.net/first_novels/main_first.htm (Nov. 11, 2006)

3. In French, to shadow someone is "*filer*," literally to spin, and a shadowing is a "*filature*," which is also a textile mill.

4. Exotic postcards of "Ouled-Naïls," these women who appear everywhere in Djebar's work, like icons of a forgotten collective memory . . .

5. *La Nouba des femmes du mont Chenoua* was shot between 1976 and 1977, and released in 1978. It won the Prix de la Critique Internationale at the Biennale de Venise in 1979. Djebar's second film, *La Zerda ou les chants de l'oubli*, was released in 1982.

6. "It is they who are writing to each other" seems to be a mistranslation, as I believe that the "cross-breeding" to which Djebar refers here is not that of the two French officers corresponding, but the hybridity produced by the transcription in French of a memory uttered in Arabic.

7. Loose trousers.

8. On the senses and the stakes of the Djebarian scene, and especially its debt to ancient Greek tragedy (the *skènè*), see Calle-Gruber, "Faire une scène au feminine," in *Assia Djebar ou la Résistance de l'écriture*. Op. cit.

9. Deianeira is no doubt the principal character in this terrible story.

10. "'En marge de ma Francophonie' annonce mon sous-titre; je serais tentée de le compléter: 'en marge' mais aussi 'en marche.' Oui, mon écriture française est vraiment une marche, même imperceptible; la langue, dans ses jeux et ses enjeux, n'est-elle pas le seul bien que peut revendiquer l'écrivain?"

11. Ruhe is right when he says that "*La Disparition de la langue française* is the first novel to place a man at its center" (Ruhe, 2005), but this privileged position becomes all the more momentous as one remembers that Djebar's preautobiographical (as in "prehistorical") novel, *Les Alouettes*, first "gave the word" (*donner la parole*) to a male narrator, who, however, unlike Berkane, remained anonymous . . .

12. "Quand Ulysse revient, après une absence moins longue que la mienne, c'est à Ithaque qu'il débarque dans l'anonymat, meme si seul le chien qui le hume le reconnaît sous ses hardes de vagabond."

13. "Je n'ai pas, moi, d'épouse fidèle à demeure, certains pourraient penser que mon retour, je m'y suis engouffré à la suite de la rupture décidée par elle, la 'Française,' comme la nommait, mélancoliquement, ma mère!" (DLF, 89)

14. And even more paradoxically is in the end, after he vanishes, instead of being at his home when he returns, she becomes the "home" he eventually inhabits as "he

returned as a ghost to inhabit his friend." And this unexpected, uncanny return happens as the actor embodies another woman on stage, Mathilde, the main character of Bernard-Marie Koltès's play *Le Retour au désert* [*Return to the Desert*], a French woman who comes back to her native French home after a fifteen-year sojourn in Algeria, at the end of the war.

15. "Je reviens donc, aujourd'hui même, au pays . . . 'Homeland,' le mot, étrangement, en anglais, chantait, ou dansait en moi, je ne sais plus: quel est ce jour où, face à la mer intense et verte, je me remis à écrire . . ." (DLF, 13).

16. Assia Djebar was elected to the Académie Française on June 18, 2005, and inaugurated on June 18, 2006. In the wakes of coincidences and paradoxes, we could add that Djebar, being the first Maghrebian to enter the Académie, thus becomes herself a founding mother. And finally, how could we resist saying that Assia, which in Arabic is the flower called "immortelle" has finally become, as are called the Académie's life members, an Immortal . . .

17. Article 24 of the original statutess of the Académie. http://www.academie-française.fr.

Works Cited

Calle-Gruber, Mireille. *Assia Djebar, ou la résistance de l'écriture. Regards d'un écrivain d'Algérie*. Paris: Maisonneuve & Larose, 2001.

Djebar, Assia. *La Disparition de la langue française*. Paris: Albin Michel, 2003. [DLF]

———. *La Femme sans sépulture*. Paris: Albin Michel/Livre de Poche, 2002. [FSS]

———. *Ces voix qui m'assiègent*. Paris: Albin Michel, 1999. [CV]

———. *Vaste est la prison*. Paris: Livre de Poche, 1995. [VP]

———. *So Vast the Prison*. Trans. B. Wing. New York: Seven Stories Press, 1999. [SV]

———. *Ombre sultane*. (1987) Paris: J. C. Lattés, 2006.

———. *A Sister to Scheherazade*. Trans. D. Blair. London: Quartet, 1988.

———. "Interview." Sept. 17, 1985. http://www.assiadjebar.net/first_novels/main_first.htm. (Nov. 8, 2006). My translation.

———. *L'Amour, la Fantasia* (1985). Paris: Livre de Poche, 1995. [AF]

———. *Fantasia: An Algerian Cavalcade*. Trans. D. Blair. London: Quartet Books, 1993. [F]

———. *Femmes d'Alger dans leur appartement*. Paris: Des Femmes, 1980. [FA]

———. *Women of Algiers in Their Apartment*. Trans. M. de Jager. Charlottesville: U. of Virginia Press, 1992. [WA]

———. *Les Alouettes naïves* (1967). Arles: Babel/Actes Sud, 1997. [AN]

Homer. *The Odyssey*. Trans. R. Fagles, New York/London: Penguin Books, 1996.

Rosello, Mireille. *France and the Maghreb. Performative Encounters*. Gainesville: University Press of Florida, 2005.

Ruhe, Ernst Peter. "'Ecrire est une route à ouvrir.' La Poétique transfrontalière d'Assia Djebar." In *Assia Djebar, Nomade entre les murs. Pour une poétique transfrontalière*. Ed. M. Calle-Gruber. Paris: Maisonneuve & Larose, 2005.

———. "Les Sirènes de Césarée. Assia Djebar chante 'La femme sans sépulture.'" In *CELAAN. Revue du Centre d'Etudes des Littératures et des Arts d'Afrique du Nord* 2, 2003.

Zimra, Clarisse. "Afterword." In Djebar. *Women of Algiers in Their Apartment*, 1992.

———. "A Woman's Memory Spans Centuries." Interview of Assia Djebar (*Ibid.*)

CHAPTER NINE

~

L'Esprit de Corps

French Civilization and the Death of the Colonized Soldier

Karl Ashoka Britto, University of California, Berkeley

The figure of the colonized soldier occupies a particularly fraught position within the colonial imaginary, both with respect to the production of hierarchies of difference and in relation to imperial practices of memory and disavowal. As Panivong Norindr has noted, images of the *tirailleurs indigènes* [native infantrymen] began to circulate widely in France during the First World War. Considered as a whole, these images can be understood to illustrate the ambivalence of French sentiment toward the *tirailleurs*, who are variously represented as fierce combattants, exotic subalterns, or buffoons.[1] While the difference of the colonized soldier may be fetishized for commercial purposes (as with Banania's *tirailleur sénégalais*),[2] Norindr argues that rituals of commemoration tend to erase that difference through a "fantasy of incorporation" in which the *tirailleur indigène* and the white French soldier are "conflated and linked together unproblematically."[3]

This essay examines another shifting boundary structuring the representation of colonized soldiers: that between life and death. The lines of demarcation between French and *indigène*, on the one hand, and life and death on the other, often met and crossed in the context of military service. In a 1920 article dedicated "A la mémoire de nos petits frères d'Asie" ["To the Memory of Our Little Asian Brothers"], *Le Figaro* succinctly articulates the intersection: "Each one of them, by dying, had saved the life of a Frenchman."[4] The brutal simplicity of this formulation is telling, but it also obscures the complex range of issues potentially at stake in the death of the colonized soldier, in the nature of that death, and in the form of its remembrance. In the discussion that follows, I will explore these issues through an analysis of *Hiên le Maboul* (1908), a colonial novel that takes as its subject the life and death of a *tirailleur indochinois*. Before turning to this text, however, I would like to take a brief detour through an unlikely source in order to clarify some of the anxieties surrounding the figure of the colonized soldier.

Walking Dead in Angkor[5]

Spaces marked by French colonialism have figured prominently in some of Hollywood's most canonical films.[6] At the opposite end of the spectrum, the same could be said about the emergence of one of Hollywood's least valorized genres: the zombie film. The first zombie films bore little resemblance to the current resurgence of movies featuring mobs of rotting corpses, hungry for the brains of the living. Nearly all contemporary zombie films take their inspiration from later works—in particular, George Romero's *Night of the Living Dead* (1968)—rather than from earlier classics of the genre such as *White Zombie* (1932) and *I Walked with a Zombie* (1943). Unlike the post-Romero films, which tend to bring horror into familiar domestic landscapes, early Hollywood zombie films were often set in the Caribbean and drew upon sensational accounts of Haitian religious practices such as those found in William Seabrook's 1929 book *The Magic Island*.[7]

Generally acknowledged to be the first Hollywood zombie film, *White Zombie* met with mixed reviews but was an enormous financial success.[8] Directed by Victor Hugo Halperin and produced by his brother Edward, the film was set in Haiti and proved to be so effective at establishing the figure of the zombie in American popular consciousness that the brothers ended up in a court battle with one of their financiers over their right to use the word "zombie" itself in the title of a later film. This was *Revolt of the Zombies* (1936), a follow-up feature that has been dismissed as shoddy and dull even by die-hard fans of *White Zombie*.[9] While it lacks the Gothic atmosphere and innovative camera work of the earlier film—not to mention the charisma of that film's star, Bela Lugosi—*Revolt of the Zombies* does offer a peculiar variation on the 1930s Hollywood zombie theme that displaces the geographic and cultural location of zombification from the Caribbean to colonial Indochina.[10]

The film opens with a scrolling textual foreword that reads: "Many strange events were recorded in the secret archives of the fighting nations during the World War . . . but none stranger than that which occurred when a regiment of French Cambodians from the vicinity of the lost city in Angkor arrived on the Franco-Austrian front . . . " In the opening scenes, we learn that this is no ordinary regiment of Indochinese colonial soldiers, who were in fact recruited to fight for the French by the tens of thousands during the First World War, but rather a regiment of zombified colonial subjects, created through a ritual discovered by French archeologists working on the restoration of the temples at Angkor. The particular form of zombification enabled by the ritual is not that of reanimating corpses, but rather of transforming living subjects into "tireless, feelingless human machines." In what is perhaps the film's most bizarre scene, we see a row of zombified Cambodian soldiers marching slowly toward an enemy trench, continuing to advance despite the bullets piercing their bodies.[11]

Immediately after this scene of combat, the film cuts to a meeting at which the military leaders of the Allied and Central Powers are addressed by a General von Schelling: "I am not here to plead the cause of the Central European Powers," he states, "but that of modern civilization! In the name of humanity, you must not go further with your experiment. It may mean the destruction of the white race!" The general does not make clear how this destruction would come about, but the implication seems to be that the French may lose control of their zombies, leading to the revolt suggested by the film's title.[12] The French, in turn, deny responsibility for the creation of the zombies—technically staying within the realm of truth, since the ritual itself was performed by a Cambodian priest—and reassure all present that the "experiment" is over. *Revolt of the Zombies* then turns away from the unsettling implications of these opening scenes and veers back to a more familiar plotline involving an unscrupulous individual who creates zombies in order to satisfy his personal desires.[13]

The cultural, political, and historical location of a decidedly B-movie from 1930s Hollywood, is, of course, rather far from that of the text I will discuss in a moment: a critically lauded novel written by a French colonial officer in the early years of the twentieth century. And yet, for all its sensational excess, *Revolt of the Zombies* does offer a striking representation, if not a critique, of colonial domination. One could certainly argue, as has Haitian author René Depestre, that "[t]he history of colonization is the process of man's general zombification."[14] What intrigues me about *Revolt of the Zombies*, however, is the particular focus in its opening scenes on the figure of the colonized soldier and the ways in which the film stages this figure simultaneously as an object of desire and horror, as an extension of European imperial power and as a force that threatens to undermine that power. The depiction of the colonized soldier as zombie, as unfeeling machine suspended in a state of death-in-life, also casts into doubt narratives of loyalty and loving devotion by raising the question of free will or ability to consent on the part of those subjects who were compelled to fight for France.

Beginning in the mid-nineteenth century, colonial military forces in Indochina began to include local recruits. From the start, policies and attitudes surrounding the *bataillons indigènes* reflected the ambivalent position of the colonized soldier. On the one hand, he was understood as a part of the united fighting forces of *la plus grande France*, as a crucial participant in the project of colonial expansion and consolidation; on the other, he embodied an always potentially treacherous element whose distance from true Frenchness had to be maintained through visible markers, such as "exotic" uniforms, that extended corporeal signs of racial difference.[15] In the second half of the nineteenth century, troops of Indochinese soldiers were repeatedly formed and disbanded by the French, reflecting anxieties not only over the potential danger of giving arms and military training to the colonized but also over the possibility that the racial hierarchy of the colonial relation could be threatened by the structure of an integrated military force. As one newspaper put it in outraged response to a late nineteenth-century proposal to reform the education received by native officers, the French ran the risk of creating such intolerable situations as that of "un sergent européen mis dans l'obligation de saluer un sous-lieutenant indigène dont un marsouin blanc dev[rait] cirer les brodequins" ["a European sergeant obliged to salute a native sublieutenant whose boots a white sailor would have to shine"].[16]

The particular kind of work demanded of the colonized soldier provoked another set of anxieties, revolving precisely around the question of obligation. Over and above the manual labor they were frequently required to perform, colonized soldiers were also expected to be ready to kill as well as to be mutilated or killed in the interests of colonial power. What sort of debt might be incurred by France's dependence on this constrained form of sacrifice? The question arises repeatedly over the first half of the twentieth century, taking on a particular urgency in the context of the two World Wars. On the one hand, a forward-looking structure of debt is articulated, one in which colonized subjects who survive military service might legitimately demand their reward in the form of political concessions, citizenship, or even independence from France;[17] on the other stands an opposite, backward-looking structure in which no amount of sacrifice on the part of the colonized could ever offset the always prior and greater debt owed to France in exchange for the gift of civilization.[18] The latter structure establishes a peculiar relationship between the body of the colonized soldier and French culture, expressed with shocking clarity by a character in Nguyen Phan Long's 1921 novel, *Le Roman de Mademoiselle Lys*. When a Vietnamese veteran who lost an arm fighting in the First World War is asked by another character how he has experienced this sacrifice, he replies,

> je n'ai donné à la France qu'un bras, et mon bras gauche encore. Somme toute, la perte n'est pas bien grande. . . . Or, ce cerveau, qui donc l'a affiné, développé, meublé, si ce n'est pas la culture que m'a dispensée généreusement la moderne Athènes, la Ville Lumière?

> I have given to France only an arm, and my left arm at that. All in all, it's not such a huge loss. . . . But this mind, what refined it, developed it, furnished it, if not the culture that the modern Athens, the City of Lights, gave to me so generously?[19]

The disturbing implication of this statement suggests that the proper value of the soldier's body lies precisely in its capacity, through mutilation or death, to offer partial repayment for the successful passage of the colonized subject into the incorporeal realm of civilization. The gift of civilization is held out to the colonized soldier, but not as a reward for faithful service; rather, it functions as the sign of a debt whose limitless claims consume his body, marking it as lost, rendering it disposable. In this sense, the body of the colonized soldier is always like that of the zombie: already dead even as it continues to serve its master.

Un personnage de chair et de sang

I would like to turn now to a discussion of the ways in which some of the tensions surrounding the figure of the colonized soldier play out in the context of *Hiên le Maboul*, an early twentieth-century novel that takes as its central character "un soldat de deuxième classe à la 11e compagnie du 1er régiment de tirailleurs annamites" ["a second-class soldier of the 11th Company of the 1st Regiment of the Annamite Infantry"].[20] Published in 1908 after having been serialized in the *Revue de Paris*, *Hiên le Maboul* was the first novel of Captain Émile Détanger, a young French colonial infantry officer who wrote a series of literary texts under the pseudonym of Émile Nolly. The novel's critical and commercial success was striking, particularly for a first book by a young and unknown author: not only was it reissued in multiple editions, it also garnered enthusiastic reviews, was considered for the *Prix Goncourt*, and was *couronné* [honored with a prize] by the Académie Française. Reviewers were particularly enthusiastic about what was perceived to be the psychological realism of the novel's depiction of its Vietnamese protagonist. "Hiên l'Annamite est un personnage de chair et de sang" ["Hiên the Annamite is a flesh-and-blood character"], wrote Lucien Maury in the *Revue bleue*, praising the novel for its ability to render this flesh-and-blood transparent to French readers: "C'est ainsi que nous pénétrons la psychologie de ces Jaunes énigmatiques; nos écrivains découvrent l'âme de ces peuples qu'hier encore nous nous contentions d'asservir; notre littérature exotique grandit merveilleusement" ["Thus we penetrate the psychology of these enigmatic yellow people; our writers are uncovering the soul of these people whom just yesterday we contented ourselves to subjugate; our exotic literature is developing marvelously."].[21]

Over the next few years, Nolly went on to write two other novels set in colonial Indochina, *La Barque annamite* (1910) and *Le Chemin de la victoire* (1913), as well as two texts set in Morocco, *Gens de guerre au Maroc* (1912) and *Le Conquérant* (published posthumously in 1916). This flurry of literary activity was cut short by the onset of World War I and the death of Captain Détanger, who was mortally wounded in the trenches of Lorraine in August 1914. Nolly's work is little read today, and his textual legacy has been almost completely overshadowed by that of other military authors such as Ernest Psichari and Pierre Loti, writers to whom he was often compared during his brief career. His novels, nonetheless, had a significant impact on the development of French colonial literature—so much so that at least one recent study proposes 1915, the year Nolly was posthumously awarded the *Grand Prix de littérature de l'Académie Française*, as the moment at which colonial literature was officially integrated into the French national tradition.[22] In the years leading up to World War I, he was widely praised for restoring a sense of pride and purpose to French literature, for reversing the cynicism and skepticism of the fin-de-siècle. His unabashedly nationalist rhetoric had a clear appeal, and his novels explicitly position colonial expansion within a larger project of French national regeneration and ongoing intra-European competition with England and, particularly, Germany. As one character in *Le Chemin de la Victoire* puts it, "Ces territoires où nous avons planté notre drapeau, d'autres peuples les guettaient, qui nous en auraient fermé les portes, qui auraient nargué plus tard notre pauvre France réduite à ses quatre-vingt-neuf départements . . . sans chantier où forger ses jeunes énergies" ["Other populations had their eyes on these territories where we have planted our flag, others who would have closed them off to us, who later would have taunted our poor France, reduced to its eighty-nine departments . . . with nowhere to forge its youthful energies."]. Later in the novel, the same character tells another French colonial officer, "Considère que tu n'es qu'un chaînon d'une chaîne immense: l'humanité. Tu n'es qu'une cellule d'un grand corps, et ce corps réclame de toi que tu coopères au travail collectif. . . .

afin que les petits Français de demain apprennent dans les écoles le français et non l'allemand!" ["Consider that you are only a link in an immense chain: humanity. You are only a cell in a large body, and this body demands of you that you cooperate in the collective work. . . . so that French schoolchildren of tomorrow will learn French and not German!"].[23]

Le grand corps, la chaîne immense, le travail collectif: there is a certain incoherence about the way these terms circulate in Nolly's texts. From one moment to the next, the *oeuvre* [work] they evoke may shift from the project of *l'humanité*, a collective work of universal improvement, to the specifically nationalist project of politically and culturally defending the French race, defined as inherently imperial: "la race de l'enthousiasme et des nobles élans . . . supérieure . . . à la race anglo-saxonne, à la race slave, à la race jaune" ["the race of enthusiasm and of noble urges . . . superior . . . to the Anglo-Saxon race, to the Slavic race, to the yellow race"].[24] If the French soldier functions as a living cell of *le grand corps*, one may well wonder what position might be occupied by the *tirailleur annamite* who serves the French imperial body even as his own is marked as belonging to the inferior *race jaune*.

In *Hiên le Maboul*, Nolly offers a peculiar narrative of the *mission civil-isatrice* in which the path toward civilization, a path that seems to offer the colonized subject access to a form of universal humanity, is simultaneously a path toward death. At the start of the novel, the title character is both set outside the realm of reason and inscribed within a colonial context, labelled not as *fou* but as *maboul*, a word of Arabic origin that entered the French language following the occupation of Algeria.[25] Hiên is presented to the reader as a barely human creature living in the grip of fear, a target of constant ridicule for his "esprit borné" ["limited mind"] and "lenteur d'intelligence" ["slow understanding"] (3). His youth is spent living in the forest, "chaque jour moins sociable et plus proche de la nature, chaque jour plus sauvage et moins pareil aux autres hommes" ["every day less sociable and closer to nature, every day more savage and less like other men"] (5). With repetitive and almost overwhelming force, the novel establishes Hiên as the embodiment of civilization's abject Other: within the first few pages, we learn that he is a "pauvre diable grotesque" ["poor grotesque devil"] (3) with the "coeur simple et fermé d'[un] enfant sauvage" ["simple heart of a savage child"] (4); his "stupidité naturelle" ["natural stupidity"] (9) and "pauvre cervelle" ["miserable brain"] are "des signes évidents d'idiotie complète" ["evident signs of complete idiocy"] (6, 7); he is "abruti" ["dazed"] (3), and in place of speech, "il gémit . . . [il] sup-pli[e] avec des mots incohérents" ["he moans . . . he implores with incoherent words"] (3, 6).

At the age of twenty, Hiên is handed over by village authorities to French military recruiters. Despite his *esprit borné*—or perhaps because of it?—he is judged fit for service by a panel consisting of a colonial administrator, a military officer, and a doctor. Hiên has no understanding of his new situation and is unable to perform the functions demanded of him. During military exercises, with his uniform constantly threatening to come undone, he tries and fails to learn to shoot his rifle; the most rudimentary elements of basic French are beyond his grasp; and, above all, "il est trop simple pour que la notion du devoir ait pénétré son cerveau" ["he is too simple for the notion of duty to have penetrated his mind"] (26). Hiên's condition is made still worse by the daily beatings he receives at the hands of Pietro, the cruel and—not incidentally—swarthy Corsican *adjutant* who rules the regiment with an iron fist in the absence of its French commanding officer.

The latter's return from a mapping expedition brings about a radical change in Hiên's existence. In stark contrast to Pietro, the French lieutenant embodies fairness in every sense: he is "galonné d'or et casqué de blanc" ["uniformed with gold stripes and a white cap"] and, as the narrator reminds us repeatedly, he has "les yeux bleus toujours souriants [et] la moustache blonde et fine . . . du justicier" ["the always laughing blue eyes and fine blond moustache of a man who fights for justice"] (39, 14). We never learn his name, since the narrator follows the reverential lead of the *tirailleurs* in referring to him only as *l'Aïeul* [the Ancestor].[26] Where Pietro is quick to dole out blows, *l'Aïeul* prefers more institutional forms of discpline: soon after his return, he tells the assembled regiment, "Le vrai tirailleur qui fait tranquillement et sans paresse son devoir quotidien doit savoir qu'il n'y aura pour lui ni salle de police ni prison" ["The true *tirailleur* who accomplishes his daily tasks quietly and without laziness should know that he will face neither police station nor prison."] (41–42). Through this displacement of the violence of the colonial relation, *l'Aïeul* is able to present himself to the *tirailleurs* as the embodiment of enlightened benevolence, and he is received by them as nothing short of divine. "L'Aïeul [est] un dieu!" ["*L'Aïeul* is a god!"], thinks Hiên, filled with a "tendresse débordante" ["overflowing tenderness"] for the blue eyes that have extinguished, "comme par enchantement [. . .] les éclairs qui flambaient dans les prunelles [de Pietro, le] tyran" ["as if by magic, the flames that shot from the eyes of Pietro, the tyrant"] (39, 38).

L'Aïeul's godlike status is confirmed when he takes on the project of civilizing Hiên. "Je lui enseignerai la vie," he tells one of his sergeants: "il saura qu'un homme en vaut un autre . . . il verra que l'abîme qui sépare de lui le reste de l'humanité n'est qu'un ruisseau . . . il sera un homme comme toi et moi" ["I will teach him life . . . he will know that one man is as good as another . . . he will see that the abyss that separates him from the rest of humanity is nothing but a stream . . . he will be a man like you and me."] (76). Under the watchful blue eyes of his commander, Hiên's inner transformation takes place with a magical speed all the more astonishing for the extreme abjection of his prior state. From one day to the next, "il fait clair dans son esprit" ["his mind is illuminated"], he develops a "facilité d'élocution" ["fluency of elocution"] (47) and tells *l'Aïeul* gratefully, "un regard de toi me donne l'intelligence et la parole" ["one look from you gives me understanding and the power of speech"] (59). Toward the end of the novel, Hiên has become "un homme civilisé, un homme pareil aux autres hommes" ["a civilized man, a man like other men"] (275).

In a posthumous tribute to Émile Nolly, Marcel Prévost described the essence of *Hiên le Maboul* as "cet humble appel de l'indigène molesté vers le juste chef français, et réciproquement l'évolution de l'âme indigène sous la protection intelligente du chef" ["this humble appeal of the mistreated native to the just French commander, and in turn the evolution of the native soul under the wise protection of the commander"].[27] The rapidity of Hiên's "evolution," the god-like powers of *l'Aïeul*, and the quasi-magical tone of the narrative ("comme par enchantement") all certainly lend themselves to a reading of the novel as a kind of colonialist fairy tale in which the gift of civilization lifts the abject native out of darkness and into the radiance of universal humanity. Unfortunately for Hiên, however, this is not in fact the whole story: at the end of the novel, the *tirailleur* undoes the red cloth belt of his uniform and uses it to hang himself. Once again, we are left with the body of the colonized soldier signifying only through its loss, but in this case the violence of death comes about not through combat but rather through the self-sacrifice of suicide. How are we to understand Hiên's death? What motivates his final act, and in the name of what ideal will his corpse be buried and his loss be mourned?

As framed by the narrative itself, the tragedy of Hiên's death comes about as a by-product of his movement toward civilization, in the sense that the formerly *maboul* soldier is unable to bear the bitterness produced by knowledge and the suffering that accompanies membership in the category of the human: "Il pleurait," the narrator tells us, "comme pleure, depuis le commencement des siècles, l'humanité penchée sur les débris de ses illusions" ["He wept . . . as humanity has wept since the dawn of time, crouched over the debris of its illusions."] (286). Even *l'Aïeul*, when confronted with Hiên's despair, confesses,

> J'ai eu tort . . . j'aurais dû laisser ton âme à sa pénombre, à son heureuse inconscience. Tu avais le bonheur, ne connaissant de l'humanité que les gestes

animaux. Je savais qu'après avoir mordu au fruit amer de la science humaine tu viendrais te rouler, quelque jour, à mes pieds, désabusé et hurlant.

I was wrong . . . I should have left your soul in its shadows, its happy unaware-ness. You had happiness, knowing nothing of humanity but animal gestures. I knew that after having bitten the bitter fruit of human knowledge you would someday come to throw yourself at my feet, disillusioned and howling. (289)

The condescending logic of the text, then, would have the reader believe that Hiên's suicide is the necessary consequence of his incapacity to shoulder the burden of civilization. I would argue that we might interpret the end of the novel differently, reading Hiên's death not as the sign of his failure to re-ceive the gift of civilization but rather as a narrative resolution to the anxi-ety produced by this gift having been offered in the first place.

If we reconsider the forward-looking structure of debt described above, we can understand how the death of the colonized soldier may be preferable, from the French perspective, to his survival: in effect, his death serves as a guarantee against the possibility of future claims. The imperial power is freed from any obligation to respond to the survivor's demands for political recog-nition and is free to mourn the colonized soldier as a loyal subject whose death is no more—indeed, is always less—than its due. In staging Hiên's death as a suicide, Nolly's text manages both to present *l'Aïeul* as the gener-ous master whose only fault lay in his overestimation of the colonized sol-dier's capacity for civilization, and definitively to foreclose any lingering debt that might have been incurred by France through a death in combat. At the same time, Hiên's suicide remains an unacknowledged sacrifice in the service of Empire, in the sense that it suspends the categorical instability implied by the phrases that circulate throughout the text in reference to his transforma-tion: "un homme en vaut un autre," "un homme pareil aux autres hommes," "un homme comme toi et moi." Even as they hold out the promise of equal-ity within universal (male) civilization, these phrases create an ideologically intolerable sense of the potential interchangeability between the subject po-sitions occupied by the French commander and the *tirailleur annamite*.

But this too is not the whole story. By way of a conclusion, I would like to offer a brief analysis of one other crucial element of *Hiên le Maboul*, an ele-ment that serves to underscore the extent to which the novel is fundamen-tally concerned with the proper maintenance of racial categories. In *Carnal Knowledge and Imperial Power*, Ann Stoler remarks that colonial sexual arrangements "were monitored if not successfully regulated early on in ways that repeatedly positioned women of different hue as desired objects and more obliquely as unruly desiring subjects as well. Connections among the making of racial categories, the prescribing of women's reproductive functions, and the managing of sexuality are hard to miss."[28] Stoler's comments are entirely relevant to a consideration of Nolly's text, the virulent misogyny of which allows for a striking displacement of the anxiety surrounding the figure of the colonized soldier onto that of the desiring woman. In an ideal world, the novel suggests, women would be confined to "le rôle de bêtes de somme et de machines à perpétuer l'espèce" ["the role of beasts of burden and of machines to perpetuate the species"] (54). Since the real world falls short of such an ideal, the most valuable form of knowledge available to the civilized man is "la connaissance du sexe ennemi" ["knowledge of the enemy sex"] (61). L'Aïeul is in full possession of this knowledge and has chosen to devote himself solely to "le culte passionné de la Patrie" ["passionate worship of the Fatherland"] (55). Hiên, on the other hand, is more vulnerable: he becomes engaged to Maÿ, a beautiful Vietnamese woman described as "une petite bête mauvaise et rusée . . . en âge déjà de ronger les coeurs des mâles et de vider leurs cerveaux" ["an evil and cunning little beast . . . old enough to gnaw at the hearts of males and to empty out their minds"] (45). His love for her brings only pain, and her power over him is conveyed in violently physical terms that figure her, and not the *tirailleur*, as armed and dangerous:

ainsi furent stupéfaits, sans doute, les sauvages d'Amérique qui entendirent pour la première fois siffler les balles . . . s'inclina[nt] avec effroi vers leurs frères blessés . . . [Hiên] ne s'éveillera de son rêve que lorsque les ongles pointus et durs de «l'Élue» se seront ensanglantés à lui déchirer le coeur!

the savages of America who heard bullets whistling for the first time, leaning with fear toward their injured brothers, might have felt the same stupefaction . . . Hiên will not wake from his dream until the sharp, hard nails of the "Chosen One" have been bloodied from tearing out his heart! (61)

L'Aïeul's lesson could scarcely be any clearer: "Il ne peut venir des femmes que deuil et malheur," he tells Hiên, urging him to forget Maÿ; "Tu l'oublieras . . . [et t]u seras grand, fort et joyeux, parce que connaissant les femmes et les méprisant" ["Nothing but mourning and sadness can come from women . . . You will forget her . . . and you will be big, strong, and happy, because you will know women and scorn them."] (162). But Hiên cannot forget her, nor can he bear this knowledge that defines the civilized man. Ultimately, it is his understanding that Maÿ not only holds him in contempt but has also betrayed him sexually that drives him to suicide. But what lies behind this inexorable narrative tragedy? What, exactly, is the nature of the "abîmes de perversion et de cruauté" ["depths of perversion and cruelty"] (71) hidden behind Maÿ's beautiful face? In a general sense, it is her status as what Stoler calls an "unruly desiring subject"—and it is worth noting here that in all three of Nolly's Indochina novels, tragedy and suffering are set in motion through the transgressive desire of female characters, both French and Vietnamese.[29] More specifically, however, Maÿ's desire reveals itself to be perverse not only in its lack of monogamous focus but also for its readiness to cut across racial difference in the service of pleasure and economic gain. Throughout the novel, we are given to understand that Maÿ dreams of sharing "le splendide lit à moustiquaire immaculée" ["the splendid bed with immaculate mosquito net"] of a Frenchman who would give her "des piastres [et] des colliers d'or" ["*piastres* and gold necklaces"] (62); when she does betray Hiên, it is with "un jeune mulâtre de la Guadeloupe" ["a young mulatto from Guadeloupe"] (201). The object of her desire is portrayed with scathing ridicule: not only is he a *dandy* whose intellectual pretensions are matched only by the "épaisse couche de fatuité" ["thick layer of self-satisfaction"] that surrounds him, but he is also, "bien entendu, antimilitariste" ["of course, antimilitarist"] (226). In one particularly grotesque scene, his white linen and silk suit ends up covered with mud, provoking hilarious laughter from the assembled townspeople, "car l'Annamite," the narrator informs us, "n'aime point le sang-mêlé" ["for the Annamite has little affection for mixed-bloods"] (227).

Far from making her a "machine à perpétuer l'espèce"—and I think that we must hear the racial undercurrent of that phrase—Maÿ's desires threaten to undermine the ideal of racial purity.[30] The anxiety over categorical instability that remains unacknowledged in relation to the *tirailleur annamite* finds full-blown expression in relation to the perversely desiring woman. When considered as a response to Maÿ's transgressive desires, Hiên's suicide might be understood finally as both the narrative resolution of his own unstable position as the civilized colonial subject, the soldier whose entry into the realm of the human has made his death a foregone conclusion, and as a sacrifice that can be openly mourned as a casualty of the struggle to defend the boundaries of racial difference.

Notes

1. Norindr names the identity produced out of this ambivalence the *drôle de zouave*. See Panivong Norindr, "Mourning, Memorials, and Filmic Traces: Reinscribing the *Corps étrangers* and Unknown Soldiers in Bertrand Tavernier's Films," *Studies in Twentieth-Century Literature* 23, no. 1 (Winter 1999): 118.

2. For more on the history of the Banania logo, see Mireille Rosello, *Declining the Stereotype: Ethnicity and Representation in French Cultures* (Hanover, NH: University Press of New England, 1998), 4–7.

3. Norindr, "Mourning, Memorials, and Filmic Traces," 121. In his fascinating discussion of the *Temple du Souvenir Indochinois* [Temple of Indochinese Remembrance] of Nogent-sur-Marne, Eric T. Jennings comes to a parallel conclusion, albeit within the context of a longer historical frame. In the 1920s, the *Temple* was "dedicated to the memory of the 1,548 Indochinese soldiers who had 'died for France' in the Great War"; its "founding logic [was] a belief that Indochinese commemoration was so radically 'other' from that of the Souvenir Français, that the unknown soldier of the Arc de Triomphe could not even begin to represent Indochinese losses, and that a separate fund, memorial, and agency need be set up to commemorate them." By the 1980s, however, the *Temple du Souvenir Indochinois* had become the *Monument du Souvenir Indochinois*, whose commemorative function was no longer primarily directed toward fallen Indochinese soliders, but rather toward French colonial soldiers killed during the wars of decolonization: "Thus conflated under the guise of egalitarianism, Indochinese soldiers of the First World War could be comfortably seen as having fought a precocious struggle to keep Indochina French. . . . This metanarrative presented a single history for France and Indochina, perceived in this way as eternally bound by colonial ties." See Eric T. Jennings, "Representing Indochinese Sacrifice: The Temple du Souvenir Indochinois of Nogent-sur-Marne," in *France and "Indochina": Cultural Representations*, ed. Kathryn Robson and Jennifer Yee (Lanham, MD: Lexington Books, 2005), 29, 31, 43.

4. Cited in Jennings, "Representing Indochinese Sacrifice," 40.

5. This section takes its lurid title from that of a *New York Times* interview with the producer of *Revolt of the Zombies*. See John T. McManus, "Walking Dead in Angkor," *New York Times*, May 24, 1936, X3.

6. Consider, for example, representations of North Africa in *Algiers* (1938) and *Casablanca* (1942), and of the French Caribbean in *To Have and Have Not* (1944). For a striking analysis of *Casablanca*'s place within the overlapping dynamics of French colonialism and U.S. foreign policy, see Brian T. Edwards, *Morocco Bound: Disorienting America's Maghreb, from Casablanca to the Marrakech Express* (Durham, NC: Duke University Press, 2005), 29–77.

7. William Seabrook, *The Magic Island* (New York: Harcourt, Brace and Co., 1929). For a brief historical overview of the zombie film, see Peter Dendle, *The Zombie Movie Encylopedia* (Jefferson, NC: McFarland & Company, Inc., 2001), 1–15. Longer discussions of the cultural and political contexts out of which early zombie films emerged can be found in Jamie Russell, *Book of the Dead: The Complete History of Zombie Cinema* (Godalming, Surrey, UK: FAB Press, 2005), and Gary Don Rhodes, *White Zombie: Anatomy of a Horror Film* (Jefferson, NC: McFarland & Company, Inc., 2001).

8. *White Zombie*, dir. Victor Halperin, Halperin Productions, distributed by United Artists, 1932. With an original budget of $62,500, the film grossed $8 million at the

box office. See Russell, *Book of the Dead*, 21. For excerpts of reviews, see Rhodes, *White Zombie*, 265–68.

9. *Revolt of the Zombies*, dir. Victor Halperin, Halperin Pictures, distributed by Academy Pictures Distributing Corporation, 1936. For more on the legal dispute between the Halperins and Amusement Securities Corporation over the use of the word "zombie," along with a representative assessment of *Revolt of the Zombies* ("a film vastly inferior to *White Zombie*"), see Rhodes, *White Zombie*, 171–77.

10. The Halperins were clearly eager to cash in on the popularity of *White Zombie* and attempted to cement in the imaginations of American moviegoers the invented connection that would link the two films. In an interview with *The New York Times*, Edward Halperin claimed: "Down in Haiti voodooism raises the zombies from their graves and sets them to work on the farms. In Asiatic Cambodia the zombies are employed as fighting creatures, and indomitable soldiers they make. You can't kill them, you see, because they're already dead." See McManus, "Walking Dead in Angkor."

11. Although Hollywood would go on to produce a number of films during the 1940s involving Nazi attempts to create zombies, to the best of my knowledge this scene is the first to show zombified subjects deployed in the service of a nation rather than an individual. Within the genre of the zombie film, one might productively trace the history of a subgenre featuring the reanimated corpses of soldiers, running from Abel Gance's 1938 remake of his 1919 film *J'accuse*, in which the dead of the First World War are called from their graves in order to remind the living of the terrible costs of war, to Joe Dante's *Homecoming* (2005), in which soldiers killed in a thinly-veiled Iraq War emerge from their coffins in order to vote in a presidential election. For a discussion of similarities between *J'accuse* and *Revolt of the Zombies*, see Russell, *Book of the Dead*, 30–31.

12. In fact, the film does ends with a revolt, but it is precisely *not* a revolt of zombies; rather, it is a group of Cambodians, newly awakened from their state of zombification, who storm the French zombie master's palace and kill him. While a full analysis of the film falls outside the scope of this essay, I would like to note how strikingly different this ending is from that of *White Zombie*, in which the plantation owner/zombie master is killed by another white character.

13. In early zombie films, including both *White Zombie* and *Revolt of the Zombies*, the desires of the zombie master are often directed both toward the production of a (usually nonwhite) pool of laborers and toward the erotic possession of a (usually white) woman. For an insightful analysis of the racial, sexual, and gendered dynamics at work in such zombie narratives, see Lizabeth Paravisini-Gebert, "Women Possessed: Eroticism and Exoticism in the Representation of Woman as Zombie," in *Sacred Possessions: Vodou, Santería, Obeah, and the Caribbean*, ed. Margarite Fernández Olmos and Lizabeth Paravisini-Gebert (New Brunswick, NJ: Rutgers University Press, 1997), 37–58.

14. Cited in Paravisini-Gebert, "Women Possessed," 39. More recently, Jean Comaroff and John Comaroff have argued that the figure of the zombie may also be un-

derstood as a postcolonial symptom produced by the workings of globalization and "millenial capitalism." See Jean Comaroff and John Comaroff, "Alien-Nation: Zombies, Immigrants, and Millenial Capitalism," *South Atlantic Quarterly* 101, no. 4 (Fall 2002): 779–805.

15. For more on the history of Indochinese colonial soldiers, see Maurice Rives and Eric Deroo, *Les Linh Tap: Histoire des militaires indochinois au service de la France (1859–1960)* (Paris: Charles-Lavauzelle, 1999).

16. Cited in Rives and Deroo, *Les Linh Tap*, 14. Throughout this essay, all translations of passages appearing in both French and English are my own.

17. While the French would prove unwilling to recognize this structure of debt in any politically significant way, the hopes it generated played an important role in the recruitement of colonized soldiers. During World War I, for example, Senegalese *député* Blaise Diagne succeeded in recruiting some 60,000 West African soldiers in part through his passionate promises of future rights to be won in exchange for military service. See Patrick Manning, *Francophone Sub-Saharan Africa 1880–1985* (Cambridge, UK: Cambridge University Press, 1988), 79–80; see also Norindr, "Mourning, Memorials, and Filmic Traces," 121.

18. Françoise Vergès has described this backward-looking structure as inherent to the dynamics of what she calls "colonial family romance": "Dependence and debt were the operative elements of the colonial family's dynamics. Its rhetoric displaced social relations determined by the symbolic and economic organization of exchange between the colony and the metropole and replaced them with the theme of continuous debt of the colony to its metropole. . . . The debt was constituted by the ideal of the French Revolution, of the French republic. In territories where feudalism, barbarism, or backwardness reigned, maternal France had brought Enlightenment and progress. She would save her children and elevate them toward full humanness . . . Precious woods, sugar, minerals, bodies to fight her wars, none of this would be enough to repay France for what she had given." See Françoise Vergès, *Monsters and Revolutionaries: Colonial Family Romance and Métissage* (Durham, NC: Duke University Press, 1997), 6, 7.

19. Nguyen Phan Long, *Le Roman de Mademoiselle Lys* (Hanoi: Imprimerie Tonkinoise, 1921), 376. For more on this novel, see Karl Ashoka Britto, *Disorientation: France, Vietnam, and the Ambivalence of Interculturality* (Hong Kong: Hong Kong University Press, 2004), 31–79.

20. Émile Nolly [pseudonym of Émile Détanger], *Hiên le Maboul*, 3rd Ed. (Paris: Calmann-Lévy, 1908), 1. Further page references will appear in the main text.

21. Lucien Maury, "Les Lettres: Oeuvres et idées—Romans," *Revue bleue* 47, no. 1, 2e sem. (3 juillet 1909): 58.

22. Denys Lombard, "Prélude à la littérature «indochinoise»," in *Rêver l'Asie: Exotisme et littérature coloniale aux Indes, en Indochine et en Insulinde*, ed. Denys Lombard, Catherine Champion, and Henri Chambert-Loir (Paris: Éditions de l'École des Hautes Études en Sciences Sociales, 1993), 128.

23. Émile Nolly, *Le Chemin de la victoire* (Paris: Calmann-Lévy, 1913), 74–75, 261, 263.

24. Nolly, *Le Chemin de la victoire*, 264.

25. While both words refer to madness or lack of reason, the "standard" French *fou*, of course, is not marked by colonial history in this fashion.

26. Nolly is of course playing here upon French understandings of Vietnamese ritual practices collectively referred to as "ancestor worship." In contrast to the death-in-life status of the zombie, the designation of the French lieutenant as *l'Aïeul* seems to afford him a kind of immortality, the potential for life beyond death.

27. Marcel Prévost, "Émile Nolly, tué à la guerre," *La Revue de Paris* 21, no. 17 (1er décembre 1914): 133.

28. Ann Laura Stoler, *Carnal Knowledge and Imperial Power: Race and the Intimate in Colonial Rule* (Berkeley, CA: University of California Press, 2002), 151.

29. For a fascinating discussion of the role of the *femme fatale* in a number of French colonial novels set in Indochina (including Nolly's *Le Chemin de la victoire*), see Jennifer Yee, "Colonial Virility and the *Femme Fatale*: Scenes from the Battle of the Sexes in French Indochina," *French Studies* LIV, no. 4 (October 2000): 469–78.

30. While the novels examined in Yee's article foreground women of European origin rather than colonized women, her analysis comes to similar conclusions regarding the structuring importance played by imperial anxieties over racial purity.

Works Cited

Britto, Karl Ashoka. *Disorientation: France, Vietnam, and the Ambivalence of Interculturality*. Hong Kong: Hong Kong University Press, 2004.

Comaroff, Jean, and John Comaroff. "Alien-Nation: Zombies, Immigrants, and Millenial Capitalism." *South Atlantic Quarterly* 101, no. 4 (Fall 2002): 779–805.

Dendle, Peter. *The Zombie Movie Encyclopedia*. Jefferson, NC: McFarland & Company, Inc., 2001.

Edwards, Brian T. *Morocco Bound: Disorienting America's Maghreb, from Casablanca to the Marrakesh Express*. Durham, NC: Duke University Press, 2005.

Homecoming. Dir. Joe Dante. Masters of Horror. Showtime. 2 December 2005.

J'accuse. Dir. Abel Gance. Forrester-Parant Productions, U.S. distribution by Arthur Mayer & Joseph Burstyn, 1939.

Jennings, Eric T. "Representing Indochinese Sacrifice: The Temple du Souvenir Indochinois of Nogent-sur-Marne." In *France and "Indochina": Cultural Representations*, edited by Kathryn Robson and Jennifer Yee, 29–47. Lanham, MD: Lexington Books, 2005.

Lombard, Denys. "Prélude à la littérature «indochinoise»." In *Rêver l'Asie: Exotisme et littérature coloniale aux Indes, en Indochine et en Insulinde*, edited by Denys Lombard, Catherine Champion, and Henri Chambert-Loir, 119–39. Paris: Éditions de l'École des Hautes Études en Sciences Sociales, 1993.

Manning, Patrick. *Francophone Sub-Saharan Africa 1880–1985*. Cambridge, UK: Cambridge University Press, 1988.

Maury, Lucien. "Les Lettres: Oeuvres et idées—Romans." *Revue bleue* 47, no. 1, 2e sem. (3 juillet 1909): 58.

McManus, "Walking Dead in Angkor." *New York Times*, 24 May 1936: X3.

Nguyen Phan Long. *Le Roman de Mademoiselle Lys.* Hanoi: Imprimerie Tonkinoise, 1921.

Nolly, Émile [pseudonym of Émile Détanger]. *Hiên le Maboul*, 3rd Ed. Paris: Calmann-Lévy, 1908.

———. *La Barque Annamite.* Paris: Charpentier, 1910.

———. *Gens de guerre au Maroc.* Paris: Calmann-Lévy, 1912.

———. *Le Chemin de la victoire.* Paris: Calmann-Lévy, 1913.

———. *Le Conquérant.* Paris: Calmann-Lévy, 1916.

Norindr, Panivong. "Mourning, Memorials, and Filmic Traces: Reinscribing the *Corps étrangers* and Unknown Soldiers in Bertrand Tavernier's Films." *Studies in Twentieth-Century Literature* 23, no. 1 (Winter 1999): 117–41.

Paravisini-Gebert, Lizabeth. "Women Possessed: Eroticism and Exoticism in the Representation of Woman as Zombie." In *Sacred Possessions: Vodou, Santería, Obeah, and the Caribbean*, edited by Margarite Ferrnández Olmos and Lizabeth Paravisini-Gebert, 37–58. New Brunswick, NJ: Rutgers University Press, 1997.

Prévost, Marcel. "Émile Nolly, tué à la guerre." *La Revue de Paris* 21, no. 17 (1er décembre 1914): 129–46.

Revolt of the Zombies. Dir. Victor Halperin. Halperin Pictures, distributed by Academy Pictures Distributing Corporation, 1936.

Rhodes, Gary Don. *White Zombie: Anatomy of a Horror Film.* Jefferson, NC: McFarland & Company, Inc., 2001.

Rives, Maurice, and Eric Deroo. *Les Linh Tap: Histoire des militaires indochinois au service de la France (1859–1960).* Paris: Charles-Lavauzelle, 1999.

Rosello, Mireille. *Declining the Stereotype: Ethnicity and Representation in French Cultures.* Hanover, NH: University Press of New England, 1998.

Russell, Jamie. *Book of the Dead: The Complete History of Zombie Cinema.* Godalming, Surrey, UK: FAB Press, 2005.

Seabrook, William. *The Magic Island.* New York: Harcourt, Brace and Co., 1929.

Stoler, Ann Laura. *Carnal Knowledge and Imperial Power: Race and the Intimate in Colonial Rule.* Berkeley, CA: University of California Press, 2002.

Vergès, Françoise. *Monsters and Revolutionaries: Colonial Family Romance and Métissage.* Durham, NC: Duke University Press, 1997.

White Zombie. Dir. Victor Halperin. Halperin Productions, distributed by United Artists, 1932.

Yee, Jennifer. "Colonial Virility and the *Femme Fatale*: Scenes from the Battle of the Sexes in French Indochina." *French Studies* LIV, no. 4 (October 2000): 469–78.

CHAPTER TEN

~

Franco-African Artistic and Cultural Cooperation

Jean-Loup Amselle,
École des Hautes Études en Sciences Sociales, Paris

France exports African artistic production.

—Ibrahim Loutou, vice-president of the A.F.A.A.[1]

What astounds me in Africa is the feeling that the world is beginning and at the same time that there is a future.

—Eric Orsenna[2]

Africa owes its place in art history to the freshness of its creativity.

—Yacouba Konaté[3]

The future of the French language will be decided along two major axes of cooperation with the Francophone countries of the Maghreb and Africa—support for systems of education and for the creative life.

—Jean-Paul Cluzel, president of Radio France International (RFI)[4]

As useful as the various books on African art may be, they all have the drawback of remaining in the rarified air of ideas and of overlooking the social conditions in which this art is produced.[5] It is not so much a question of examining African art in all its diversity as of grasping its genealogy and reinserting it in the public and private networks that shape it. In other words, there is nothing spontaneous about the genesis of contemporary African art—on the contrary, this art is the product of an encounter between certain kinds of actors and institutions and a milieu that can be likened to virgin territory. The term *Afriche*[6] used to account for this situation seems particularly appropriate given that it refers to the dual nature of Africa as both a continent to be deciphered ("déchiffrer") and a continent to be cultivated ("défricher"). Indeed, in cultural and artistic terms, as in many other areas, Africa has often been seen as a land of adventure, a field of experimentation open to all those—adventurers, conquerors, artists, ethnologists, builders of empire, or kings of the bush—eager to penetrate to the heart of darkness, at the risk of burning their wings. We should thus not be surprised that the romantic figure of the officer in the "Service des affaires indigènes," fascinated by the idea of going native, continues to haunt the imagination of many a cultural operator working on African soil, nor that the specter of "African freshness" continues to inform the representations and practices of Franco-African actors on the artistic and cultural scene.

Paradoxically, African artistic and cultural development is far from having been the exclusive property of the institutions that first come to mind when the question of development is raised. With the exception of a few colonial administrators such as Emile Biasini, for example, who during the 1950s implemented a sort of prototype of "choc électif" in Africa, which by bringing those under his authority—"les administrés de la brousse"—into contact with the classics of European high culture, intended to forge contemporary African art and culture in the crucible of European high culture,[7] the majority of actors working in this direction belonged to the private sector. Indeed, by introducing technological innovations and Western aesthetic models, both played the role of catalysts and midwives for contemporary African art. The terms "catalyst" and "midwife" seem justified here because the debate over who really "invented" contemporary African art (was it Georges Thiry, Meiring, Pierre Lods, Pierre Romain-Desfossés, Frank McEwen, the Beier husband and wife team?) seems to me particularly futile. Even if easel painting is obviously the result of a European import in Africa, it is nonetheless true that the African artistic forms that emerged from the Poto-Poto School or in the studios of Pierre Romain-Desfossés and Frank McEwen are better seen as the result of the arrival of an art that already existed *in potentia* or as the revival of already existing forms. From this perspective, the "white prophets" of African art invented nothing at all, if by invention is meant starting with a lump of clay or a blank slate—they simply encouraged the blossoming or the transfer of artistic patterns that were already there, waiting only to appear. The begetting of contemporary African art under the influence of an external gaze, which can be compared to an incubator, also explains the progression which led African art to be taken in by outsider art ("art brut") and its various avatars—popular art, naïve art, *arte povera, art modeste*, ready made, etc. The result of the asymmetrical encounter between the white artist and his black counterpart could only be a form of art given either a positive or negative charge according to one's point of view, but in any case not a neutral art. Indeed, the artistic and cultural cooperation that has been ongoing for several decades between France and Africa[8] must be analyzed and contextualized within the framework of this inaugural gesture (constantly renewed since) featuring the European artistic expert and his African interlocutor. Is not this process, by which the artistic skills of the Robinsons of Fine Art are grafted onto the "African freshness" of their Fridays, a process reinforced by the European artist's reinjection of primitivity[9] into the indigenous culture, emblematic of the relationship between France and its former colonies? In this light, does not the artist's gift of brushes, colors, paper, and canvases to the "nativeness" of the place, rapidly generating wonders of ingenuity and spontaneity, resemble a sort of primal scene of contemporary African art, an allegory of what could be called "Françafriche"?[10] At any rate, this is the meaning that should be given to the following story, told by Pierre Lods, one of the chief promoters of primitivity in the domain of contemporary African art, a function that he first fulfilled in Brazzaville and then in Dakar in the context of a Senegalese cultural policy focused on "negritude":

Je n'oublierai jamais la joie d'Ossali, mon domestique, lorsque je le découvris après deux jours d'absence, en train de peindre des oiseaux bleus sur une vieille carte de balisage de l'Oubangui. Ils étaient inquiétants et cocasses ces oiseaux avec leur forme de couteau de jet; ils avaient un présence égale à celle des plus beaux masques africains. Je n'avais rien vu de semblable dans tous les arts d'Afrique mais ils étaient incontestablement nègres par leur efficacité dans le choc, la grandeur et la magie qui s'en dégageaient.[11]

I will never forget the joy of my servant, Ossali, whom I discovered—after being absent for two days—in the process of painting blue birds on an old explorer's map of Oubangui. These birds, shaped as throwing knives, were at the same time disquieting and comical. Their presence equaled that of the most beautiful African masks. I had never seen such a thing in all the Arts of Africa, but they were unquestionably negro in the effectiveness of the shock, greatness and magic that emanated from them.

French Cultural and Artistic Action in the "Field" Countries

To understand French artistic and cultural action in the "pays du champ" (literally "field" countries), that is to say in the former French colonies of black Africa, we must go back to the tradition of administrating "African populations" such as it was expressed and taught within the École coloniale and then the École Nationale de la France d'Outre-Mer (ENFOM). In parallel to the French "civilizing mission" and the politics of assimilation associated with it, another current, represented by the "association" and indirect administration of the "natives," also occupied a prominent place in the training of colonial administrators. In fact, for several decades the *Ecole coloniale* and then the *ENFOM* were privileged centers of expression for a vision that could be qualified as "indigenist" or "ethnological." In a filiation that can be traced back to Baron Roger, to the Saint-Simonian *Bureaux arabes*, and to Faidherbe, the great figures of this institution—notably Georges Hardy and Robert Delavignette—were keen observers of African cultures, passionate advocates of their traditions, and the kindly godfathers of French ethnology between the wars and immediately after World War II.[12] Nor should we be surprised that the last graduating classes of the ENFOM produced the men, or rather the man, who was to become the principal architect of the definition and implementation of the "cultural action" policy associated with the name André Malraux. Indeed, it was a colonial administrator in Benin and a fervent admirer of "African popular cultures" named Emile Biasini who, having been entrusted with the mission of developing the material for the public relations campaign for the 1958 constitutional referendum in the overseas territories, took the reins of a "cultural action" in Africa under the tutelage of André Malraux (named Minister of Culture in 1959).[13] For Malraux, Africa had a special status—as opposed to the United States and the USSR, seen as too "materialistic," Africa, and especially certain African countries such as Chad, the Congo, Senegal, and Gabon, represent a source of spiritual enrichment or a reservoir of energy. In hopes that his "cultural action" policy might be extended to the overseas territories, he confided this mission to Biasini, who in 1959 returned to Chad and, as a gesture of thanks for the support offered by this country to the Free French, worked for the creation of a cultural center. The center, which aimed to ensure the presence of French culture in Africa, would never see the light of day, but it provided the model for Malraux's "Maisons de la culture," the foundation for his "cultural action" policy in Metropolitan France.[14] It also prefigures the numerous "Centres culturels français" that would be created in the former French colonies of Black Africa, starting with the center in Dakar, in 1959.[15] The twofold guiding principle that governs the functioning of the centers was present starting in this period: on the one hand, ensure the cultural influence of France, while on the other, encourage local cultural life. Under the auspices of the policy of cultural and artistic cooperation between France and its former African holdings, of particular note is the existence of a plan for developing the "théâtre du Palais" in Dakar, a project aimed at transforming the theater into a "Maison des Arts," offering classes in African plastic arts taught by Africans trained in France. The arrival of Pierre Lods in Dakar in 1961 at the behest of Léopold Sédar Senghor can be seen as part of the same broad trend, so strong is the link between the initiatives of the Senegalese president-poet and those of André Malraux, French Minister of Culture. The groundwork having been laid by sending ethnologist Rolf Italiaander to Brazzaville, Pierre Lods's invitation to Dakar and his nomination as the head of the African Section of the School of Fine Arts helped shape the first generation of Senegalese painters. There, under the influence of the head of the Poto-Poto School, a primitivist current emerged, one of whose best-known exponents, Papa Ibra Tall, would see his works recognized by André Malraux at the first Festival mondial des arts nègres in 1966.[16]

The French Cultural and Artistic Network in Africa

Building on the foundation of a "cultural action" policy largely inspired by Biasini and Malraux, the French cultural and artistic network emerges in Africa at the dawn of independence. The network rests on two main axes— "Centres culturels" and Fine Arts Schools.[17] Until 1980–1981, the principle underpinning French cultural and artistic policy rests on the idea of the specificity of sub-Saharan African cultures,[18] which is expressed by the notion of "*champ*" ("field"). Indeed, in contrast to French cultural and artistic action in the "traditional foreign domain," overseen by the Ministry of Foreign Affairs and the Association Française d'Action Artistique (A.F.A.A)[19] and interacting with cultures viewed as being of equal force, the French policy in "black" Africa is supposed to build ties between a dominant culture, the French culture—which is furthermore that of the former colonial power—and "a" weaker culture, "the one" African culture which must be made to "evolve" or even be regenerated. In the agglomerating discourse of the experts on cooperation, most of whom in this period are former colonial administrators, what goes for one goes for all, such that there exists this abstract entity, "African culture," at once symbol and symptom of a cultural action envisaged as a technology to be applied on fallow cultural soil, a terrain that is itself ripe for development. This explains why, given that the watchword of the "Centres culturels français" of Africa during the 1960s is, as in "traditional foreign domains," to further the promotion of French culture ("La vitrine France"), cultural action also aims in theory to "susciter une culture africaine qui intègre l'apport français et les valeurs de la civilisation traditionnelle" ("bring forth an African culture that integrates the French contribution and the values of traditional civilization").[20] In other words, its gaze fixed on tradition, and thus on the past, African culture can only nourish itself through contact with French culture, which gives it access to universal values.[21] This encounter is thus grasped in terms of crossbreeding ("métissage")[22]: by means of the fertilization undertaken in the "Maisons franco-africaines de la culture," the cultural clash induced by the cultural action of France is supposed to favor the awakening of African culture and galvanize development. This cultural action is first and foremost intended to reach the middle managerial classes, the new crop of "evolved" Africans of the colonial period. It was hoped that the latter category would spread this model to the masses by example.[23]

Nonetheless, the "Vitrine France" model triumphs over Franco-African artistic and cultural cooperation up until the 1980s, all the more so because the French expatriates ("coopérants") working in Africa and private sector employees formed a powerful lobby and were above all concerned to benefit from the French cultural presence. The behavior of the actors involved in French cultural policy in Africa did not make any recognizable strides until the 1980s and the setting up of reforms establishing the fiscal independence of the CCF as well as the accountability of their directors.[24] At this time the need emerged to offer a yearlong calendar of artistic and cultural events. This, in combination with the arrival of a new generation of cultural executives and impresarios more steeped in African culture, fostered renewed interest in the efforts of precursors such as Pierre Lods, Pierre Romain-Desfossés, or Frank McEwen and encouraged the burgeoning of young local artistic and cultural "talent."[25] Thus, at the end of the 1970s, spurred on by the staff of the "Centres culturels français," a favorable climate existed for the creation of the first cultural and artistic projects in the domains of theater, music, and the plastic arts. The natural extension of this process of cultivating ("défricher") and deciphering ("déchiffrer") young African talents was the setting up in 1990 of the association "Afrique en créations" and in 1991 of the journal *Revue noire*.

Franco-African Artistic and Cultural Coproduction

By Franco-African artistic and cultural coproduction is meant the process of fostering an emerging "contemporary African art" scene by French public, private, or combined operators with the support of subsidies provided by all three. This process marks the dawning of a new age in Franco-African artistic and cultural cooperation. Henceforth it is no longer a question of shoring up and preserving the influence of "Vitrine France" in her former colonies or in her larger sphere of action but indeed of promoting a far subtler form of domination, one that gives its blessing to the failure of economic and especially of agricultural development policies implemented in Africa since independence and which takes over the artistic and cultural domain as a sector capable of yielding maximum returns. In other words, moving away from the classical French model (Molière, Corneille, Racine), a new Franco-African tendency comes to the fore as a means of revamping French culture via Africa or of cogenerating a Franco-African culture as a substitute for a crumbling French culture and for a French language in worldwide decline. Whether this process occurred in cooperation with or in opposition to the private sector and other influential countries or in a supranational context (the European community) had no impact on the fact that the fate of French culture—and thus of the greatness of France—was seen from this point forward as being essentially decided not only in Africa (though primarily there) but also in all countries where French cultural entities work for cultural revival by identifying and enriching cultural and artistic forms more vibrant than those of France herself in order to benefit from the positive effects of this grafting process.

One of the first milestones in the establishment of this new Franco-African artistic and cultural configuration was born with the 1972 creation of the FESPACO, the African Film Festival in Ougadougou, Burkina Faso. Originally envisioned in the form of a film society by the director of the "Centre culturel français" and his Burkinabe friends, it met with great success and was then handed over to the country's authorities. Thanks to FESPACO, a high-quality African cinema emerged graced by the names of such directors as Idrissa Ouédraogo, Souleymane Cissé, and Cheik Oumar Sissoko. For lack of sufficient funds, however, its development remained in the French orbit. In this regard, FESPACO no doubt looks ahead to the model of the new Franco-African artistic and cultural configuration, on which France was counting to renew the luster of its reputation. It is indeed Africa, but also the Caribbean and in general the entire "Zone de Solidarité Prioritaire"[26] (ZSP), understood as an artistic and cultural fallow—"friche"—which seems to offer the best opportunities for capitalizing on the artistic and cultural investments of France. Shaken by the forces of globalization, and in particular by the dominant status of North American art and culture, (see the Quemin report),[27] is not French culture now condemned to seek salvation in the least developed regions, that is to say the planet's wildest, in which case her taste for primitivism, tinged by paternalism, is little more than a way of making a virtue of necessity?

This process of Franco-African cultural fermentation carries on in an underground fashion until 1990, a watershed year that sees the founding of "Afrique en créations." The creation of a certain number of associations and events over the course of the 1980s prepares the ground for this fermentation process and testifies to the need to move forward with an aggiornamento of the uses to which African artistic cultures are put by France.

One of these groundbreaking events was the 1984 creation of the "Association pour le développement des échanges interculturels" (ADEIAO) under the aegis of "Musée des arts africains et océaniens de la Porte Dorée." Though the museum's activities were traditionally oriented toward "primitive" art, the ADEIAO sought to organize temporary exhibits focusing on "les sociétés actuelles et l'art vivant du Maghreb, de l'Afrique noire et de l'Océanie" ("Present-day societies and living Art in the Maghreb, Black Africa, and Oceania").[28] By the same token, the ADEIAO looked to "révéler des artistes contemporains, montrer leur créativité et leur donner une juste place aux côtés de leurs pairs européens" ("discover contemporary artists, display their creativity and provide them with the position they deserve alongside their European peers").[29] Between 1985 and 1993, the association thus organized twenty or so exhibits, which offered the occasion for acquiring, via purchase or donation, the works of art that would henceforth constitute its legacy. Though the ADEIAO failed to make a name for itself as a major factor in the discovery and promotion of contemporary African art, and although its persistent behind-the-scenes work was largely ignored by the most high-profile groups and events, it is nevertheless true that it played a pioneering role in the arrival of contemporary African art on the world artistic scene and that it continues, under the leadership of its president Lucette Albaret, to maintain its position in the enshrining machinery of current African art.[30] The relative marginalization that the ADEIAO suffered must surely be seen in relation to the aesthetic choices that it made and which led it to privilege academic art at the expense of the art of self-taught artists.[31] And yet, as will be seen later, as of today it is essentially nonacademic art that has brought Africa recognition as the foremost artistic continent on the world stage.

At about the same time (1986) the A.F.A.A. (Association Française d'Action Artistique)[32] created a program that was to enjoy great success, and which consisted in sending French artists to Africa, not only to exhibit their work but also to serve as educators through contact with local African artists. Based on a tried-and-true model, that of the exchange of technical know-how for "freshness," this was the spark for a policy that would be implemented in the context of artistic residencies set up under the auspices of "Afrique en creations."[33]

Although almost forgotten today, another important milestone of contemporary Franco-African art and cultural coproduction is the 1987 *Ethnicolor* exhibit and the subsequent eponymous work published under the supervision of Bruno Tilliette and Simon Njami.[34] In the book's preface, which gave prominent billing to the reflections of major figures of the contemporary African art of the period, as well as to those who were on the rise,[35] Bruno Tilliette and Simon Njami deplored the fact that the West and France in particular were

> contentés de continuer à porter sur la culture du continent noir un regard essentiellement ethnographique . . . les critiques s'empressant de souligner si, par hasard, émergeait quelque production contemporaine, avec une condescendance teintée de paternalisme, sa 'spécificité africaine', la reléguant ainsi dans le ghetto d'une sous-culture régionale.

> contend to continue looking at the culture of the Black continent from an essentially ethnographic point of view . . . If, by any chance, some contemporary production emerged, critics would hasten to underline its specifically African nature, with a condescension tinted by paternalism, thereby consigning it to a ghettoized regional subculture.[36]

The year 1989 was one to remember for it was then that a major exhibit took place for the shaping of contemporary African art. Organized for the bicentennial of the French Revolution, the exhibit "Les Magiciens de la terre," held in parallel with Jean-Paul Goude's July 14 "multicolored" parade on the Champs-Elysées, marks the true birth of multiculturalism in contemporary art. Based on a belief in the inanity of contemporary art, as organizer Jean-Hubert Martin put it, the exhibit looked to spark a veritable rebirth in Western art through the discovery and display of a large number of artifacts from the countries of the South. Thanks to a team of traveling curators gathered around Jean-Hubert Martin, and notably André Magnin, who, as has been seen, was to become the big boss of contemporary African art, a whole series of artifacts were recognized on the international art market, whether works of art in the traditional sense[37] or "artworks," that is to say objects taken from their context and promoted as works of art for the good of the cause (ready made). Producers considered until then as popular, naïve, or outsider artists, such as Frédéric Bruly-Bouabré, Seni Camara, Bodys Isek Kingelez, Esther Mahlungu, and Cheri Samba were thus magically elevated to the rank of artists next to recognized professionals.[38] With "Magiciens de la terre" Africa's vocation as mainly a generator of "art de la friche" ("fallow art") was decided, followed by a corresponding decline of African academic art.[39] From this moment forward, the "outcasts" of official art take center stage, namely in the context of the real powerhouse on the contemporary African art scene, Jean Pigozzi's "collection d'art africain contemporain" (C.A.A.C) with André Magnin as adviser.

Following on the heels of "Magiciens de la terre," in 1990 and 1991, two major events would also take place: the founding of "Afrique en créations" on the one hand and of *Revue noire* on the other.

Let us focus first of all on the second event, which, although linked to the first, is the less important of the two, at least in institutional terms.[40] The founding of *Revue noire* took place largely in reaction to "Magiciens de la terre." Confronted with an art seen as ethnological,[41] such as it had been promoted by Jean-Hubert Martin and André Magnin, and which had already been criticized during the "Ethnicolor" exhibit, Jean-Loup Pivin and Simon Njami seek to encourage the emergence of artists who think of themselves as such rather than that of artisans transfigured into artists at the touch of some curator-expert's magic wand.[42] This no doubt explains why the first issue of the journal should be devoted to Ousmane Sow, a sculptor who, it is true, never received formal academic training but whose artistic intentions are undeniable and whose work is deeply inspired by the photographs of the Nuba taken by Leni Riefenstahl as well as by a group of prestigious sculptors such as Rodin, Bourdelle, and Giacometti.[43] In fact—and this would be confirmed in the following issues of *Revue noire*—the choices made by Jean-Loup Pivin or Simon Njami, particularly in the presentation of Rotimi Fani-Kayode's photographs,[44] tend to sketch a sort of neoclassical aesthetic that could also be qualified as "Greco-negro" and certain characteristics of which can be found in the sulfurous work of Robert Mapplethorpe.[45] All of this to say that the aesthetic of the founders of *Revue noire*, far from being some primitivism or other, is concerned rather to find in contemporary African art (a notion itself conceived as problematic) features that it is no doubt possible to locate in other cultures and which could thus be seen as invariable or universal traits.

This universalizing conception of contemporary African art and of the "black" diaspora is reflected in the review's sumptuous layout, which is made possible by the support of the Fonds d'aide et de coopération (FAC) and aims to bring *Revue noire* up to the level of other art journals and, in this way, to place African productions on equal footing with the rest of contemporary art.

The review,[46] publications, CD-ROMS, exhibits, a digitized collection of photographs, etcetera, enabled the *Revue noire* staff to play an important role in Franco-African cultural and artistic development as well as in the shaping of a field specific to contemporary African art, all the more so because the semi-independent status of its members allowed them to benefit from public funding while at the same time maintaining their distance vis-à-vis official institutions.[47] This is true of Simon Njami, a freelance expert who served as organizer for several exhibits and biennials and notably for the latest Rencontres photographiques africaines de Bamako in 2001, 2003, 2005, and 2007 supported and financed by the A.F.A.A. and "Afrique en creations."[48]

"Afrique en Créations"

The founding of "Afrique en créations" in 1990 represented an important stage in the setting up of "Françafriche" and in the creation of a cultural space specific to contemporary African art. Indeed, until this date, even if the A.F.A.A. (the only institution in the world devoted to spreading French artistic and cultural creation) interceded periodically in Africa, there existed no institution devoted to the production and promotion of Franco-African art and culture. The founding of "Afrique en créations" reflects a growing recognition among aficionados of Africa of the emergence of new young talent in African art and culture. "Afrique en créations" assumes the mantle of the A.F.A.A., which had been created after World War I to frustrate the hegemonic ambitions of the United States. Relying on its ties with Africa, France now looks to coproduce an African art and culture capable of thwarting American domination in these fields.

The founding moment in the history of "Afrique en créations" was a series of gatherings held on the 15 and 16 of January, 1990, in Paris, on the theme "Création artistique, dialogue des cultures, développement : les enjeux de la coopération et du développement"—"Artistic creation, dialogue of cultures, developments: the stakes of cooperation and development."[49] Michel Rocard, Prime Minister at the time, was behind these gatherings, which were initiated by Jacques Pelletier, Minister of Cooperation, and were organized throughout the year 1989 by Bernard Mounier,[50] a member of the Société Eurékam, in collaboration with the association Africréation. They were preceded by the television program *Afriques Passions*[51] broadcast by Antenne 2 and distributed in Africa by Canal France International, as well as by missions carried out in several African countries to meet with cultural envoys, heads of "Centres culturels français," as well as artistic creators and producers. Further groundwork was laid in France, notably at the Festival d'Avignon, and resulted in gatherings that brought together more than 300 participants and enabled the display of about sixty works solicited from creators and producers in Africa and France.

Among the big names to play a role in this "Françafriche" high mass, apart from those mentioned above, are Alfa Oumar Konaré, President of

I.C.O.M.,[52] former Minister of Culture and future president of Mali; Hervé Bourges, CEO of SOFIRAD; Jack Lang, Minister of Culture and Communications, of Public Works, and of the Bicentennial; Catherine Tasca, undersecretary in charge of Communications; Eric Orsenna, cultural adviser to François Mitterrand; Pierre Gaudibert, curator of the Grenoble Museum of Sculpture and Painting; Souleymane Koly, director of the Koteba ensemble of Abidjan; and Manu Dibango, as well as many others.

After the fashion of other events of this type, the founding gatherings of "Afrique en créations" were a veritable toolbox, a laboratory out of which emerged some of the ideas that were to give form to Franco-African cultural and artistic cooperation in the years that followed. The watchword of these meetings was the "cultural dimension of development." Jacques Pelletier, Minister of Cooperation, first used it in reference to André Malraux,[53] and it was taken up by Alfa Oumar Konaré and then by Jack Lang.[54] The theme "cultural dimension of development" was the main thread running through the conference in concert with the notion of cultural métissage, foundation of the regeneration or cogeneration of Franco-African art and culture. For it really was from this profound ambiguity that—in the wake of festivals in Limoges and Nantes, of the FESPACO and of the "Magiciens de la Terre"—"Afrique en créations" was born, an institution that established the emergence of African cultures and arts on the international scene, and in particular of music, and which, besides, and without announcing its intentions, sought to take advantage of this cultural boom to polish the escutcheon of French culture.[55] It is thus in terms of a Franco-African cultural and artistic coproduction that the proposals that were made during these gatherings as well the projects that emerged from them must be analyzed.

Thus the idea put forth by Alfa Oumar Konaré according to which "Centres culturels français" must assert themselves as centers for Franco-African exchange and open up to African popular culture, in particular to the craft industry, marks the end of the policy of exclusive presence of French culture in Africa ("Vitrine France"), and takes cognizance of an African culture open to the world. By the same token, all proposals for the creation of mixed residencies or exchanges for artists and writers, whether in France or Africa, and the corresponding desire to move forward with a decrease in the number of French expatriates ("coopérants") teaching in the Schools of Fine Arts, show that a new age had begun in the life of the cooperation, one in which it was no longer so much a question of imposing external models as of cogenerating a Franco-African culture. In this regard, all of the cultural and artistic institutions that would emerge from this conference, in particular all festivals, biennials, and gatherings, would (because of a clear financial and organizational preeminence) provide the basis for French domination over Franco-African art and culture. From this point of view, if there is such a thing as a French "cultural state," as Marc Fumaroli[56] would have it, the notion should apply first and foremost to the Franco-African cultural state, without forgetting that the latter is at the same time the precondition for the existence of a Franco-African cultural exception.

Achievements

Among the numerous achievements and examples of aid and support for which "Afrique en créations" can be credited since its founding, two major events stand out clearly on the Franco-African artistic and cultural landscape: "Rencontres de la création chorégraphique africaine" in the area of performance arts, and "Rencontres photographiques africaines" in the visual arts.

African Choreography—
"Rencontres de la chorégraphie africaine"

The title of pioneer—"défricheur" of African choreography—indubitably goes to Maurice Béjart, who in 1977, at the behest of President Senghor and with the support of UNESCO and of the Fondation Calouste Gulbenkian, created the École Mudra Afrique in Dakar. The son of Franco-Senegalese philosopher Gaston Berger and great-grandson, on his father's side, of a "signare" of Saint-Louis,[57] Maurice Béjart developed an artistic project based on the idea that the Western choreographic tradition had run dry, opening up the possibility for renewal through the contributions of African and oriental sources.[58] In this regard, Africa, or Islam (to which he converted), represented for him, besides Indian dance, an opportunity for Western choreography to be regenerated, and thus his student Germaine Acogny would become director of the École Mudra Afrique, where she would develop a synthetic vision of African dance before later directing the Rencontres de chorégraphie africaine in Luanda in 1998.

The other pioneer of contemporary African dance is no doubt the dancer and researcher Alphonse Tiérou, originally from Côte d'Ivoire. In order to counter criticisms of African dance, directed first and foremost against the latter's lack of a codified tradition, Tiérou went about theorizing it in order to ensure that it would have its place in the world choreography heritage and that it would serve as a reference point for new choreographers. This universal language, which assumes codes recognized by all, was laid out in his *Dooplé, loi éternelle de la danse africaine*, a work in which emerge ten basic movements regarded as common to all African dances.[59]

In 1992, responding to the polemical discourses, "Afrique en créations" decided to launch a project entitled: "Pour une danse africaine contemporaine." The project consisted in locating young talent on the African Continent interested in inventing a new repertory of gestures and finding means of self-expression without copying either traditional or foreign models and in exposing them to a program to heighten their awareness about contemporary dance. Thus a series of exhibits, conferences, and workshops were organized in Africa under the guidance of Alphonse Tiérou.[60] The idea of creating a Pan-African competition in contemporary dance that would allow dance troupes to meet and compete with one another then came to the fore. This would give birth to the "Rencontres de la création chorégraphique africaine," the first edition of which took place in Luanda, in Angola, at the end of 1995, with Alphonse Tiérou as artistic director.

The competition was the occasion for a veritable explosion of new choreographic talents, notably the winners of the "Rencontres": the South African troupe "Moving into Dance" as well as troupes from Zimbabwe, "Tumbuka," and Madagascar, "Tsingory."

The second "Rencontres," which also took place in Luanda in 1998, were entrusted to Germaine Acogny. Both Senegalese and French, from 1977 to 1982 the latter filled the role of artistic and educational director of Mudra-Afrique, which, as already mentioned, was created by Maurice Béjart. At the same time, Acogny put on performances and tours in Europe, the United States, China, and Africa. In 1980, she published *Danse africaine*, which describes her own technique of modern African dance, based on a synthesis of traditions from West Africa and classical and contemporary "modern" dance—that is to say, Western dance.[61] In the 1980s, she worked in Brussels with Maurice Béjart and conducted numerous international workshops. From 1987 to 1995, she created several choreographies (Biennials in Lyon in 1994 and in Sao Paulo in 1995). In 1995, she decided to create a "Centre international de danses traditionnelles africaines" in Toubab Dialaw, in Senegal.[62]

Germaine Acogny expresses her conception of choreography in the following terms:

Pour que la nouvelle danse africaine puisse continuer à vivre, pour qu'elle garde en même temps toute sa force tellurique, pour qu'elle reste puissante et vraie, il faut continuer à la stimuler en favorisant des échanges entre créateurs d'Afrique et d'ailleurs, en créant en Afrique des centres de formation de danses traditionnelles et contemporaines, parce que sans une base solide physique et intellectuelle, il ne peut y avoir de développement durable.

In order for the new African dance to carry on living, while keeping all of its telluric force, for it to remain powerful and true, we need to continue stimulating it by promoting interaction among creators from Africa and from elsewhere, by creating traditional and contemporary dance training centers in Africa, because without a solid physical and intellectual base, there cannot be any sustainable development.[63]

This second "Rencontres," placed beneath the banner of métissage, signals the arrival of African choreography on the international stage. New troupes take away prizes: "N'Soleh" (Ivory Coast), "Gaara" (Kenya) and especially two dancers from Burkina Faso, "Salia Nï Seydou," who, trained by Mathilde Monnier in her Center for Choreography in Montpellier, could look forward to a promising career. Mathilde Monnier herself was present in Luanda where she put on her piece "Pour Antigone." After the "Rencontres," she went on to lead a workshop in Windhoek, Namibia, and continued to collaborate with both African and Western choreographers at the "Montpellier-Danse" festival, which took place that same year with the participation of the prize-winning troupes from Luanda.

In this period, then, a veritable policy of choreographic cooperation was established between France and Africa, through the efforts of those who present themselves as "métis" as well as those who focus their artistic practice on "métissage," or both.[64] This policy, oriented toward "métissage," is reflected in the choice of Tananarive as the site of the third "Rencontres" in 1999 whose organizers saw Madagascar as the crossroads par excellence of dance traditions from Africa, Malaysia, and Polynesia, and is reinforced with an eye toward outreach by the place given to North Americans alongside African and European operators. Entrusted once more to Germaine Acogny, these "Rencontres" are intended to allow African choreographers and dancers to build an international career, but they are also seen as an opportunity "d'engendrer des affinités, d'inscrire des marques tangibles, de susciter le désir . . ." ("create affinity, leave tangible traces and arouse desire").[65] At the conclusion of the preceding "Rencontres" in Luanda, a boomerang effect occurred in what can be called the "Metropole" when Mathilde Monnier invited artists who had been discovered at Tananarive to the 2000 edition of the "Montpellier-Danse" festival, "instaurant de fait une diagonale chorégraphique entre le Sud et le Nord" ("establishing a de facto choreographic diagonal between North and South").[66]

The 2001 edition of the "Rencontres," which were held in Tananarive once again, established the international reputation of Mathilde Monnier's students, Salia Nï Seydou, as is demonstrated by the decision to entrust Salia Sanou, one of the duo's members, with the responsibility of directing the festival. The fifth edition, held once more in Madagascar in 2003, was the setting for a scandal and a near diplomatic incident with the awarding of second prize to the Mozambican troupe Augusto Cuvilas, which showed female bodies in a state of complete nudity.[67] This incident, which left the Malgache government, the "Rencontres" jury, and the French embassy in a deadlock, is representative of the ambiguous status of African art within contemporary art and of the limits within which the patronage of the A.F.A.A. obliged that art to operate. In attempting to transgress the boundaries of artistic etiquette, Augusto Cuvilas's troupe insofar as it is African was forced to endorse the worst stereotypes of African fallow. What would have been perfectly acceptable of a "white" choreographic troupe performing in any festival was not in Tananarive because nothing is neutral when it comes to African art, and it is thus impossible for African artists to behave as global adult artists. But it was perhaps also at this moment that the limits of the "Rencontres de la chorégraphie africaine" appeared. After having succeeded in promoting African dance on a world scale, the "Rencontres" had perhaps reached the crossroads insofar as the adjective "African" could now be seen as constituting a hindrance to their development.

Only time will bring an answer to this question, but as of now it can be observed that the success of the "Rencontres de la chorégraphie africaine" would doubtless not have been as complete without the synergy that was produced between this biennial event and the other "flagship" artistic event of "Afrique en créations," namely the "Rencontres de la photographie africaine de Bamako."[68]

The "Rencontres de la Photographie Africaine"

The creation of Rencontres de la photographie africaine is indissolubly bound to the discovery or rediscovery of African photography by certain Western operators, who by relying on the above-mentioned principle of the recycling of African kitsch, fostered the emergence of a new category of artifacts on the art market.

The whole story, unless it is a founding myth, began when André Magnin located two portraits taken in 1955 by an unknown photographer from Bamako, the prints of which were hung from the molding at the "Africa Explores: 20th Century Art" exhibit organized by Susan Vogel in New York in

1991.[69] Struck by the beauty of the prints, and willing to identify the photographer, André Magnin supposedly paid a visit in Bamako to Malik Sidibé, who, as the story goes, asserted that the photograph was the work of a colleague, his "older brother" Seydou Keita[70] . . . The story, even if it is too good to be true (since the person who sent the anonymous prints to Susan Vogel would still have to be identified) says a great deal about the process of mythification that occurs in the production of contemporary works of art, especially when applied to the mode of production of outsider art.

In any case, this little story leaves out the role played by photographer Françoise Huguier, whom some consider as the "inventor" of Seydou Keita and Malik Sidibé and who was no doubt chosen for this reason, and independently of the quality of her work, as one of two organizers, along with Bernard Descamps, of the "Premières Rencontres de la photographie africaine," held for the first time in Bamako in 1994. Besides, in this case, it is less a question of knowing to whom the paternity (or the maternity) of the "discovery" of Seydou Keita's work belongs than of bringing to light the process by which an artistic heritage was produced, a process which has nothing original about it, but which, where Africa is concerned, takes place in the domain of a new "primitivity," the very one that replaces the defunct primitivism of "tribal art." In this sense, these first "Rencontres," mainly devoted to the "rediscovery" of studio artisan-photographers from the 1950s and 1960s, that is to say to their transubstantiation into artists, were the means by which these artifacts were endowed with prestige on the international art market, whereas their impact on the local public was minimal. The second "Rencontres," which also took place in Bamako, with Robert Pledge, Robert Delpire, as well as Cameroonian photographer Bill Akwa Bétaté at the helm, continued this process of canonization of artisan-photography, notably with the transubstantiation of the family photos of Cornélius Yao Augustt Azaglo into a work of art.[71]

The 1998 edition, entrusted to Louis Mesplé,[72] and especially the 2001 and 2003 editions, with Simon Njami as director, break decisively with the preceding events: indeed they open up the "Rencontres de la photographie africaine" to new countries and new generations of African photographers, whether the latter are labeled as activist photographers, diaspora photographers, or above all as art photographers. The emergence of the category of art photography applied to African photography in concert with the theme of the Black diaspora indeed reflects the aestheticisation of African photography and thus crowns its true entry into the world art market. The arrival on the market of professional artist photographers means that African photography has now reached adulthood, but at the same time begs the question of its perpetuation or dissolution as such. In this regard, the film made by

"Afrique en créations" about the 2001 "Rencontres" is a good illustration of this ambiguity. It asks relevant initial questions such as: what makes African photography African? Is it the fact that the subject is African? That an African takes the photo? Is it the African technique used to take the photo? However, the rest of the film is devoted exclusively to "Black," "Sub-Saharan" or Diaspora African photographers to the exclusion of those from the north of the continent whose work was nonetheless displayed at the same event.[73] This focus on "Black" African photography is a good indicator that the idea of African cultural specificity is a loaded one, certainly linked to that of "freshness" and which, as has been seen, was one of the topoï of colonial thought. That this idea should be defended by certain African artists, who in an utterly contradictory fashion pose as photographers of the "Black race" while at the same time denying the existence of an "African photography," in no way changes the fact that this nationalist posture is perhaps at the same time the condition of access to the international art market.[74]

The 2003 edition of the "Rencontres" which saw African "art" photography take to the streets for the first time, strengthens without any doubt the status of the event as a flagship of the politics of cultural and artistic cooperation promoted by "Afrique en créations." It also strengthened the status of Bamako and Mali as centers for African photography, a status that had already been established when the "Hasselblad" prize—the highest distinction in photography—was awarded to the most illustrious exponent of "photonostalgie," Malick Sidibé.[75] Is Africa the spring at which Western contemporary art can slake its thirst, and will this regeneration depend upon the use of the freshness of the African fallow?—that in any case is the question that defines the workings of the Franco-African artistic and cultural landscape.

Conclusion

In Lille, ten years after the original "Rencontres" in Paris, a new "high mass" was celebrated in the context of the "Mission 2000" presided over by Jean-Jacques Aillagon, crowning a decade of cultural and artistic action undertaken by "Afrique en créations." Entitled "Territoires de la création. Artistes, institutions et opérateurs culturels. Pour un développement durable," ("Territories of Creation. Artists, institutions and cultural executives. Toward sustainable development")[76] the conference aimed at summing up artistic and cultural development in Africa for the benefit of an audience of officials, including some who had participated in the "Rencontres" in 1990. The entirety of the performance and visual arts, and not only choreography and photography, provided fodder for reflection and commentary which was accompanied by a long series of artistic events, the most important of which, in the context of Fest'Africa, returned to the works of art displayed at the Dakar Biennial (Dak'art). Even if the quality of the papers and projects presented at the conference left something to be desired, the fact remains that the repercussions of the event, notably in the domains of the plastic arts and design, helped to jumpstart the recognition of the works of certain African artists such as Aboudlaye Konaté, Amahiguere Dolo, Viyé Diba, Ndary Lô, Antonio Ole, Kwesi Owusu-Ankoma, Nicolas Cissé, etc.[77]

In ten years, "Afrique en créations" has thus fully succeeded in playing the role of "seed-planter," in the words of Ibrahim Loutou,[78] vice-president of A.F.A.A., that is to say in cultivating young African cultural and artistic talent. But to continue to extend this biological metaphor, has "Afrique en créations" for all that fulfilled the mission at the foundation of any project for development, that of nourishing and spreading the offspring of the African fallow? Examining two areas in which the results of "Afrique en créations" are the most tangible—choreography and photography—seems to be a good indicator of its ability to spawn, in its own terms, "sustainable development."

After taking a quick inventory of the projects undertaken by "Afrique en créations" in choreography, an initial observation springs to mind—the success of the various editions of the "Rencontres de la chorégraphie africaine" as events able to shape African dance troupes. It is incontestably the case that during this event and the tours that followed, dancers and troupes alike emerged and enjoyed growing success on the international stage. It is enough to cite the names of Salia Nï Seydou to be convinced of this. This enfranchisement of choreographic entrepreneurs has led the latter to consider moving on to another stage of production, that of training African dancers in Africa. By the same token, Germaine Acogny wishes to transform her "Centre de danses traditionnelles et contemporaines africaines" in Toubab Dialaw in Senegal into a veritable "Maison de la danse africaine" conceived as "lieu d'enseignement, de rencontres et d'échanges culturels et chorégraphiques entre l'Afrique, sa diaspora et le monde entier"—"a site for teaching, encounters, cultural and choreographic exchange between Africa, the diaspora and the whole world."[79] In addition, this site, which already hosts a space devoted to theater, painting, and sculpture, in Acogny's mind should allow for the development of an industry linked to cultural tourism, a concept that no doubt has a promising future in Africa. A similar pattern can be observed with regard to Salia Nï Seydou troupe's plan to create a "Centre chorégraphique de Ouagadougou," which would function in collaboration with that of Germaine Acogny, the former in the creative domain, the latter as a training center.[80]

The grooming of young choreographic talent thus really did take place, even if it could not help raising questions about the identity of the performances. Indeed, some worried about the authenticity of African choreographic productions that are faced with the influence of Western operators, as if African dance had not always been constructed, as has already been underlined, through contact with European dance.[81] Worrying about the possible contamination of the one by the other comes down to postulating the existence of a "pure" African dance whose model exists solely in the minds of the very people who are at the origin of the synthesis of the disparate elements that have produced this choreography.

This choreographic primitivism was fully expressed, for example, in a Heddy Maalem performance that was intended to allow dancers of African origin, living in France, to meet their counterparts on the African continent, in this case Senegal.[82] Without leaving any room for doubt about the intentions of its promoter, this "transnationalist" project nonetheless leaves one wondering about Heddy Maalem's ability to produce a purely "African" performance when the true nature of the "operator" ("Afrique en créations," Montpellier-Danse) overseeing its realization remains unclear. As long as the French cultural network, whether "Afrique en créations" or the "Centres culturels français" in Africa, are in control of the production, the distribution, and the networking of various African artistic and cultural initiatives, it is the latter that will give its stamp of approval to the authentic "Africanity" of these projects.[83]

It is thus in terms of control and even sometimes of competition between French and African cultural producers that the question of "Françafriche's" future will be posed. The border between competition and partnership is in any event often rather blurry, which sometimes has the result, notably in the domain of exhibits, of making the French cultural network an operator exercising its functions in Africa in a market in which Africans also participate. The fact that Africans are alienated, relatively speaking, from the product of their artistic and cultural activities also raises the question of the nature and location of the authority that valorizes this artistic and cultural production.[84]

The Franco-African Artistic and Cultural Landscape/Le paysage artistique et culturel franco-africain (PACAF)

Franco-African artistic and cultural landscape is understood by the process of instantiation, the effect of which is to bring into being in France, and beginning with this country, the concept of Franco-African art and culture. It is a question of a hierarchy of power relationships, a unified competitive space defining a series of positions that can be occupied in turn by the same actors both discursively and in the art market.

The conditions under which this space is deployed are defined (1) by the link between public and private with the extension of the private sector[85] within the context of liberalization as a backdrop, (2) in contrast to the international art market, controlled by the United States, Switzerland, Germany, and Japan as well as to supranational institutions (the European community), (3) by the joining of the French national identity with "Francophonie," (4) in the difference from contemporary and global art in general. In short, what we have been referring to as "Françafriche" or again "Afriche" conceived as the "first" continent of art has its niche within this space.

In order to sketch a quick outline of PACAF's features, the example of the visual arts can be used since this is the most active and best-functioning market.

In this sector, "Afrique en créations" turns up again, since this association, which as has been seen, operates for the most part in the photographic domain, but also makes its presence known in the domain of the plastic arts with the support it gives, along with other backers, to the Dakar Biennial (Dak'art), and notably, within the Biennial, to the design sector.[86] "Afrique en créations" also has several high-profile public projects to its credit, in particular the exhibit organized in Paris in 1999 on the Pont des Arts. This open-air exhibit, which "welcomed" several million visitors, represents the pinnacle of one of the biggest promotional undertakings of African art ever embarked upon by France. Indeed, the sculptor Ousmane Sow, who made his first appearance in the bosom of the CCF in Dakar and who was promoted by *Revue noire*, had the opportunity to see his work gain international recognition at this event. But this landmark success overshadows the relatively low-profile nature of the other events organized by "Afrique en créations" in the domain of the plastic arts, apart from the Lille "Fest'Africa," which was itself linked to the Mission 2000, the latter having also supported the exhibit of works of the Malian sculptor Amahiguire Dolo in the Jardin de Tuileries in Paris. If such is the case, this is because the domain of the plastic arts, and especially of painting and of "photo-nostalgie," is in large part monopolized by the private sector. Within this sector, the André Magnin-Jean Pigozzi duo and the Collection d'Art africain contemporain (CAAC), a sort of semiprivate museum located in Geneva, along with several associates of whom more will be said later, play the most important part. Indeed, it is the CAAC that fixes the market price of contemporary African plastic art and that thus establishes its boundaries. Holding the place of preference in the market for African outsider art along with several stars such as Frédéric Bruly Bouabré, Cheri Samba, Bodys Isek Kingelez, Moke, Seydou Keita, and Malick Sidibé, among others, the Franco-Swiss consortium leaves other forms of contemporary African art little chance for success, and in particular art considered as academic. Indeed the contemporary African art market functions today based on principles similar to those that govern so-called "tribal" art, that is to say according to the principle of pedigree. It is because an artifact has passed through the hands of such-and-such a collector, art critic, or curator that it acquires its value and not in virtue of its intrinsic properties. This quasi-monopolistic control over taste and the market exerted by the André Magnin-Jean Pigozzi tandem is explained by the disappearance of a certain number of rivals and in particular of Jean-Hubert Martin, and of the driving forces behind *Revue noire*, Jean-Loup Pivin and Simon Njami.

After having drafted the birth certificate of contemporary African art along with a number of curators, including André Magnin, thanks to "Magiciens de la Terre," and after having given a second life to this landmark event with "Partages d'exotismes" in 2000, Jean-Hubert Martin has now left French territory, if not the French artistic scene, to assume the position of director at the Kunst Palast Museum in Düsseldorf, Germany, where he continues to put on exhibits of a thematic nature.[87] Although still very much present on the international art market as a reference or as a resource for valuation purposes, he no longer truly belongs to PACAF.

The same is true of the collaborators of *Revue noire* and in particular of Jean-Loup Pivin and Simon Njami who, through their publications and public appearances, have played a leading role in the fashioning of "Françafriche," as has been seen with regard to the work of Ousmane Sow. This is because, even as they initially held important positions in the Franco-African cultural network and notably within the Ministry for Cooperation, these major players in PACAF marginalized themselves or were progressively marginalized. *Revue noire* stopped being published in 1999, and the editorial team was distanced from the African events of Mission 2000. By the same token the merger between the A.F.A.A. and "Afrique en créations" was accomplished without *Revue noire*, and Simon Njami, even if he still directs several important "Afrique en créations" events such as the Rencontres de la photographie africaine de Bamako (2001, 2003, 2005, and 2007) for instance, is now just an African freelance organizer among others.[88]

The other players within PACAF have had a foothold in the market for a long time, either in collaboration with the Magnin-Pigozzi tandem, such as the Fondation Cartier or Agnès B for African outsider art, or independently, as is the case for FNAC in the domain of photography.[89] The existence of new venues such as the Musée Dapper must also be mentioned. The evolution of the Fondation-Musée Dapper is in this regard particularly revealing of the blossoming of the African contemporary art sector within the market for African art and art in general. Having gotten her start, fifteen years ago, on the market for "tribal" or "art premier" destined for museums, its founder Christiane Falgayrettes-Leveau has increased the breadth of her palette so as to touch upon other areas. The result has been several landmark events: the display of the "métisse" work of Cuban artist Wifredo Lam, then that of Senegalese sculptor Ndary Lô, of the Antillean artist Serge Hélénon, and finally the exhibit devoted to tribal and contemporary art of Ghana, made possible by the support of Magnin and Pigozzi's CAAC.[90] This broadening of Christiane Falgayrettes-Leveau's field of influence is indicative of the degree to which the theme of recycling African kitsch has made headway within PACAF. Those pieces of "tribal art" catalogued or endowed with a pedigree having become inaccessible to the vast majority, a new museum market has emerged at the intersection of "art premier" and contemporary African art. But what is above all worth noting is that the market itself maps out a new commercial market that is emerging in the layer right below its point of reference, the museum market. Here is meant what has come to be known as "Afro-bobo" art, which is often anonymous and which can be found at the Pop Galerie, on the Rue d'Orsel in Paris, at the Halle Saint-Pierre, at the Musée international des arts modestes in Sète ("Incredible Movie Posters du Ghana") or at the CSAO on the Rue Elzévir in the Marais.[91] This "Afro-bobo" art will be diversified in its turn, transformed into a version destined for the *pecus vulgum* ("African" plastic kettles with zebra patterns, matchbox cars in derelict soup cans, plastic corn rows, etc.) or, on the contrary, rebranded by "trendy" designers and elevated or promoted, in the near or distant future, to the status of a veritable work of art.[92]

Finally, the landscape of "Françafriche" would not be complete if the media and its role as the bellwether in fixing the value of contemporary African art was not mentioned. It can be noted first off that the French media had to make an effort to adjust in "accommodating" contemporary African art. Apart from the journals that had made this sector their specialty, such as, for example, *Revue noire*, but whose failure may have been due precisely to this specialization, the other art journals have only recently begun to devote significant space to the PACAF in their columns, and many of them, especially the most traditional ones, still devote the majority of their articles only to "tribal" or "art premier."[93] It is the most modern or "fashionable" journals, such as *Art Press* or *Beaux Arts Magazine*[94] or again *Mouvement* and *Art absolument* that devote a significant portion of their analyses to contemporary African art envisioned as an element of global art or in the wake of reports devoted to big "ethnological," "culturalist," or "postcolonialist" artistic events. On the editorial valuation circuit a special place certainly goes to the publication that presents itself as a TV Guide but which is in reality far more: *Télérama*. Targeted to the cultured, upscale viewer, *Télérama* devotes a significant portion of its pages to culture and the arts, and notably to African culture and arts. Recent years have indeed seen this weekly magazine feature reports and articles on important personalities and events related to "Françafriche": the Ousmane Sow exhibit on the Pont des Arts, "Afrique en créations" in Lille, Rencontres de la photographie africaine in Bamako, a special report on African cultural diversity, etc.[95] . . . In short, *Télérama* wants to be considered as a major player on the Franco-African artistic and cultural market valuation circuit. By the same token *Le Monde*, to which *Télérama* is linked, seems eager, especially of late, to make a place for itself in the "Françafriche" niche and to supplant, in this area as in others, *Libération*, whose political as well as aesthetic opinions quite naturally give an important role to the editorial treatment of PACAF.

In order to finish sketching the outlines of PACAF in the media realm, the role of radio and television remains to be dealt with. In radio, first prize obviously goes to RFI, a partner with A.F.A.A. and co-organizer of the Rencontres chorégraphiques d'Afrique et d'océan Indien. RFI, due to the absence of Pan-African media, but perhaps also thanks to this very absence, can ensure, like "Afrique en créations," that South/South ("Sud/Sud") cultural events are linked up and thus acts as a universalizing operator.[96] Far behind RFI, "France Culture" devotes some of its programs to contemporary African art, while insofar as television is concerned, Arte and channel 5 occupy the foreground, notably with the series devoted to "Afrique en créations" in the domain of photography, dance, and the plastic arts, or to Nurith Aviv's film devoted to Frédéric Bruly Bouabré's alphabet.[97]

Translated from the French by Mireille Le Breton and Trevor Merrill.

Notes

1. Interview, April 11, 2003.
2. "Afriques Passions," Antenne 2, 1990.
3. Yacouba Konaté, "L'Afrique n'est pas une table rase . . . ," in *Territoires de la création, artistes, institutions, et opérateurs culturels. Pour un développement durable en Afrique*, Actes des Rencontres internationales de Lille, 26, 27, et 28 septembre 2000, A.F.A.A. ("Programme Afrique en créations"), Culture et Développement, pp. 96-97. Yacouba Konaté is professor of philosophy and aesthetics at the University of Abidjan/Cocody and is an important figure of "Françafriche."

4. "La Parole à Jean-Paul Cluzel, président de RFI," Interview with Jérôme Neutres, *Rézo International*, n. 9, 2002, p. 20. Jean-Paul Cluzel is currently president of Radio-France.

5. This text is translated from chapter VII of my book *L'Art de la friche, essai sur l'art africain contemporain*, Paris, Flammarion, 2005.

6. The term is a play on words combining the French "friche," meaning "fallow," and "Afrique." *–translators' note.*

7. For further information on Emile Biasini's colonial and French career, the reader is invited to consult his autobiography (*Grands Travaux. De l'Afrique au Louvre*, Paris, Odile Jacob, 1995) as well Marie-Ange Rauch's *Les Administrateurs de la France d'Outre-mer et la création du Ministère des Affaires culturelles*, "Comité d'histoire du ministère de la Culture," Paris, ministère de la Culture et de la Communication, 1998. I thank Philippe Urfalino for having drawn my attention to this figure. Emile Biasini, with André Malraux, the father of the "Maisons de la culture" of the "Centres culturels français" in Africa, in large part conceived the so-called policy of "cultural action" and of "choc électif," which is linked to his name (The expression is Philippe Urfalino's in his book, *L'Invention de la politique culturelle*, Paris, La documentation française, 1996.). A passage from his autobiography deserves to be cited here *in extenso*:

> Dans ma brousse, j'avais beaucoup lu, écouté infiniment de musique, m'étais passioné à faire des copies de Cézanne ou de Van Gogh, et beaucoup impliqué à en offrir la découverte aux Africains.

> In the bush, I read a lot, listened extensively to music, and enthusiastically reproduced paintings by Cezanne and Van Gogh, and was very involved in sharing what I had discovered with Africans. *Grands Travaux*, op. cit., p. 137. The same goes for classical music, ibid., p. 145.

8. We will focus here on Franco-African artistic and cultural cooperation because there is no equivalent example in Africa.

9. Pierre Lods invites "his" African Congolese artists to paint in the presence of traditional African objects, but like Emile Biasini he also brings them into contact with paintings by Raphaël. Pierre Lods, "Les peintres de Poto-Poto," *Présence africaine*, 1959, 24–25, pp. 326–30. Susan Vogel for her part recounts that Georges Thiry made the painters he was training remove any evidence of modernity (bicycles, European clothing) from their canvases. Susan Vogel, *Africa Explores, Twentieth Century Art*, New York, The Center for African Art, Munich, Prestel, 1991, p. 187.

10. This topos is omnipresent in the machinery for cultivating and promoting contemporary African art. We see it with Meiring who gave cans of paint to the Ndébélé (chapter 5 of *L'Art de la friche*, the book from which this essay has been taken), with Georges Thiry who distributed paper and paint in the Belgian Congo in the 1930s (Bogumil Jewsiewicki, mentioned in my seminar on March 8, 2001), with Pierre Lods in Congo-Brazzaville (Pierre Lods, *infra*). In the same way, Karl-Heinz Krieg encouraged Kolouma Sovogui to transfer paint onto cardboard and plywood,

using new colors, toma body-paintings, which until then had been executed in black, ochre, and rust red. Catalogue from *Partages d'exotismes*, op. cit. t. 2, p. 43. The same machinery is also present in the Australian context (chapter 5 of the book from which this essay has been taken). This theme of the gift and of sharing is also expressed in an interview with dancers from the Didier Théron team working in Mozambique. Cécile Canut and Ludwig Trovato's film, *Contre-temps*, October 2002.

11. Cf. "Congo Zaire, Thango de Brazza à Kin," *Cahiers de l'ADEIAO*, 10, 1991, p. 12. In this regard, Pierre Lods' career is particularly significant. Pierre Lods was born in 1921. After studying the sciences, his preparation for the Naval Academy was interrupted by the war, and he joined the Resistance. After the war, he pursued studies in ethnology, archeology and linguistics at the Sorbonne, and at the same time enrolled at the Art Academy of the "Grande Chaumière." In 1946, he organized documentary and scientific missions to Spitzburg, Morocco, Algeria, Sudan and Niger. He also participated in the "Mission Ogooué Congo" in the pygmy tribe Babinga de la Sangha (Congo-Brazzaville) in the company of Raoul Hartweg and Gilbert Rouget, professors at the Musée de l'Homme. The following year, he continued, alone this time, to pursue his studies in linguistics with the Babenzele pygmies and with the Bakwélé, and at the same time embarked on some painting projects. He then returned to Brazzaville to paint in a personal studio located in the Poto-Poto quarter and inspired many Congolese acquaintances to take up painting in his footsteps. I thank Lucette Albaret for having given me this information.

12. On Robert Delavignette's indigenism and "colonial humanism," see Bernard Mouralis and Anne Piriou's (dir.) book, *Robert Delavignette, savant et politique (1897–1976)*, Paris, Karthala, 2003, pp. 125–35. Maurice Delafosse, Henri Labouret, Marcel Griaule, Michel Leiris, Léopold Sédar Senghor, Jacques Soustelle, among others, taught at the École coloniale and at the ENFOM.

13. Within the last graduating classes of the ENFOM, Guy Georgy should also be mentioned. Georgy was colonial administrator and later ambassador to France in China and a connoisseur of primitive art, a category which for him extends from prehistoric art to contemporary African or Oceanian art. See his preface to the book commemorating the tenth anniversary of the founding of the ADEIAO, *Art Contemporain d'Afrique et d'Océanie*, ADEIAO, 1984–1994, Paris, ADEIAO, 1995. On the ADEIAO, see infra.

14. The story of the to-ings and fro-ings between African "Centres culturels" and French "Maisons de la culture" is expressed in an exchange between Gaëton Picon, then director of Arts and Letters, and André Malraux as reported by Emile Biasini. André Malraux: "I found a guy (Biasini) who is going to make us some cultural houses in Africa. And Gaëton (Picon) replied: Why not in France?" Emile Biasini, *Grands Travaux . . .* op. cit., p. 139.

15. Jacques Bonnamour, et al. *Les Centres culturels français en Afrique, Evaluation de l'action des CCF dans les pays du Champ*, Evaluations n. 5, Paris, Ministère de la Coopération et du Développement, 1991, p. 244. Infra, CCF. The idea of creating Cultural Centers in fact goes back to the 1950s: on March 14, 1953, in AOF, a de-

cree calls for "the creation of cultural centers whose vocation would be to serve as meeting places for African and European elites in the urban centers and local capitals of the circle." In 1954, the first issue of *Trait d'union* appears, an entity linking the "Centres culturels" of the AOF. The bulletin's objective was to "establish as close a partnership as possible among all the Africans who, 'évolués' or not, want to put their culture into action and to ceaselessly build knowledge," ibid., p. 242.

16. "As André Malraux told me at the inauguration in Dakar of the Premier Festival Mondial des Arts Nègres: 'You have, here, in Senegal, five or six artists who can match the greatest European artists for stature.' I am thinking of Ibou Diouf and Papa Ibra Tall, of Bokar Diong and El Hadji Sy. These painters have done away with the effects of perspective in order to play on color, on colors: a tapestry by Papa Ibra Tall which hangs in my house in Dakar contains as many as ten different hues." Léopold Sédar Senghor, from "Ce que je crois," *in* Clementine Deliss (ed.), *Seven Stories*, Paris, Flammarion, 1995, op. cit., p. 218 (italics mine, J.-L. A.). André Malraux's narrative figures in his "Anti-Mémoires," *Oeuvres complètes III*, Paris, Gallimard (Bibliothèque de la Pléiade), 1966, pp. 487–515.

17. The question of the history of the Fine Arts Schools in the countries of Francophone Africa will be addressed here only incidentally, given that it could itself form the subject of an entire study.

18. "Convinced of the need to respect African cultural specificity, the cultural advisers considered the way in which to accomplish the sea change that would lead the mentality of the traditional world to the ever-evolving modern world," CCF, p. 198, "L'Afrique est un pays (*sic*) différent," Biasini, *Grands Travaux*, op. cit., p. 115.

19. At present, they are called "Cultures France," which clearly shows the asymmetrical relationship between French culture and other cultures.

20. CCF, op. cit., p. 178.

21. "For in these countries France, her culture, and her language already belong to the national heritage. They are not an intellectual luxury, but allow access to universal values. Today, through the play of mutual influences, French culture has become and continues to be Franco-African culture, and truly belongs to Africans," CCF, ibid., p. 183; "The true ties to the Africans were conditional on the certainty that self-interest was not involved: we gave them a key which would enable them to unlock the world. Beyond political change and possible upheaval, they could only benefit from our giving them access to a universal way of thinking. We ourselves had a great deal to derive from their virtues," Biasini, *Grands Travaux*, op. cit., p. 146.

22. "Métissage is inevitable, and it's an opportunity, but it must come about in a tranquil fashion," CCF, op. cit., p. 180.

23. "If we can enter into direct contact with the elites, have an impact on the intermediary social categories, and in particular the junior managers, who speak and read French but need to improve their skills, the latter, being in close touch with the masses, will act as ad hoc intermediaries on our behalf. Given our concern to contribute to economic development, action undertaken 'for the middle manager' can reconcile high yield and low cost," CCF, ibid., p. 186.

24. CCF, ibid., p. 210 and those that follow.

25. Yves Bourguignon, Ministère des Affaires étrangères, Interview, March 12, 2003. Bernard Mounier, founder of "Afrique en créations," was both witness to and one of the precursors of this transformation when he directed the CCF in Tananarive from 1964 to 1967. Interview, La Rochelle, April 25, 2003. On Bernard Mounier and "Afrique en créations," see infra.

26. The "Zone de solidarité prioritaire" (ZSP) financed by the "Fonds de solidarité prioritaire" (FSP) of the Ministry of Foreign Affairs, embraces the entirety of sub-Saharan Africa, Tunisia, Morocco, Vietnam, Laos, and Cambodia, Haiti, Santo Domingo, Cuba, Saint Lucia, Lebanon, and Yemen.

27. Alain Quemin, L'Art contemporain international entre les institutions et le marché (le rapport disparu), Editions Jacqueline Chambon/Artprice, 2002.

28. ADEIAO, op. cit.

29. Ibid.

30. Since 1996, the ADEIAO is housed in the offices of the Centre d'études africaines at the EHESS.

31. See in particular the first exhibit organized by the ADEIAO, "Arts africains: sculptures d'hier—peintures d'aujourd'hui" centered on the Ivoirian current known as "vohou vohou" and which was accompanied by a gift of thirty-six works by young Ivoirian painters, former students of Professor Yankel at the Ecole Nationale Supérieure des Beaux-Arts de Paris. This statement should be qualified in light of the exhibits organized around the "naïf" Dogon painter Alaye Atô (See "Alaye Atô, dessinateur dogon," Cahiers de l'ADEIAO, n. 14, 1999) on the one hand, and on the other Moke and Cheri Samba (April 1 to 30, 2004). All of these exhibits put on by the ADEIAO took place at the Maison des Sciences de l'Homme.

32. A few chronological markers may help to situate the redeployment of the A.F.A.A. In 1981, Jack Lang became Minister of Culture. In 1982, Catherine Clément became the director of the A.F.A.A. and "reoriented the compass southward, toward the most disadvantaged countries . . . there are numerous directors who are packing their bags for Africa, Latin America, or Asia." See Guy Lacroix and Benjamin Bibas, Artistes sans frontières, une histoire de l'AFAA, Paris, A.F.A.A., 2002, p. 45.

33. See the artist studios organized by Yves de la Croix, then director of the Cultural Center of Niamey in Niger. These consisted of a "bivouac on the banks of a river of artists who had come from Africa and France." "Lettre de la Fondation d'Afrique en creations," Revue noire, juillet-juin-août 1994, p. 63. See also his presentation on March 20, 2003, at my seminar.

34. Bruno Tilliette and Simon Njami (eds.), Ethnicolor, Paris, Autrement, 1987.

35. In addition to precursors such as Pierre Gaudibert, these included Bruno Tilliette, Simon Njami, and Jean-Loup Pivin, future founders of the Revue noire and essential figures in "Françafriche."

36. Ethnicolor, op. cit., p. 8.

37. By work of art is understood works produced intentionally with an artistic goal. In this sense, all art, insofar as it is art, is "art for art's sake."

38. I am thinking here of, among others, Cildo Meireles, renowned Brazilian artist whose works have already been displayed at the Musée d'Art moderne et contemporain de Strasbourg (mars-mai 2003, organized by Cécile Dazord). It seems this artist had intentionally produced "primitivist" works for the "Magiciens de la Terre." Interview with Cécile Dazord, Strasbourg, April 1, 2003.

39. See the comments of André Magnin regarding Frédéric Bruly-Bouabré in whom he sees an artist of "freshness" and "necessity" and whom he thus places in opposition to Ivoirian academic artists guilty in his eyes of practicing "decorative" art and content to reproduce the works of Leonardo da Vinci or Picasso. "Aujourd'hui l'art africain contemporain," France Culture, Marie-Laure Bernadac, March 27, 2003.

40. From the start the two structures were linked since editing of "La lettre de la Fondation Afrique en créations" was entrusted to *Revue noire* and published in its pages. *La lettre de la Fondation Afrique en créations*, 1991, n. 1.

41. Simon Njami, "Regards anthropométriques," *Revue noire*, n. 5, *see* also his remarks during the above-cited France Culture radio program.

42. "The point of view of the 'noble savage' is to say to a carpenter from Ghana: 'You are a contemporary artist.' I wouldn't see any problem if one said the same about a Lubéron potter. A genuine artist has a plan first of all, it's not a matter of chance, what he does differs from mere production." Remarks by Simon Njami reported by Henrik Lund, "Simon Njami, gourou malgré lui," *Rézo international*, 3, autumn 2000.

43. See the interview with Ousmane Sow in the first issue of *Revue noire*: "Isn't there a parallel to be drawn between the Greeks and this aesthetic obsession? Ousmane Sow: At the risk of shocking a good many people, I must say that there are very few Greek sculptures I like. Because there the aesthetic takes precedence over life. Perhaps because of their choice of materials . . . The three Europeans who have most inspired me are Rodin, Bourdelle, and Giacometti. Giacometti is the sparest of forms, and as Bernard Schaeffer at RFI rightly pointed out to me, I begin my sculpture, its skeletal structure 'with Giacometti,' and I finish 'with Rodin.' "Ousmane Sow, interview with Pierre Gaudibert and Simon Njami," *Revue noire*, 1, 1991, p. III.

44. *Revue noire*, 3, 1991, Rotimi Fani-Kayode and Alex Hirst, *Photographs*, Paris, *Revue noire*; London, Autograph, 1989.

45. The *Revue noire* team's perspective is here very close to that of Stuart Hall and the "Black British" diasporic current. See Stuart Hall and Marc Sealy (eds.), *Different: A Historical Context, Contemporary Photographers and Black Identity*, London, Phaidon, 2001.

46. *Revue noire* stopped appearing in 1999 but maintains an online site at www.revuenoire.com.

47. Jean-Loup Pivin was the architect of the Musée national de Bamako and an adviser to President Alfa Oumar Konaré. He belonged to the team that evaluated the

"Centres culturels français" of Africa for the Ministry of Cooperation in 1991, see CCF, op. cit.

48. He was also an organizer associated with the Dakar Biennial in 2001, the "El Tiempo de Africa" exhibit (Madrid, 2001) and belongs to the team of organizers of "Africa Remix." (2005). See infra.

49. Actes des rencontres, Afrique en créations, Paris, 15–16 janvier 1990, "Création artistique, dialogue des cultures, développement: les enjeux de la coopération culturelle," Paris, Focal Coop, Ministère de la Coopération et du Développement, 1990.

50. Bernard Mounier, whose career path is particularly sinuous, came out of the Secrétariat à la Jeunesse et aux Sports, where he worked from 1961 to 1962 before assuming the role of director of the Service culturel of the "Association pour les stages et l'accueil des techniciens d'Outre-Mer" of the Ministry of Cooperation (1963-64). He was then director of the Centre culturel français at Tananarive (1964-67), then director of the Maison de la culture of Le Havre (1967–1975), of that of La Rochelle (1975–1983), and was finally assigned to FR3 (1983–1986). During the period from 1986–1990, he created the production company Eurékam, participated in the making of "Afriques Passions," and then prepared the founding "Rencontres" of "Afrique en créations." From 1990 to 1994, he was at France 3 Sud. Retired since 1994, he formed a team with Bérangère Casanova within the production company "Equipage." He was vice-president of "Afrique en créations," directed the "Bouillon de culture" TV show at Bamako with Bernard Pivot, entitled "Spécial Mali," on France 2 (1998), as well as the series "Afrique en créations" which was broadcast in April 2003 on channel 5 and TV5. He is currently administrator of the A.F.A.A. and a member of the advisory board of the program "Afrique en créations." He is a key figure in Franco-African artistic and cultural cooperation. Interview, La Rochelle, April 25, 2003.

51. The program hosted by Frédéric Mitterrand gave a broad overview of Franco-African art and culture in the deliciously obsolete context of the Musée des Arts africains et océaniens de la Porte Dorée, inviting as guests Eric Orsenna, Germaine Acogny, Manu Dibango, Papa Wemba, Claude Nougaro, Idrissa Ouedraogo, Johnny Clegg, Ousmane Sow, etc.

52. Organisation internationale des musées.

53. Reference is made in his speech to André Malraux's idea according to which art is an "anti-destiny."

54. For more on Jack Lang's ideas about the economic dimension of culture and linked to the economic crisis and his anti-Atlanticist positions, see Philippe Urfalino's book, L'invention de la politique culturelle, op. cit.

55. In this regard should be mentioned the role as founder or precursor of the "Musiques métisses" Festival in Angoulême, which was devoted to popular musics from the Francophone world as well as non-Francophone Southern Africa. Created by Christian Mousset in 1976, the Festival d'Angoulême, organized by the Association Musiques métisses, devoted itself primarily to French and European jazz for five years. During a trip to Bamako, in Mali, Christian Mousset became a passionate fan

of Mandigue music, a taste that would lead to numerous Malian artists coming to An-goulême in 1982, then to a special West Indies event. The turn toward métisse mu-sics was definitively taken by the Festival de jazz d'Angoulême at this point but for some time the festival continued to recycle the former glory of the African music of the 1960s and 1970s (see chapter 1). Christian Mousset did not participate in the founding gatherings of "Afrique en créations," but he is a member of the institution's Board of Trustees and Artistic Board. *Afriques en scènes*, 4, 1995, 9 March 1998.

56. Marc Fumaroli, *L'Etat culturel. Essai sur une religion moderne*, Paris, Ed. de Fal-lois, 1991.

57. She was called Fatou Diagne. After having seen a performance of Stravinsky's "The Rite of Spring, " Senghor supposedly said to Béjart that he would not have been able to bring off such a staging if he hadn't had "this little bit of black blood." "Afrique en créations, Noire attitude," Channel 5, April 13, 2003.

58. "Béjart did more in integrating with the forty or so 'steps' of classical dance, other movements emerging from South Asia—I am thinking of Dravidian India—and from Mother Africa." Léopold Sédar Senghor, "Le nouveau ballet africain" (1980), preface to a book by Germaine Acogny, *Danse africaine*, Weingarten Kunstverlag, 1994, 4th edition, p. 5. For a brief historical survey of contemporary African choreog-raphy, one can refer to Corinne Moncel's article "Et l'Afrique recréa sa danse. . . ," *Afrique en scènes*, 9, 1998, pp. 11–19. In the following lines I am largely indebted to this article.

59. Alphonse Tiérou, *Dooplé, loi éternelle de la danse africaine*, Paris, Maisonneuve et Larose, 1989. In this sense, Alphonse Tiérou really is, along with Germaine Acogny, and for better or for worse, the inventor of a *standard* contemporary African dance, like certain linguists who "invent" or rather deduce a *standard* Dogon language from the multiple languages and dialects spoken in or around the Bandiagara cliff. For a critique of the notion of "African dance," see Mahalia Lassibille's article, "'La Danse africaine, une catégorie à déconstruire. Une étude des danses des WooDaaBe du Niger," *Cahier d'études africaines*, 175, 2004, 680–90.

60. The latter thus presents his exhibit and leads workshops and conferences in Ouagadougou in December 1993, in Yaoundé in December of the same year, and in Abidjan in March and April 1994. "Lettre de la Foundation Afrique en créations," *Revue noire*, n. 12, mars-avril-mai 1994, p. 60.

61. "*Danse africaine* has as its goal the correct execution of the various dance movements invented by Mme Acogny based on popular Negro-African dances. In doing so she proceeds exactly as European choreographers did when they invented the movements of classical ballet." Léopold Sédar Senghor, op. cit., p. 6.

62. *Afriques en scènes*, n. 9, mars 1998, p. 8.

63. Ibid., p. 9. See the comments of Léopold Sédar Senghor: "In using the word 'step,' the Europeans make dance a play of abstraction, to take man up from the earth and project him into the sky. In preferring the word 'movement,' Mme Acogny puts the emphasis on the symbolic value of the figure of dance and on the adherence of the dancer to the earth: to Mother Earth, which gives the dancer his soul," op. cit.,

p. 6. See also the reference made by Germaine Acogny to the kapok tree to symbolize at once opening toward the exterior (the branches) and being rooted in the ground. "Afrique en créations, Noire attitude," ibid.

64. See the already-cited declarations of Mathilde Monnier, chapter II, as well as her contribution to Chantal Pontbriand's book, in which she expresses regret at not being African . . . "Antigone l'étrangère," in Chantal Pontbriand (ed.), Danse: langage propre et métissage culturel, Montréal, Parachute, 2001, op. cit., pp. 191–97. True, Mathilde Monnier challenges, furthermore, the problem of métissage, preferring a conception that foregrounds the clash of cultures resulting from the encounter of African and European dancers. Lettre de Fondation Afrique en créations, sept–nov. 1993. But is not to refuse métissage the same as assuming, at the same time, the existence of an "African dance" on the one hand and a "Western dance" on the other? It would be equally fitting to examine the artistic collaboration between Mathilde Monnier and the philosopher Jean-Luc Nancy and the properly "telluric" or "archetypal" (Senghorian) vision of African dance that the latter embraces. Jean-Luc Nancy, "Séparation de la danse," ibid., pp. 199–205. See also "Allitérations," Mathilde Monnier's proposal along with Jean-Luc Nancy, Seydou Boro et al., Centre Pompidou, April 10, 2003.

65. "L'Afrique réinvente la danse, elle arrive à Tana. . . ," Zéro international, issue O, octobre-novembre 1999, p. 11.

66. Jérôme Neutres, "Afrique en créations. De l'association au programme," Rézo International, n. 5, printemps-été, 2001, pp. 17–18.

67. See the report compiled by Laurent Goumarre, "Ils n'ont rien vu à Tananarive!," Art Press, n. 299, mars 2004.

68. This point is underlined by Bernard Mounier in "Comment l'esprit vient aux Biennales," Rézo International, n. 6, automne 2001, pp. 17–18.

69. Please refer to Cat. 59, "Portrait of a Man, 1955," unknown photographer (Bamako, Mali), from original negative, 19 by 13 cm, private collection, and Cat. 60, "Portrait of Two Men, 1955," unknown photographer (Bamako, Mali), silver print, 1974, from original negative, 18 by 13 cm, private collection, in Susan Vogel (ed.), Africa Explores, 20th Century Art, op. cit., pp. 160–61.

70. Malik Sidibé told me that Françoise Huguier discovered him as an artist before André Magnin organized the exhibit of his works at the foundation Cartier, in 1995. Interview, Bamako, May 20, 2002. Around the same topic, refer to Jean-François Werner's catalogue's account of the exhibition of Seydou Keïta's work at the Fondation Cartier (1994), in Cahiers d'études africaines, 141–142, 1996, pp. 313–16.

71. Erika Nimis, Photographes de Bamako de 1935 à nos jours, op. cit., p. 117. The pictures taken by Cornélius Yao Augustt Azaglo appear in this veritable encyclopedia: Anthologie de la photographie africaine et de l'Océan Indien, edited by Revue noire in 1998.

72. Louis Mesplé was the director of the "Rencontres photographiques" in Arles.

73. "Afrique en créations, Merci pour la photo," April 5-6, 2003. Mémoires intimes d'un nouveau millénaire, IVèmes Rencontres de la photographie africaine 2001, Paris, Editions, Eric Koehler, 2001.

74. See Angèle Etoundi Essamba's words in the film quoted above.

75. The international photography prize of the Hasselblad Foundation—50 000 öre prize money and a gold medal—was awarded to him on October 25, 2003, in Göteborg, Sweden.

76. *Territoires de la création*, *artistes*, op. cit.

77. Consult the catalogue of the exhibition *L'Afrique à jour, 10 ans de création contemporaine à la Biennale de Dakar*, Afrique en créations.

78. Interview, April 11, 2003.

79. "L'Afrique réinvente la danse," *Rézo international*, oct-déc. 1999, pp. 11–12, Germaine Acogny; "Faire bouillir la marmite: se professionnaliser pour devenir un maillon de la chaîne," in *Territoires de la création . . .* , op. cit., pp. 40–41.

80. This center opened in December 2006.

81. Michel Chialvo, "Former les artistes . . . et les techniciens," ibid., p. 42. Michel Chialvo is in charge of the production at the "Centre chorégraphique national de Montpellier," directed by Mathilde Monnier.

82. "Aix, Avignon, Montpellier, Terres d'accueil," *Rézo* international, n. 2, été 2000, p. 14.

83. One may think, at the moment when I am writing these lines (November 2004), that African choreographic troupes have become increasingly autonomous thanks to the organization, in Ouagadougou, of the Festival "Dialogue des Corps" by the troupe Salia Nï Seydou, if it were not for the fact that this festival takes place within the framework of the 10ème sommet de la Francophonie, henceforth within France's sphere of influence.

84. The first rumblings were heard at the last "Rencontres de la photographie africaine" in Bamako. Emmanuel de Roux, "Tensions franco-maliennes autour des choix de programmation," *Le Monde*, 11 octobre 2003.

85. While already engaged in a process of liberalization, the French cultural network (A.F.A.A., CCF in Africa) holds to the idea of confronting the market to defend its identity, either by taking up the defense of the public sector, or by nationalism, or both.

86. Ibrahim Loutou, interview, April 11, 2003.

87. Jean-Hubert Martin directed the "musée national des Arts d'Afrique et-d'Océanie" (MAAO). He was curator of the "musée national d'Art moderne de Paris" from 1971 to 1982, commissioner for numerous exhibits, and also directed the Kunsthalle in Berne between 1982 to 1985, before taking on leadership of the "musée national d'Art moderne" (centre Georges Pompidou) from 1987 to 1990. He also belongs to the team of commissioners of "Africa Remix," the traveling exhibit that started in Düsseldorf in July 2004.

88. And it is also, as has already been said, one of the commissioners of "Africa Remix" (2005). We wrote these lines in 2003. Since then, it seems that the situation has radically changed and that Simon Njami has become one of the major players on the contemporary African art stage. Indeed, he is in charge of the "Pavillon africain" at the Biennale de Venise (2007) and of the exhibit "Check List, Luanda Pop" which

is meant to be an autonomous artistic African event, while remaining one of the pillars of "Françafriche," since Njami is also "high commissioner" of Rencontres africaines de la photographie de Bamako, 2007 edition.

89. On the role played by gallery owner Agnès B, please refer to chapters 1 and 3 of *L'Art de la friche*, op. cit. (the book). André Magnin organized the retrospective of the work of Cheri Samba at the Fondation Cartier during the 2004 first semester ("J'aime Cheri Samba"). The FNAC is partner with "Rencontres de la photographie africaine" in Bamako and displays photographs from Africa in the network of galleries associated with its bookstores. The FNAC directing body particularly appreciates "l'originalité, la spontanéité et la vitalité de la photo africaine" (A.F.A.A. documents about "Les Troisièmes rencontres de la photographie africaine").

90. "Ghana, hier et aujourd'hui" exhibit, Musée Dapper, Paris, 2003, and especially works by Almighty God lent by André Magnin.

91. See Anne Deguy, "La rue de la petite Afrique," *Libération*, April 18, 2003.

92. The pearl-encrusted furniture, ornamented with zebu horns and calabasa, with which Philippe Stark decorated his new restaurant on top of the Samaritaine department store, ibid.

93. It would be worth mentioning here the cultural journal *Africultures*, influenced by postcolonial and afro-centrist theories, which devotes some issues to African contemporary art but whose impact is difficult to assess.

94. From this point of view, it is obvious that *Beaux Arts Magazine* devotes the entirety of its article dealing with the musée Dapper exhibit: "Ghana, hier et aujourd'hui" to Akan mortuary tribal art in terra cotta whereas not a single line is devoted to Ghana's contemporary art. Bérénice Geoffroy-Schneiter, "Les faces cachés du Ghana," *Beaux Arts Magazine*, 227, 2003, pp. 72–76. *Télérama* TV guide, although more open to contemporary African art, only devotes a few sentences to the contemporary works exposed during that exhibit. Michel Daubert, "Pour tout l'or des Akan," *Télérama*, n. 2782, May 7, 2003.

95. See especially, "la diversité culturelle face à la mondialisation (3/5): le Mali. L'Empire mandingue contre-attaque" by Luc Desbenoît, *Télérama*, n. 2781, May 3–9, 2003.

96. "La parole à Jean-Paul Cluzel, president de RFI," interview by Jérôme Neutres, *Rézo International*, op. cit.

97. Screened on channel Arte. January 15, 2005.

~

Conclusion

My Mother Tongue, My Paternal Languages

Michel Serres, Member of L'Académie Française

We Francophones speak along a circlet or circuit that, reaching from Quebec to Belgium, runs from Switzerland to Africa and on to Haiti. Being as here on this circuit, we turn to a center, located in Paris, toward which we emit our various voices and from which we look for a reaction, often with a feeling of resentment at Paris's old arrogance.

For my part I would like to outline another circlet, this one of long standing and inconspicuous: it runs from Alsace to the Piemonte, from Corsica to the Pyrenees, from the Basque Country and Brittany to Picardy. My mother tongue—Occitan, Gascon—hums on this second circlet.

Rural Circuits

Before the Second World War, at least half of the French population spoke the language of Gide no more than did the natives of the first circlet. When the wicked Fathers decided to murder their sons by the millions, in hideous battles in 1914–1918, they sorted the young peasant men into infantry regiments region by region, so that they would understand, in languages as different as Gallo or the Provençal of the Nice area, the orders they received to commit suicide while butchering the boys on the other side. The murder of the sons took place in local dialects. And so the way was prepared to teach, later on, the murder of the fathers in the dominant language. At the time,

197

the central language had not yet reached the fullness of its historical and spatial age. Demographically speaking, French is not yet a hundred years old. What in the classical age was referred to as "la cour et la ville" [the court and the capital] excluded the common people; ordinary people spoke dialect. My parents still spoke it.

Consider me a refugee from those times—times more checkered than people tend to think. Coming back from Tokyo recently, I saw on the airplane's movie screen an announcement telling us that we were directly above Königsberg, followed by the label: Paris, 730 kilometers. I then realized that the randomness of fate had set my birthplace at the same distance from the capital as the city where Immanuel Kant lived and thought! The remoteness of Paris from my childhood world can be evaluated on the same scale and at an analogous ratio to the distances experienced by my colleague and friend Elisabeth Boyi, born in Zaïre. Francophonie is not just a product of the former colonies, as I will now try to explain.

Having spent my formative years there, I speak as a witness of a composite, disparate, heterogeneous France, divided by borderlines, sprinkled with languages, and with no bridge to connect them all: Basque, indeed, stands outside the Indo-European family of languages. In that France, you could not count on the first person you met being always or definitely a pure French-speaker.

My friend Philippe, who comes from Château-Thierry, in the Aisne department of the Champagne region, came to see me in my home region of Gascony. He had to ask his way eleven times and still was unable to make himself understood or to understand what the aborigines—my countrymen—were telling him in response. That was in 1954, a little over half a century ago. The year 1954, for the people of 2006, may sound like a historical date, but it still belongs to living memory—at least mine, whatever the statute of limitations for such a case may be. In the Jura, on the lowlands of the Pas-de-Calais, in Rennes or Nancy, or even for that matter among the châteaux of the Loire, I was, linguistically speaking, as far from home as if I had been at Berlin or Warsaw.

When, in 1940, the Blitzkrieg scattered on the banks of my Garonne tens of thousands of refugees, we got a sense of the diversity of France in terms of opacity of speech, of habits, of customs, of religion, and law. "They eat butter!" said my grandfather in amazement, never having seen that before. Later, he affixed the name *estoquère* to the vehicle known as a *scooter*, observing, despite his lack of diplomas, the most subtle rules of phonetics, in this case, as you will have noticed, metathesis. When I read Montaigne today I can still hear my Gascon-speaking grandfather, saying *méchant* ("wicked") where others would say *mauvais* ("bad") or describing a pretty girl as *gorgias*; and yet I can't make head or tail of Rabelais with his Anjou dialect. Our throats could do no better than to designate as Charcot a man whom they called Schwartzkopf in his hometown on the wine-growing plains of the Lower Rhine.

In 1949 I took the viva-voce entrance exam to the Naval Academy in a building that, as I did not know at the time, belonged to the Collège de France. At the same time doctors tested our powers of sight and hearing. The tests occurred in public, with the whole class looking on. The examiners murmured, faintly, a number that we, the candidates, had to repeat from across the room; and when they heard the way I pronounced the last syllables of *trente* or *quarante* they dragged out the session so that everyone could have a turn at play, while the other candidates laughed themselves silly over my accent. With a clown like me in their grasp, how could they let go? A few years later—in 1955, to pin down the interminable brevity of this half-century—at the conclusion of the oral examination for the *agrégation* in philosophy, the chairman of the jury sat me down to discuss the results and confessed to me with embarrassment that, despite my good performance, he was unable to give me this or that top mark because I could not be employed throughout the whole territory of France. Today that judgment would seem scandalously unfair, but at the time I thought he was correct. Would anyone have understood my lectures north of Limoges or eastward from Clermont-Ferrand? I spoke French with an accent whose strength derives from the power one language exerts over another.

Meanwhile, every Wednesday morning, just outside our front door in Agen, in the Lot-et-Garonne, a market was held in the Calf Stockyard where everybody spoke Gascon. Once in a while the veterinarian appeared and gave a speech in French about a possible livestock infection. The farmers roared with laughter, without being sure whether they failed to understand what he was saying on account of the science or the language. And on the Poultry Market square, every Sunday morning, I followed my mother as she bargained for eggs and roosters in what we called our patois. Before the war I doubt I had ever heard French spoken in the grocery store owned by my uncle in Montaigu-de-Quercy, in the Tarn-et-Garonne. I learned French at school, of course; and that explains the difficulty I had answering the requests for dried codfish and spaghetti uttered by certain aged and toothless clients who spoke in a strange mixed language, part precise Cahors dialect and part a French extracted from the grammar book which they had memorized under the schoolteacher's guidance. I had in this way my first experience of foreign languages right in the middle of France. My second experience, during the occupation, regrettably put me in contact with German, an ordeal that caused me such pain that I lost forever the ability to express myself in a language other than that of the Resistance.

I first saw Paris in the years around 1948—again, that decisive half-century. No one could understand what I said, neither in the ticket booth of the Gare Saint-Lazare, nor in the box office of the Comédie Française, nor in the stores. My sister, a lively dark-haired girl of fifteen, went one morning to the hardware store to buy a *monk*: that's what we called a wooden handle with an opening to hold the charcoal brazier with which we warmed the sheets before going to bed, necessary in those days without heating. The Parisian shopkeeper: "You want to buy a *monk*, miss? To do what, may I ask?" And my little sister replied with an innocent smile: "To put in my bed, of course." The store immediately turned into a comic show. Everyone mocked our accents and exaggerated their inability to make sense of what we said. I memorized their way of intoning: "un aller-retour Bois-Colombes" ("a return ticket to Bois-Colombes") and repeated it silently to myself five times before performing it as best I could at the station window. How many times have I made an engagement for lunch or dinner with a Parisian couple and waited for them in vain because the words "lunch" and "dinner" had different meanings in the France that was high on the latitude charts and the France down below?

When boarding at the Lycée Montaigne in Bordeaux I lived in dormitories and dining halls loud with the talk of mutual foreigners, foreign to each other in language, accent, and habits: Charentais, Landais, Pyreneans, Basques, Garonnais, and so forth, whose gestures and shouts only emphasized their differences, sometimes greater differences than those I observed later on when boarding again at Louis-le-Grand in Paris, where the same students, Berrichons from Berry, Mokos from Toulon, Tunisians and Martiniquians, represented the whole of France.

I've compared notes with them many times: I doubt that any Arab, Senegalese, Walloon, or Québecois friend of today has endured more hazing, mockery, and humiliation than we provincials got at the time from Parisians. Just as readily as the passers-by, our professors at the university classed us as peasants barely off the farm, in the same way that they called the Québecois "Iroquois" or called the Oceanian or African students "savages": all three groups had in common our relation to nature, be it tundra, bush, or plowed fields. They, on the other hand, considered themselves civilized people, proprietors of culture.

I've drawn lessons in patience from this experience, which brought together, more and more effectively than can be imagined today, the speakers of the first circlet and those of the second. I present myself to you today, once more, as a Francophone, an interior Francophone. The distinction between nature and culture, a stupid and cruel invention by some city dweller, caused us so much pain that I wonder now if its purpose had not been, precisely, to separate, in a silently racist way, two groups of human beings on the basis of their remoteness from rain, trees, plowing, and pastures. It allowed those who boasted of having a history to distinguish themselves from those whose ethnology would become the object of subsequent research. On the day that the university set aside funds for the participant-observer study of my ruined Occitan culture, I began to dream, with some vengefulness, I admit, of gathering a team of Pyrenean shepherds who would take the train for Paris and study the customs of the professors of the Collège de France, their cuisine (raw or cooked?), and their sexual habits. Why should social studies be forced to operate with nothing more than semiconductors?

Moreover, does not that same nature-culture distinction help to delineate an objective field where culture can, without hindrance or regret, destroy nature? I cannot imagine a place for culture's emergence other than nature.

In sum, I hear the ringing of what we call Francophonie not only from the outer, greater circlet of its extension but also from the inside too: from the edge of the second circlet, from the hollows of my ears, from the depths of my chest, from the well of my memories, from the internal borders of France.

We are talking, of course, about the most unified country on the planet, far more so than England (distinct from Scotland and Ireland), more than Italy (burdened with its scorn for the South), more than Spain (tormented by its Basques and Catalans), more than Germany with its mosaic of Länder, more than the United States (periodically surprised to rediscover that Texas has indeed had six flags)—but I am here to testify to a France that was motley, striped, pocked with toll stations, where routine travel was an exploration. In one trip you might go from butter to oil, from tile to slate, from dry heat to foggy humidity, from militant atheism to social Catholicism, from concentrated ranching to vineyard monoculture, from the softness of Atlantic moss to the sharpness of Mediterranean pines, from composite Latinities to striated Germanicities, from Flemish-inflected northern speech to half-Breton dialects. French by no means provided the harmonic synthesis of all these, nor did it lead the orchestra.

Now it happens that times change, sometimes abruptly, in far less than a half-century: pride isn't what it used to be. Even Parisians travel. An accent becomes fashionable, be it Gascon, Québecois, or Franco-Arab. The very capital begins to contemplate with pleasure the influence exerted upon French by another language. City people become activists on behalf of the protection of a nature that they conceive in amiably Arcadian terms and experience only while on vacation. They line up to pay court to José Bové.

How can things have changed so suddenly?

Wars, according to some, melted the kaleidoscope of French variety. Television flattened it. Historical and technical explanations, diabolically clever. In this connection the primary schoolteachers of the Third and Fifth Republics are often celebrated or denigrated for their efficiency. This legend—which amounts to a lesson in how to read history—seems to me to belong to the public-relations side of education: we, professors, are apt to overstate our own importance. You will discover these truths in your books, just as you will find their socioeconomic and political conditions, which are deep enough to explain everything.

In reality it was the death of agriculture as the main model of human activity that liquidated once and for all the linguistic patchwork. At the start of the twentieth century, 75 percent of Frenchmen were peasants; at its end, only 2.3 percent: here is the great event, more a matter of anthropology than of history, that has shaped my life and our times; a circumstance so enormous that we forget to name it as a cause; so powerful that we are not done with its consequences yet. My mother tongue comes to its end at the same time, then, as does the Neolithic era, some thousands of years after its beginning with the selective domestication of a few species of fauna and flora, now to finish at the conclusion of the twentieth century with the mastery of genetic mutation, the second gear of our relation to life. We have experienced the end of an era tens of thousands of years in duration, a vanished time when words rose from the soil or wandered in from the woods, like beasts and religions, a time when writing, like plowing, was done in boustrophedon fashion. The crisis of the page starts from the disappearance of the *pagus*. No more peasants, no more peaceful pastures, no more paganism, no more pages well spoken before being written down. And so I have lived through the end of rural languages and cultures. What language or culture, by the way, was ever not rural?

We, the peasants, the savages, the Iroquois . . . we bore on our shoulders, unperceived, what city people called, for a short moment, culture, the better to mask its emergence from agriculture: both culture and agriculture vanished at the same time as my agrarian religion and my mother tongue.

Even though standing on the rim of the Pacific, should I have delivered this eulogy today in Gascon? Now that my brother has died, no one understands its turns of phrase. I will die with a thorax full of words that no one else shares. Even more, I wear mourning for a certain worldwide landscape, for the ancient contract with nature, mourning for a universally peasant humanity.

But Paris still has a way of blowing off provincials like me, just as Paris infuriates you, better Francophones than I will ever be. One example: six million French people continue, despite the aforementioned mourning, to say *Adischats* or something similar to take leave of each other, but this signal has never been recorded in the dictionary—while a Parisian journalist using the word *winglet* in place of *aileron*, one snobby day among others, succeeds in lodging the term in the *Dictionnaire Robert*. The fake Anglo-American slang of *Libération* wins out over what the French Academy's dictionary calls "provincial regionalisms, archaic and obsolete." There is more English in our glossaries now than words that according to me are French, words still in use, though far from Paris.

A beloved person who has not been glimpsed for a long time, we say, is "to speak of" [*à dire*]; we contemplate a fine prospect from a spot we call "being as here" [*d'ici étant*], the locative phrase from which I began to weave my two circlets and which I've heard said in Haiti, where many people are born with the family name Serres and the first name Michel. This is where our two circlets meet.

Corpus Circlets

However, with a sob in my throat, I am of two minds about the use and supposed protection of local languages. I feel as if I have spent my life losing a mother tongue the better to learn another, paternal, tongue, which too is all but ready to vanish. Just as I lament the loss of songs I heard as a child in fields and stables, so too I would feel castrated in my own work if some ideologue had obliged me, from primary school onwards, to do all my learning in the language of my mother. No one will ever make Gascon—or Iroquois, for that matter—into a scientific language ready to discuss pertinently DNA or climate; no one will ever train an exclusively Breton-speaking person to be a geophysicist . . . in short, education dispensed in these languages, first on the demand of activists and more recently in response to central decrees, becomes quickly counterproductive, from the moment the language blocks the people who speak it from access to sciences taught, but also invented, in other languages. But where should the line of language protection fall? I do not know how to answer this question.

Surrounded by my ten hesitations—uneducated guesses—about the future of languages, here I must recall the second "Francophonie" of my life: no longer the speech of my fleshly mother, but that of my intellectual fathers.

After the death of the mother tongue, must I also bewail that of the paternal language? Has anyone pointed out that the teaching of science and the carrying out of research in the one exclusive communicative idiom may well cause the disappearance, like a cathedral sinking under the waves, of the whole corpus, four centuries in the making and hundreds of volumes in size, namely the works of Viète, Pascal, Desargues, Descartes himself, the *Encyclopédie* of d'Alembert, Laplace, Lavoisier, Pasteur, not to mention Jean Perrin, Hadamard, or Henri Poincaré? Here is a "Francophonie" even more deeply lost than the one we have been discussing over these two days.

I hope not to be misunderstood. The world and its history have never lacked for an idiom of communication. For centuries, the Mediterranean spoke a Greek koiné whose vividness made the Jews say "synagogue" and the Egyptians, "pyramid"; then the inhabited world used Latin for almost two millennia. After that, Arabic (for a long time), French (for three centuries), English (for now), successively became convenient media for merchants, sailors, doctors, and astronomers. We cannot predict who will take the next stage. The heavens unfold the history of communicative idioms to the dimensions of space: Antares and Arcturus, two stars with Greek names, shine far from the Latin Sirius and the blue and red supergiants Rigel and Betelgeuse, labeled in Arabic. I am not so silly as to deny the use of a koiné, especially today as we dash from colloquia to symposiums in every latitude. But does it require the disappearance of such beautiful cathedrals?

When we speak of "French," we refer most often to a literary language, perhaps to a political or historical one; but like every language, French is made up of many corpora, many of which elude the linguist's notice. The common language lives in its special corpora. I would even like to offer this definition: a language is the interior koiné of these numerous, singular, differentiated bodies. Ordinary language uses vaguely the rigorous or precise terms of sciences, arts, and trades. For example, if you write "post" or "cable," everyone will understand you, except sailors, who say *aussière* [hawser], and carpenters, who say *arbalétriers* [rafters]. Yet if you use the exact terms, nobody will understand you. If, on the other hand, you decide to use the vague word—"flower" instead of *myosotis* or *cyclamen*, "rope" instead of lines, sheets, or shrouds—the specialists will say you don't know what you're talking about. A writer's vocation, indeed his function, is to open up, in real time, a path of communication between these two discourses, to create a koiné in the interior of his language. A language truly lives by this continuous movement, instigated by good stylists, unifying these corpora to the common language.

What happens, then, if no one reads any more, as is the case in France today, and if no one safeguards, if no one protects these special subsets of language, technical, scientific, practical, or handicraft languages? Laplace, for example, writes in a vastly purer style than that of ten of his contemporaries whose platitudinous poetry is still studied in French departments. Yet his work survives only as long as the knowledge of which it was a part survives.

I will plait, then, ten more circlets or wreaths, no longer across the space of the globe but within languages, including my own language, French, whose usual idiom masks the specialized dialects of the exact sciences, law, philosophy, arts, and trades. These are my paternal languages. These are the paternal languages of the writer, the novelist, the scriptwriter, the philosopher . . . if they will keep faith with their craft. I repeat, a language develops on the basis of many subsets of which linguists often know nothing, since linguists are people who never talk stone-masonry, electricity, algebra, chemistry, pediatrics, cooking, cello, or civil procedure. But a writer worth his salt will never fall back on vague words: such a writer will gladly collect specialized words, even at the price of becoming difficult. The writer's stylistic task, I insist, is to create an exchanger between these two blocks. I see the writer as more organist than pianist. The pianist presses previously aligned keys, as if the ordinary words were there to begin with; but the organist creates his sounds by pulling out the various stops, each of which reaches to one of the corpora I have mentioned: he pulls the sailing stop, the soccer stop, the protein stop, the color stop. . . . The writer's language comes from these submerged corpora. Should they disappear, what will become of language? Language lives through its less-frequently spoken idioms.

Everyone knows that in Chinese France is known as the "Land of Laws," no doubt because we have produced so many systems of law and constitutions? The judicial corpus in French exceeds in volume and importance even the enormous corpus of natural sciences. Neither of these corpora has found a publisher. I pass over the music composed by Francophones which is never published either in the way that German music is published; it stands to reason that music that is never published will never be played. The enterprise I began two decades ago of publishing the Corpus of Philosophical Works in the French Language has taught me much that few know, in particular the existence of these many orphan corpora.

A language gives voice to a small part, visible and audible to all, a vague part, as I just said; restricted in size, this part conceals, below it, like an iceberg, enormous and dense volumes of vital importance, many corpora constructed by specialists, sailors, shipbuilders, instrument-makers, geometers, judges, gynecologists . . . precisely those people who use exact words or authentic language, language that opens the best pathway to the things themselves. If these volumes should melt, the iceberg tips over and the spoken part of language, too, sink into the black waters of oblivion.

We try to save the temples of Angkor and the Aztec pyramids; is this not the same concern? Should we save these linguistic corpora threatened by progressive Sanskritization, rather than Picard or Gascon? I do not have the answer to these questions either.

Francophonie? Besides the Francophonie that we are here to celebrate today, I propose two versions that you may not have expected: a Gascon Francophonie and a learned Francophonie, both endangered, both precious; one precious to my ears and to the love I felt for the mother who bore me, that is, the soil where I was born; the other precious to my head and to the passion I feel for the crafts and disciplines that I had to enter before I could begin to think.

Close to the other threshold, that of departure from life and work, must I begin my mourning labor so early? Farewell, equations and patois, sciences and agriculture, genitals and brains, body and soul, pathos and reflection; *adischats*, my foster-mother; adieu, my fathers of thought.

Stanford University, April 9–15, 2006

Translated from the French by Haun Saussy

Bibliography

Acogny, Germaine. *Danse africaine*, 4th edition. Weingarten Kunstverlag: 1994.
———. "L'Afrique réinvente la danse, elle arrive à Tana . . . " *Zéro international*, issue O, (Octobre–Novembre 1999), p. 11.
Actes des rencontres, Afrique en créations, Paris, 15–16 janvier 1990, "Création artistique, dialogue des cultures, développement: les enjeux de la coopération culturelle," Paris: Focal Coop, Ministère de la Coopération et du Développement, 1990.
Almassy, Eva. *Tous les jours*. Paris: Gallimard, 1999.
———. *Comme deux cerises*. Paris: Stock, 2001.
Amselle, Jean-Loup. *Branchements: Anthropologie de l'universalité des cultures*. Paris: Flammarion, 2001.
———. *L'Art de la friche, essai sur l'art africain contemporain*. Paris: Flammarion, 2005.
Anderson, Christiann and Monique Y. Wells. *Paris Reflections: Walks Through African American Paris*. Blacksburg, VA: McDonald and Woodward, 2002.
Anthologie de la photographie africaine et de l'Océan Indien. Edited by *Revue noire*, 1998.
Archer-Shaw, Petrine. *Negrophilia: Avant-Garde Paris and Black Culture in the 1920s*, New York: Thames & Hudson, 2000.
Aristotle, *Poetics*. Richard Janko (trans.). Indianapolis: Hackett Publishing Company, 1987.
Arkoun, Mohamed. *Histoire de l'Islam et des Musulmans en France. Du Moyen Age à nos jours*. Paris: Albin Michel, 2006.
Art contemporain d'Afrique et d'Océanie, Aideiao, 1984–1994. Paris: ADEIAO, 1995.
"Au Revoir, Freedom Fries!" *New York Times* (August 4, 2006).
Badiou, Alain. "Derrière la loi foulardière, la peur." *Le Monde* (22–23 March 2004).

Balibar, Étienne. *Nous, Citoyens d'Europe? Les Frontières, l'État, le peuple*. Paris: La Découverte, 2001.

———. *We, the People of Europe? Reflections on Transnational Citizenship*. Trans. James Swenson. Princeton: Princeton University Press, 2004.

———. *Abdelkader*. Paris: Hachette, 2003.

Baubérot, Jean. *Laïcité 1905–2005, entre passion et raison*. Paris: Seuil, 2004.

———. *Vers un nouveau pacte laïque*. Paris: Seuil, 1990.

Bédouelle, Guy (ed.). *Une République, des religions. Pour une laïcité ouverte*. Paris: L'Atelier, 2003.

Begag, Azouz. *Ethnicity and Equality: France in the Balance*, edited and translated by Alec G. Hargreaves. Lincoln: University of Nebraska Press, 2007.

———. *Béni ou le paradis privé*. Paris: Seuil, 1989.

———. *Le Marteau pique-cœur*. Paris: Seuil, 2004.

Belal, Y. *Le Réenchantement du monde: autorité et rationalisation en Islam marocain*, PhD thesis. Paris: Sciences Politiques, 2005.

Benmakhlouf, Ali (ed.). *Routes et déroutes de l'universel*. Rabat: Le Fennec, 1998.

Bennasser, B. and L. *Les Chrétiens d'Allah. L'histoire extraordinaire des rénégats (XVI et XVIIe siècle)*. Paris: Perrin, 1987.

Beresniak, Daniel. *Laïcité, pourquoi?* Saint-Estève: Cap Béar éditions, 2005.

Berliner, Brett. *Ambivalent Desire: The Exotic Black Other in Jazz-Age France*. Amherst: University of Massachusetts Press, 2002.

Bernabé, Jean. Patrick Chamoiseau, and Raphaël Confiant. *Eloge de la créolité*. Paris: Gallimard/Presses Universitaires Créoles, 1989.

Bertrand, R. "Les Cimetières des 'esclaves turcs' des arsenaux de Marseille et Toulon au XVIIIe siècle" in *Revue des mondes musulmans et de la Méditerranée*, 99–100, (2002) p. 205–17.

Biasini, Emile. *Grands Travaux. De l'Afrique au Louvre*. Paris: Odile Jacob, 1995.

Blake, Jody. *Le Tumulte Noir: Modernist Art and Popular Entertainment in Jazz-Age Paris*. University Park, Pennsylvania: Pennsylvania State University Press, 1999.

Blanchard, Pascal and Ali Blanchard. *Paris Noir*. Paris: Hazan, 2001.

Blérald, Alain. *La Question nationale en Guadeloupe et en Martinique: essai sur l'histoire politique*. Paris: L'Harmattan, 1998.

Bol, Victor. *Lecture de Stèles de Victor Segalen*. Paris: Lettres Modernes, Minard, 1972.

Bonnamour, Jacques et al. *Les Centres culturels français en Afrique, Evaluation de l'action des CCF dans les pays du Champ*, Evaluations 5. Paris: Ministère de la Coopération et du Développement, 1991.

The Book of Songs (*Shi Jing*). Trans. Arthur Waley. New York: Grove Press, 1996.

Bory, Jean-Louis. *Eugène Sue: le roi du roman populaire*. Paris: Hachette, 1962.

Bourdieu, Pierre. *Distinction: A Social Critique of the Judgment of Taste*. Trans. Richard Nice. Cambridge: Harvard UP, 2002.

———. *Sociologie de l'Algérie*. Paris: PUF, 1958.

Branch, Taylor. *Parting the Waters*. New York: Simon and Schuster, 1988.

Brenner, Emmanuel (ed.). *Les Territoires perdus de la République: antisémitisme, racisme et sexisme en milieu scolaire*. Paris: Mille et Une Nuits, 2002.

Brezault, Eloïse. "Visages Francophones dans l'édition française." *Lettre du Bureau International de l'édition française* (8 March 2006), pp. 7–8.

Brion-Davis, David. *Inhuman Bondage: The Rise and Fall of Slavery in the New World*. New York: Oxford University Press, 2006.

Britto, Karl Ashoka. *Disorientation: France, Vietnam, and the Ambivalence of Interculturality*. Hong Kong: Hong Kong University Press, 2004.

Burton, Richard D. E. *La Famille coloniale: la Martinique et la mère patrie, 1789–1992*. Paris: L'Harmattan, 1994.

———. *Assimilation or Independence? Prospects for Martinique*. Montreal: McGill University, 1978.

Butler, Kim D. "Abolition and the Politics of Identity in the Afro-Atlantic Diaspora: Toward a Comparative Approach," in *Crossing Boundaries: Comparative History of Black People in Diaspora*. Hine, Darlene Clark and Jacqueline McLeod (eds.). Bloomington: Indiana University Press, 1999.

Calle-Gruber, Mireille. *Assia Djebar, ou la résistance de l'écriture. Regards d'un écrivain d'Algérie*. Paris: Maisonneuve & Larose, 2001.

——— (ed.). *Assia Djebar, Nomade entre les murs. Pour une poétique transfrontalière*. Paris: Maisonneuve & Larose, 2005.

Camus, Albert. *Noces à Tipaza*. Paris: Folio, 23.

———. *Le Premier homme*. Paris: Gallimard, 1994.

Canto-Sperber, Monique and Paul Ricoeur. "Les Philosophes en parlent." *Le Monde*, 10 (December 2003).

Carmichael, Stokeley and Charles V. Hamilton. *Black Power: The Politics of Liberation in America*. New York: Vintage, 1967.

Castoriadis, Cornelius. *Une Société à la dérive: Entretiens et débats, 1974–1997*. Paris: Seuil, 2005.

Césaire, Aimé. *Une Tempête, d'après "La tempête" de Shakespeare*. Paris: Seuil, 1969.

Chafer, Tony. *The End of Empire in French West Africa: France's Successful Decolonization?* New York: Berg, 2003.

Chafer, Tony and Amanda Sackur (eds.). *French Colonial Empire and the Popular Front: Hope and Disillusion*. New York: Palgrave, 1999.

Chaïb, Y. *L'Islam et la mort en France. Introduction à l'islam en France: le rapatriement des dépouilles mortelles entre la France et la Tunisie*, thèse doctorale. Aix-en-Provence: 1992.

———. *L'Emigré et la mort: la mort musulmane en France*. Aix-en-Provence: Edisud, 2000.

Chapman, Herrick and Laura Frader. *Race in France: An Interdisciplinary Approach to the Politics of Difference*. New York: Berghahn Books, 2004.

Chirac, Jacques. "Eriger la diversité en principe du droit international." *Le Monde*, 4 (February 2003).

Chouaki, Aziz. *Baya*. Alger: Laphomic, 1988.

Cochin, Auguste. *L'Abolition de l'esclavage*. Paris: Désormeaux, 1979.

Comaroff, Jean and John Comaroff. "Alien-Nation: Zombies, Immigrants, and Millenial Capitalism." *South Atlantic Quarterly* 101, no. 4 (Fall 2002): pp. 779–805.

Condé, Maryse. *La Traversée de la Mangrove*. Paris: Mercure de France, 1989.

———. "Habiter ce pays, la Guadeloupe." *Chemins critiques* 1.3 (1989): 5–13.

Conklin, Alice. *Mission to Civilize: The Republican Idea of Empire in France and West Africa*. Stanford: Stanford University Press, 1997.

Constant, Fred. "Talking Race in Colorblind France: Equality Denied, 'Blackness' Reclaimed." Unpublished paper presented at the conference, "Black Europe and the African Diaspora." Northwestern University, April 2006.

Cooper, Frederick, Thomas C. Holt, and Rebecca Scott. *Beyond Emancipation: Explorations of Race, Labor, and Citizenship in Postemancipation Societies*. Chapel Hill: University of North Carolina Press, 2000.

Cornille, Jean-Louis. "Glissant est-il égal à Segalen?" *French Studies in Southern Africa*, 32 (2003): 1–13.

Dakhlia, Jocelyne. *Islamicités*. Paris: PUF, 2005.

———. "Islam et nationalisme: la fin des Etats de grâce," "Le Religieux dans le politique." *Le Genre humain* (May 1991), pp. 19–32.

———. "Du 'tapis maghrébin' au 'polygone étoilé': retour sur le motif." *Revue des Mondes musulmans et de la Méditerranée* 83-84, (1997/1–2), pp. 125–34.

———. "L'Historien, le philosophe et le politique" in *La Colonisation, la loi et l'histoire*, pp. 145–50. Claude Liauzu and Gilles Manceron (eds). Paris: Syllepse, 2006.

Daubert, Michel. "Pour tout l'or des Akan," *Télérama*, 2782, (7 May 2003).

Davis, F. James. *Who Is Black? One Nation's Definition*. University Park, Pennsylvania: Pennsylvania State University Press, 1991.

Davis, Natalie Zemon. *Trickster Travels. A Sixteenth-Century Muslim between Worlds*. New York: Hill & Wang, 2006.

Debray, Regis. "L'enseignement du fait religieux dans l'École laïque." *Rapport* (Feb. 2002).

Deguy, Anne. "La Rue de la petite Afrique," *Libération*, (April 18th, 2003).

Deleuze, Gilles and Guattari, Felix. *A Thousand Plateaus*. Trans. Brian Massumi. Minneapolis: University of Minnesota Press, 1987. Originally published as *Mille Plateaux*. Paris: Minuit, 1980.

Dendle, Peter. *The Zombie Movie Encyclopedia*. Jefferson, NC: McFarland & Company, Inc., 2001.

Deny, Jean. "Chansons des janissaires turcs d'Alger" in *Mélanges René Basset. Etudes, tudes nord-africaines et orientales*. Paris: Leroux, 1923–1925.

Desbenoît, Luc. "La Diversité culturelle face à la mondialisation (3/5): le Mali. L'Empire mandingue contre-attaque." *Télérama*, 2781 (May 3–9, 2003).

Désir, Harlem. *Touche pas à mon pote*. Paris: B. Grasset, 1985.

Dewitte, Philippe. *Les Mouvements nègres en France, 1919–1939*. Paris: L' Harmattan, 1985.

Dib, Mohammed. *L.A. Trip: A Novel in Verse*. Paul Vangelisti (trans.). Copenhagen: Green Integer, 2003.

Diouf, Abdou. "La Francophonie, une réalité oubliée." *Le Monde* (March 19, 2007).

Dirèche-Slimani, Karima. *Histoire de l'immigration kabyle en France au XXe siècle: réalités culturelles et politiques et réappropriations identitaires*. Paris: L'Harmattan, 1997.

Djaïdani, Rachid. *Boumkoeur*. Paris: Seuil, 1999.

Djebar, Assia. *La Disparition de la langue française*. Paris: Albin Michel, 2003.

———. *La Femme sans sépulture*. Paris: Albin Michel, Livre de Poche, 2002.

———. *Ces Voix qui m'assiègent*. Paris: Albin Michel, 1999.

———. *Vaste est la prison*. Paris: Albin Michel, Livre de Poche, 1995.

———. *So Vast the Prison*. Betsey Wing (trans.). New York: Seven Stories Press, 1999.

———. *Ombre sultane*. (1987) Paris: J. C. Lattés, 2006.

———. *A Sister to Scheherazade*. D. Blair (trans.). London: Quartet, 1988.

———. *L'Amour, la Fantasia* (1985). Paris: Livre de Poche, 1995.

———. *Fantasia: An Algerian Cavalcade*. D. Blair (trans.). London: Quartet Books, 1993.

———. *Femmes d'Alger dans leur appartement*. Paris: Des Femmes, 1980.

———. *Women of Algiers in Their Apartment*. M. de Jager (trans.). Charlottesville: U. of Virginia Press, 1992.

———. *Les Alouettes naïves* (1967). Arles: Babel/Actes Sud, 1997.

———. *Villes d'Algérie au XIXème siècle*. Paris: Centre Culturel algérien, 1994.

———. "Interview." Sept. 17, 1985 http://www.assiadjebar.net/first_novels/main_first .htm. (accessed Nov. 8, 2006).

Donadey, Anne and Adlai Murdoch (eds.). *Postcolonial Theory and Francophone Literary Studies*. Gainesville: University of Florida Press, 2005.

Dubois, Laurent. *Avengers of the New World: The story of the Haitian Revolution*. Cambridge: Harvard University Press, 2004.

Dupin, Jacques. *Dehors*. Paris: Gallimard, 1975.

Duras, Marguerite. *L'Amant*. Paris: Editions de Minuit, 1984.

Dyer, Ervin. "Passage to Paris: A New Wave of Black Americans Is Calling The French Capital Home." *The Crisis* (January/February 2006).

Edsall, Thomas Byrne and Mary D. Edsall. *Chain Reaction: The Impact of Race, Rights, and Taxes on American Politics*. New York: Norton, 1992.

Edwards, Brent Hayes. *The Practice of Diaspora: Literature, Translation, and the Rise of Black Internationalism*. Cambridge: Harvard University Press, 2003.

Edwards, Brian T. *Morocco-Bound: Disorienting America's Maghreb, from Casablanca to the Marrakesh Express*. Durham: Duke University Press, 2005.

Estivalèzes, Mireille. *Les Religions dans l'enseignement laïque*. Paris: Presses Universitaires de France, 2005.

Ezra, Elizabeth. *The Colonial Unconscious: Race and Culture in Interwar France*. Ithaca: Cornell University Press, 2000.

Fall, Mar. *Les Africains noirs en France: des tirailleurs sénégalais aux . . . blacks*. Paris: L'Harmattan, 1986.

Fani-Kayode, Rotimi and Alex Hirst. *Photographs: Revue noire*. London: Autograph, 1989.

Fick, Carolyn. *The Making of Haiti: The Saint Domingue Revolution from Below*, Knoxville: University of Tennessee Press, 1990.

Fisher, Philip. *Hard Facts: Setting and the Form in the American Novel*. New York: Oxford University Press, 1987.

Forsdick, Charles. "Colonial History, Postcolonial Memory: Contemporary Perspectives." *Francophone Postcolonial Studies*, 5, 2, (Autumn-Winter 2007), pp. 101–18.

Forsdick, Charles and David Murphy (eds.). "France in a Postcolonial Europe: Identity, History, Memory." *Francophone Postcolonial Studies*, 5, 2 (Autumn-Winter 2007). Special issue.

Franklin, John Hope. *From Slavery to Freedom: A History of African Americans*. New York: McGraw-Hill, 1994.

Frederickson, George M. *The Arrogance of Race: Historical Perspectives on Slavery, Racism, and Social Inequality*. Middletown, CT: Wesleyan University Press, 1988.

Freeman, Bryant C. and Jowel C. Laguerre. *Haitian-English Dictionary*. Lawrence, KS: Institute of Haitian Studies, 1996.

Fumaroli, Marc. *L'Etat culturel. Essai sur une religion moderne*. Paris: De Fallois (ed.), 1991.

Garrow, David. *Bearing the Cross: Martin Luther King, Jr., and the Southern Christian Leadership Conference*. New York: Vintage, 1986.

Gatewood, Willard B. *Black Americans and the White Man's Burden, 1898–1903*. Urbana: University of Illinois Press, 1975.

Geoffroy-Schneiter, Bérénice. "Les Faces cachées du Ghana." *Beaux Arts Magazine*, 227, (2003), pp. 72–76.

German, Félix. "Dangerous Liaisons: The Lives and Labor of Antilleans and sub-Saharan Africans in 1960s Paris," PhD dissertation, University of California, Berkeley, forthcoming.

Gibbs, Jewelle Taylor. *Race and Justice: Rodney King and O. J. Simpson in a House Divided*, San Francisco: Jossey-Bass, 1996.

Gilroy, Paul. *The Black Atlantic: Modernity and Double Consciousness*. London: Verso, 1993.

Giraud, Michel. *Races et classes à la Martinique*. Paris: Editions Anthropos, 1979.

———. "Les enjeux présents de la mémoire de l'esclavage" in Patrick Weil and Stéphane Dufoix, *L'Esclavage, la colonisation, et après . . .* Paris: Presses Universitaires de France, 2005.

Glissant, Edouard. *Les Indes*. Paris: Seuil, 1956.

———. *L'Intention poétique*. Paris: Seuil, 1969.

———. *Introduction à une poétique du Divers*. Paris: Gallimard, 1996.

———. *Poétique de la Relation*. Paris: Gallimard, 1990.

———. *Poetics of Relation*. Betsy Wing (trans.). Ann Arbor: University of Michigan Press, 1997.

———. *Traité du Tout-Monde*. Paris: Gallimard, 1997.

———. "La Langue qu'on écrit fréquente toutes les autres." *Le Monde des livres* (16 March 2006).

Gondola, Ch. Didier. "'But I Ain't African, I'm American!': Black American Exiles and the Construction of Racial Identities in Twentieth-Century France" in Heike, Raphael-Hernandez, *Blackening Europe: The African American Presence*. New York: Routledge, 2004.

Grossman, James R. *Land of Hope: Chicago, Black Southerners, and the Great Migration*. Chicago: University of Chicago Press, 1989.

Goumarre, Laurent. "Ils n'ont rien vu à Tananarive!" *Art Press*, n. 299 (March 2004).

Gruson Luc (ed.). *L'Islam en France*. Paris: la documentation française, 2000.

Guène, Faïza. *Kiffe kiffe demain*. Paris: Hachette, 2004.

Hadj-Moussa, Ratiba. "New Media, Community and Politics in Algeria." *Media Culture and Society*, 25.4 (2003): pp. 451–68.

Haitian Creole-English-French Dictionary. Bloomington: Indiana University Creole Institute, 1981.

Hall, Stuart and Marc Sealy (eds.). *Different: A Historical Context, Contemporary Photographers and Black Identity*. London: Phaidon, 2001.

Hargreaves, Alec. "Ships Passing in the Night? France, Postcolonialism and the Globalization of Literature." *Francophone Postcolonial Studies*, 1, 2, (2003): pp. 64–69.

———. (ed.). *Memories of Empire and Postcolonialism: Legacies of French Colonialism*. Lanham: Lexington Books, 2005.

———. "French, Francophone or Maghrebian? Maghrebian Writers in France" in Nicki Hitchcott and Laïla Ibnlfassi (eds.), *African Francophone Writing: A Critical Introduction*, Oxford: Berg, 1996, pp. 33–43.

Hargreaves, Alec and Mark McKinney (eds.). *Post-Colonial Cultures in France*. New York: Routledge, 1997.

Hélénon, Véronique. "Les Administrateurs coloniaux originaires de Guadeloupe, Martinique et Guyane dans les colonies françaises d'Afrique, 1880–1939." PhD thesis, École des Hautes Études en Sciences Sociales, Paris, 1997.

Helgason, D. "Historical Narrative as a Collective Therapy: The Case of the Turkish Raid in Iceland." *Scandinavian Journal of History*, 22, (1997), pp. 75–289.

Hollinger, David A. *Cosmopolitanism and Solidarity: Studies in Ethnoracial, Religious, and Professional Affiliation in the United States*. Madison: University of Wisconsin Press, 2006.

———. *Postethnic America: Beyond Multiculturalism*. New York: Basic Books, 2000.

Holt, Thomas. "*From Slavery to Freedom* and the Conceptualization of African American History." *Journal of Negro History*, vol. 77/#2 (Spring 1992).

Homecoming. Dir. Joe Dante. Masters of Horror. Showtime. 2 December 2005.

Homer. *The Odyssey*. R. Fagles (trans.). New York: Penguin Books, 1996.

Hughes, Langston. *Collected Works of Langston Hughes*, vol. 16: *Translations: Federico García Lorca, Nicolas Guillén, and Jacques Roumain*. Columbia: University of Missouri Press, 2002.

Hutchinson, George. *The Harlem Renaissance in Black and White*. Cambridge: Harvard University Press, 1989.

Huttman, Elizabeth et al. *Urban Housing Segregation of Minorities in Western Europe and the United States*. Durham: Duke University Press, 1991.

J'accuse. Dir. Abel Gance. Forrester-Parant Productions, U.S. distribution by Arthur Mayer & Joseph Burstyn, 1939.

James, C. L. R. *Black Jacobins: Toussaint L'Ouverture and the San Domingo Revolution*. New York: Random House, 1963.

Jennings, Eric T. "Representing Indochinese Sacrifice: The Temple du Souvenir Indochinois of Nogent-sur-Marne." *France and "Indochina": Cultural Representations*. Kathryn Robson and Jennifer Yee (eds.). Lanham: Lexington Books, 2005, pp. 29–47.

Jennings, Lawrence. *French Anti-Slavery: The Movement for the Abolition of Slavery in France*. Cambridge: Cambridge University Press, 2000.

Jordi, J-J and Hamoumou, M. *Les Harkis, Une mémoire enfouie*. Paris: Autrement, 1999.

Jules-Rosette, Bennetta. "Black Paris: Touristic Simulations." *Annals of Tourism Research* 21, no. 4 (1994).

Kaussen, Valerie. "Slaves, *Viejos*, and the *Internationale*: Modernity and Global Contact in Jacques Roumain's *Gouverneurs de la rosée*." *Research in African Literatures* 35, no. 4 (2004), pp. 121–41.

Keaton, Trica. "The Interpellation of 'Black American Paris': Migration Narratives of Inclusion and Social Race in the Other France," unpublished paper presented to the conference "Paris Is Burning," Museum of the African Diaspora, San Francisco, April 2006.

Kessas, Ferudja. *Beur's Story*. Paris: L'Harmattan, 1990.

Kesteloot, Lilyan. *Black Writers in French: A Literary History of Negritude*. Washington, D.C.: Howard University Press, 1991.

Khatibi, Abdelkebir. *Figures de l'étranger dans la littérature française*. Paris: Denoël, 1987.

Konaté, Yacouba. "L'Afrique n'est pas une table rase . . ." in *Territoires de la création, artistes, institutions, et opérateurs culturels. Pour un développement durable en Afrique*. Actes des Rencontres internationales de Lille, 26, 27, et 28 septembre 2000, A.F.A.A. ("Programme Afrique en créations"), Culture et Développement, pp. 96–97.

Kristeva, Julia. *Etrangers à nous-mêmes*. Paris: Fayard, 1988.

Lacroix, Guy and Benjamin Bibas. *Artistes sans frontières, une histoire de l'AFAA*. Paris: A.F.A.A., 2002.

L'Afrique à jour, 10 ans de création contemporaine à la Biennale de Dakar, Afrique en créations.

Lallaoui, Mehdi. *Du Bidonville aux HLM*. Paris: Diffusion Syros, 1993.

Laroui, Fouad. *Les Dents du topographe*. Paris: Julliard, 1996.

———. *De quel amour blessé*. Paris: Julliard, 1998.

———. *Méfiez-vous des parachutistes*. Paris: Julliard, 1999.

————. *La Meilleure façon d'attraper les choses*. Rabat: Yomad, 2001.

————. *Le Maboul*. Nouvelles. Paris: Julliard, 2001.

————. *Chroniques des temps déraisonnables*. Casablanca: Tarik éditions-Paris: Emina Soleil, 2003.

————. *La Fin tragique de Philomène Tralala*. Paris: Julliard, 2003.

————. *Tu n'as rien compris à Hassan II*. Paris: Julliard, 2004.

Laroussi, Farid and Christopher Miller (eds.). "French and Francophone: The Challenge of Expanding Horizons." *Yale French Studies*, 103, (2003).

Lassibille, Mahalia. "'La Danse africaine, une catégorie à déconstruire. Une étude des danses des WooDaaBe du Niger." *Cahier d'études africaines*, 175, (2004), pp. 680–90.

Le Bris, Michel and Jean Rouaud (eds.). *Pour une littérature-monde*. Paris, Gallimard, 2007.

Lemann, Nicholas. *The Promised Land: The Great Black Migration and How It Changed America*. New York: A. A. Knopf, 1991.

Lewis, David Levering. *When Harlem Was in Vogue*. New York: Oxford University Press, 1989.

Levi, Primo. *Si c'est un homme*. Paris: Poche, 1988.

Levy, Daniel, et al. *Old Europe, New Europe, Core Europe: Transatlantic Relations after the Iraq War*. London: Verso, 2006.

Lewis, David Levering. *When Harlem Was in Vogue*. New York: Oxford University Press, 1989.

Lingis, Alphonso. *The Community of Those who Have Nothing in Common*. Bloomington: Indiana University Press, 1994.

Lionnet, François and Dominic Thomas (eds.). "Francophone Studies: New Landscapes." *Modern Language Note*, 118, 4, (September 2003).

Litwack, Leon. *Been in the Storm So Long: The Aftermath of Slavery*. New York: Knopf, 1979.

————. *Trouble in Mind: Black Southerners in the Age of Jim Crow*. New York: Vintage, 1999.

Locke, Alain. *The New Negro*. New York: Atheneum, 1989.

Lods, Pierre. "Les Peintres de Poto-Poto." *Présence africaine*. 24–25 (1959), pp. 326–30.

Lombard, Denys. "Prélude à la littérature «indochinoise»." *Rêver l'Asie: Exotisme et littérature coloniale aux Indes, en Indochine et en Insulinde*. Denys Lombard, Catherine Champion, and Henri Chambert-Loir (eds.), pp. 119–39. Paris: Éditions de l'École des Hautes Études en Sciences Sociales, 1993.

Lund, Henrik. "Simon Njami, gourou malgré lui." *Rézo international*, 3, (Autumn 2000).

Lunn, Joe. *Memoirs of the Maelstrom: A Senegalese Oral History of the First World War*. Oxford: James Currey, 1999.

Lyotard, Jean-François. *La Condition postmoderne*. Paris: Minuit, 1979.

Maalouf, Amin. *Les Identités meutrières*. Paris: Grasset, 1998.

————. "Contre la littérature Francophone." *Monde des livres* (March 2006).

Malraux, André. *Oeuvres complètes III*. Paris: Gallimard (Bibliothèque de la Pleïade), 1966.

Manet, Eduardo. *La Sagesse du singe*. Paris: Grasset, 2001.

———. *Mes années Cuba*. Paris: Grasset, 2004.

Mann, Gregory. *Native Sons: West African Veterans and France in the Twentieth Century*. Durham: Duke University Press, 2006.

Manning, Patrick. *Francophone Sub-Saharan Africa 1880–1985*. Cambridge: Cambridge University Press, 1988.

Marable, Manning. *Living Black History: How Reimagining the African American Past Can Remake America's Racial Future*. New York: Basic Civitas, 2006.

Marc, Michel. *L'Appel à l'Afrique: Contributions et Réactions à l'Effort de Guerre en A.O.F. (1914–1919)*. Paris: Publications de la Sorbonne, 1982.

Marcellesi, Jean-Baptiste. "Les 'langues régionales' de France, langues minorées," in Wolfgang Bandhauer and Robert Tanzmeister (eds.). Romanistik Integrativ: Festschrift für Wolfgang Pollack, *Wiener Romanistische Arbeiten*, Wien, Wilhelm Braumüller, 13, (1985), pp. 363–71.

Maury, Lucien. "Les Lettres: Oeuvres et idées—Romans." *Revue bleue* 47, 1, 2e sem. (3 juillet 1909), p. 58.

McCloy, Shelby. *The Negro in France*. Louisville: The University of Kentucky Press, 1961.

McKay, Claude. *Banjo: A Story without a Plot*. New York: Harcourt, Brace, and Jovanovich, 1957.

McManus. "Walking Dead in Angkor." *The New York Times* (24 May 1936), X3.

Memmi, Albert. *Portrait du colonisé précédé du portrait du colonisateur*. Paris: Payot, 1973.

Mémoires intimes d'un nouveau millénaire, IVèmes Rencontres de la photographie africaine 2001. Paris: Editions Eric Koehler, 2001.

Michel, Marc. *L'Appel à l'Afrique. Contributions et réaction à l'effort de guerre en AOF (1914–1919)*. Paris: Publications de la Sorbonne, 1988.

Middel, Matthias. "Francophonia as a World Region?" *European Review of History*, 10, 2, (2003), pp. 203–20.

Miller, Christopher. "Francophonie." *Columbia History of Twentieth-Century French Thought*. Lawrence Kritzman (ed.). New York: Columbia UP, 2005, pp. 235–38.

Miomandre, Francis de. *Le Pavillon du Mandarin*. Paris: Emile-Paul Frères, 1921.

Mirville, Solon. *L'Ecole primaire et la lutte contre l'analphabétisme en Haïti*. Port-au-Prince: La Phalange, 1959.

Monnier, Mathilde. "Antigone l'étrangère." Chantal Pontbriand (ed.). *Danse: langage propre et métissage culturel*. Montréal: Parachute, 2001, pp. 191–97.

Mounier, Bernard. "Comment l'esprit vient aux Biennales," *Rézo International*, 6 (Automne 2001), pp. 17–18.

Moura, Jean-Marc. *Littératures Francophones et théorie postcoloniale*. Paris: Presses Universitaires de France, 1999.

Mouralis, Bernard and Anne Piriou (ed.). *Robert Delavignette, savant et politique (1897–1976)*. Paris: Karthala, 2003.

Mudimbe-Boyi, Elisabeth. *Essais sur les cultures en contacts. Afrique, Amériques, Europe*. Paris: Karthala, 2006.

————. (ed.). *Beyond Dichotomies: Histories, Identities, Cultures, and the Challenge of Globalization*. Albany: SUNY Press, 2002.

Multitude, War, and Democracy in the Time of Empire. London: Penguin 2004.

Murdoch, Adlai. "Making Frenchness Plural: How France Contends with Its 'Others'," *Francophone Postcolonial Studies*, 5, 2, (Autumn-Winter 2007), pp. 41–68.

Myard, Jacques (ed.). *La Laïcité au cœur de la République*. Actes du Colloque du 23 mai 2003. Paris: L'Harmattan, 2003.

Nancy, Jean-Luc. "Séparation de la danse." *Lettre de Fondation Afrique en créations*. (Sept.-Nov. 1993), pp. 199–205.

Ndiaye, Pap. "Pour une histoire des populations noires en France: préalables théoriques." *Mouvement social* (Fall 2005).

Negri, Antonio and Michael Hardt. *Empire*. Cambridge: Harvard University Press, 2001.

Nguyen, Phan Long. *Le Roman de Mademoiselle Lys*. Hanoi: Imprimerie Tonkinoise, 1921.

Nickerson, Colin. "Youths' Poverty, Despair fuel Violent Unrest in France." *Boston Globe* (November 6, 2005).

Nicolas, Armand. *Histoire de la Martinique*, vol. 3. Paris: L'Harmattan, 1998.

Nimis, Erika. *Photographes du Bamako de 1935 à nos jours*. Paris: Éditions Revue Noire, 1998.

Njami, Simon. "Regards anthropométriques." *Revue noire*, 5.

Nolly, Émile. *Hiên le Maboul, 3rd Edition*. Paris: Calmann-Lévy, 1908.

————. *La Barque Annamite*. Paris: Charpentier, 1910.

————. *Gens de guerre au Maroc*. Paris: Calmann-Lévy, 1912.

————. *Le Chemin de la victoire*. Paris: Calmann-Lévy, 1913.

————. *Le Conquérant*. Paris: Calmann-Lévy, 1916.

Norindr, Panivong. "Mourning, Memorials, and Filmic Traces: Reinscribing the *Corps étrangers* and Unknown Soldiers in Bertrand Tavernier's Films." *Studies in Twentieth-Century Literature* 23, no. 1 (Winter 1999): 117–41.

Ogbonna, Jeffrey and Ogbar Green. *Black Power: Radical Politics and African American Identity*. Baltimore: Johns Hopkins University Press, 2005.

Ottley, Roi. *No Green Pastures*. New York: Scribner, 1951.

Paravisini-Gebert, Lizabeth. "Women Possessed: Eroticism and Exoticism in the Representation of Woman as Zombie." *Sacred Possessions: Vodou, Santería, Obeah, and the Caribbean*, pp. 37–58, Margarite Ferrnández Olmos and Lizabeth Paravisini-Gebert (eds.). New Brunswick: Rutgers University Press, 1997.

Peabody, Sue. *"There Are No Slaves in France": The Political Culture of Race and Slavery under the Ancien Régime*. New York: Oxford University Press, 1996.

Peabody, Sue and Tyler Stovall (eds.). *The Color of Liberty: Histories of Race in France*. Durham: Duke University Press, 2003.

Péna-Ruiz, Henri. *Histoire de la Laïcité, genèse d'un idéal*. Paris: Gallimard, 2005.

————. *La Laïcité*. Paris: Domino Flammarion, 1998.

Peniel, Joseph E. (ed.). *The Black Power Movement: Rethinking the Civil Rights-Black Power Era*. New York: Routledge, 2006.

Périna, Mickaëlla L. "Construire une identité politique à partir des vestiges de l'esclavage? Les départments français d'Amérique entre héritage et choix." *L'Esclavage, la colonisation, et après . . .* Patrick Weil and Stéphane Dufoix (eds.). Paris: Presses Universitaires de France, 2005.

Petek, Gaye. "Les Elco, entre reconnaissance et marginalisation." *Hommes et migrations*, no 1252, (November–December 2004), pp. 45–55.

Prevos, Andre. "Postcolonial Popular Music in France: Rap Music and Hip-Hop Culture in the 1980s." *Rap and Hip-Hop Outside the USA*. Tony Mitchell, (ed.). Middletown: Wesleyan University Press, 2001.

Prévost, Marcel. "Émile Nolly, tué à la guerre." *La Revue de Paris* 21, 17 (December 1, 1914): pp. 129–46.

Qin, Hai Ying. "*Stèles*: épigraphes chinoises et stratégie d'une écriture transculturelle." *Lectures de Segalen:* Stèles et Equipée. Marie Dollé (ed.). Rennes: Presses Universitaires de Rennes (1999), pp. 113–23.

Quemin, Alain. *L'Art contemporain international entre les institutions et le marché (le rapport disparu)*. Editions Jacqueline Chambon/Artprice, 2002.

Rauch, Marie-Ange. *Les Administrateurs de la France d'Outre-mer et la création du Ministère des Affaires culturelles*. "Comité d'histoire du ministère de la Culture." Paris: Ministère de la Culture et de la Communication, 1998.

Reinhardt, Catherine. "Slavery and Commemoration: Remembering the French Abolitionary Decree 150 Years Later." *Memory, Empire, and Postcolonialism: The Legacies of French Colonialism*. Alec Hargreaves (ed.). Lanham: Lexington Books, 2005.

Revolt of the Zombies. Dir. Victor Halperin. Halperin Pictures, distributed by Academy Pictures Distributing Corporation, 1936.

Rhodes, Gary Don. *White Zombie: Anatomy of a Horror Film*. Jefferson: McFarland & Company, 2001.

Rives, Maurice and Eric Deroo. *Les Linh Tap: Histoire des militaires indochinois au service de la France (1859-1960)*. Paris: Charles-Lavauzelle, 1999.

Roediger, David C. *The Wages of Whiteness: Race and the Making of the American Working Class*. London: Verso, 1991.

———. *Colored White: Transcending the Racial Past*. Berkeley: University of California Press, 2002.

Rose, Phyllis. *Jazz Cleopatra: Josephine Baker in Her Time*. New York: Doubleday, 1989.

Rosello, Mireille. *Declining the Stereotype: Ethnicity and Representation in French Cultures*. Hanover: University Press of New England, 1998.

———. *France and the Maghreb. Performative Encounters*. Gainesville: University Press of Florida, 2005.

Roumain, Jacques. *Gouverneurs de la rosée*. Coconut Creek: Educa Vision, 1999.

Roux, Emmanuel de. "Tensions franco-maliennes autour des choix de programmation." *Le Monde* (11 Octobre 2003).

Ruhe, Ernst Peter, "'Ecrire est une route à ouvrir.': La Poétique transfrontalière d'Assia Djebar." *Assia Djebar, Nomade entre les murs. Pour une poétique transfrontalière*. M. Calle-Gruber (ed.). Paris: Maisonneuve & Larose, 2005.

———. "Les Sirènes de Césarée. Assia Djebar chante 'La femme sans sépulture.'" In *CELAAN. Revue du Centre d'Etudes des Littératures et des Arts d'Afrique du Nord 2*, (2003).

Russell, Jamie. *Book of the Dead: The Complete History of Zombie Cinema*. Godalming. Surrey: FAB Press, 2005.

Saada, Emmanuelle. *Les Enfants de la colonie. Les métis de l'empire français entre sujétion et citoyenneté*. Paris: La Découverte, 2004.

Sage, Adam. "A National Idea Goes up in Flames. Observations on France." *The New Statesman* (November 14, 2005).

———. "Paris is Burning." *Maclean's*, November 14, 2005.

Sala-Molins, Louis. *Dark Side of Light: Slavery and the French Enlightenment*. Minneapolis: University of Minnesota Press, 2006.

Sand, George. *François le Champi*. Paris: Éditions Gallimard, 1976.

Sartre, Jean-Paul. *Qu'est-ce que la littérature?* Paris: Éditions Gallimard, 1948.

Seabrook, William. *The Magic Island*. New York: Harcourt, Brace and Company, 1929.

Segalen, Victor. *Essai sur l'exotisme*. Paris: Poche, 1986.

———. *Essay on Exoticism: An Aesthtetics of Diversity*. Rachel Schlick Yaël (trans.). Durham: Duke University Press, 2002.

———. *Les Immémoriaux*. Paris: Seuil, 1985.

———. *A Lapse of Memory*. Rosemary Arnoux (trans.). Brisbane: Boombana Publications, 1995.

———. *Les Origines de la statuaire de Chine*. Paris: Editions de la Différence, 1976.

———. *Stèles*. Edition critique d'Henry Bouillier. Paris: Mercure de France, 1982.

———. *Stèles*. Présentation et notes de Christian Doumet. Paris: Poche, 1999.

———. *Stèles*. Michael Taylor (trans.). Santa Monica: The Lapis Press, 1987.

———. *Stèles, Peintures, Equipée*. Paris: Club du Meilleur Livre, 1955.

Segalen, Victor and Henry Manceron. *Trahison fidèle: Correspondance 1907–1918*. Paris: Seuil, 1985.

Sharpley-Whiting, T. Denean. *Negritude Women*. Minneapolis: University of Minnesota Press, 2002.

Senghor, Léopold Sédar. "Ce que je crois," *Seven Stories*. Clementine Deliss (ed.). Paris: Flammarion, 1995.

Silverman, Maxim. *Deconstructing the Nation: Immigration, Racism and Citizenship in Modern France*. London: Routledge, 1992.

Silverstein, Paul. "'Why Are We Waiting to Start the Fire?' French Gangsta Rap and the Critique of State Capitalism." *Black, Blanc, Beur: Rap Music and Hip-Hop*

Culture in the Francophone World. Alain-Philippe Durand (ed.). Lanham: Scarecrow Press, 2002.

———. "Black: Africains, Antillais . . . Cultures noires en France." special issue of *Autrement*, 49 (April 1983).

Simek, Nicole J. "The Past Is Passé: Time and Memory in Maryse Condé's *La Belle Créole*." *Memory, Empire and Postcolonialism: Legacies of French Colonialism*. Alec G. Hargreaves (ed.). Lanham: Lexington, 2005.

Smith, Timothy. *France in Crisis: Welfare, Inequality, and Globalization since 1980*. New York: Cambridge University Press, 2004.

Song, Min Hyoung. *Strange Future: Pessimism and the 1992 Los Angeles Riots*. Durham: Duke University Press, 2005.

Spencer, Jon Michael. *The New Colored People: The Mixed-Race Movement in America*. New York: New York University Press, 1987.

Stoler, Ann Laura. *Carnal Knowledge and Imperial Power: Race and the Intimate in Colonial Rule*. Berkeley: University of California Press, 2002.

——— (ed.). *Haunted by Empire: Geographies of Intimacy in North American History*. Durham: Duke University Press, 2006.

Stoler, Ann and Frederick Cooper (eds.). *Tensions of Empire: Colonial Cultures in a Bourgeois World*. Berkeley: University of California Press, 1997.

Stovall, Tyler. *Paris Noir: African Americans in the City of Light*. Boston: Houghton-Mifflin, 1996.

Stovall, Tyler and Georges Van Den Abbeele (eds.). *French Civilization and Its Discontents: Nationalism, Colonialism, Race*. Lanham: Lexington Books, 2003.

Sue, Eugène. *Les Mystères de Paris*. Paris: Éditions Robert Laffont, 1989.

Sugrue, Thomas. *The Origins of the Urban Crisis: Race and Inequality in Postwar Detroit*. Princeton: Princeton University Press, 1996.

——— (ed.). *The Great Migration in Historical Perspective: New Dimensions of Race, Class, and Gender*. Bloomington: University of Indiana Press, 1991.

Targète, Jean and Raphael G. Urciolo. *Haitian Creole-English Dictionary*. Kensington: Dunwoody Press, 1993.

Tate, Greg (ed.). *Everything But the Burden: What White People Are Taking from Black Culture*. New York: Broadway Books, 2003.

Thomas, Martin. *The French Empire between the Wars: Imperialism, Politics, and Society*. Manchester: Manchester University Press, 2005.

Tiérou, Alphonse. *Do   oplé, loi éternelle de la danse africaine*. Paris: Maisonneuve et Larose, 1989.

Tilliette, Bruno and Simon Njami (eds.). *Ethnicolor*. Paris: Autrement, 1987.

Todorov, Tzvetan. *La Conquête de l'Amérique, la question de l'autre*. Paris: Seuil, 1982.

Toynbee, Arnold J. *Civilization on Trial*. Oxford University Press: 1948.

Tribalat, Michèle. *De l'immigration à l'assimilation: enquête sur les populations d'origine étrangère en France*. Paris: La Découverte, 1996.

Trotter, William Jr. *Black Milwaukee: The Making of an Industrial Proletariat, 1915–1945*. Urbana: University of Illinois Press, 1985.

———— (ed.). *The Great Migration in Historical Perspective: New Dimensions of Race, Class, and Gender.* Bloomington: University of Indiana Press, 1991.

Urfalino, Philippe. *L'Invention de la politique culturell.* Paris: La Documentation Française, 1996.

Valdman, Albert. *A Learner's Dictionary of Haitian Creole.* Bloomington: Indiana University Creole Institute, 1996.

Vergès, Françoise. *Monsters and Revolutionaries: Colonial Family Romance and Métissage.* Durham: Duke University Press, 1997

Vigneault, Guillaume. *Chercher le vent, 2nd Edition.* Paris: Seuil, 2006.

Vogel, Susan (ed.). *Africa Explores, Twentieth Century Art.* New York: The Center for African Art, 1991.

"War on Terror—Battleground France." *National Review* (December 5, 2005).

Wei-Wei. *Fleurs de Chine.* Paris: Aube, 2001.

————. *Une fille Zhuang.* Paris: Aube, 2006.

White, Owen. *Children of the French Empire: Miscegenation and Colonial Society in French West Africa, 1895–1960.* Oxford: Oxford University Press, 1999.

White Zombie. Dir. Victor Halperin. Halperin Productions, distributed by United Artists, 1932.

Wieviorka, Michel. *Une Société fragmentée? Le multiculturalisme en débat.* Paris: La Découverte, 1996.

Wilder, Gary. *The French Imperial Nation-State: Negritude and Colonial Humanism between the Wars.* Chicago: University of Chicago Press, 2006.

Winders, James. *Paris Africain: Rhythms of the African Diaspora.* New York: Palgrave Macmillan, 2006.

Wolton, Dominique. *Demain la Francophonie.* Paris: Flammarion, 2006.

Woodward, Vann C. *The Strange Career of Jim Crow.* New York: Oxford University Press, 1965.

Yee, Jennifer. "Colonial Virility and the *Femme Fatale*: Scenes from the Battle of the Sexes in French Indochina." *French Studies* LIV, no. 4 (October 2000): 469–78.

Zack, Naomi (ed.). *American Mixed Race: The Culture of Micro-Diversity.* Lanham: Rowman & Littlefield, 1995.

Zimra, Clarisse. "Afterword." *Women of Algiers in Their Apartment.* M. de Jager (trans.). Charlottesville: U. of Virginia Press, 1992.

————. "A Woman's Memory Spans Centuries." *Women of Algiers in Their Apartment.* M. de Jager (trans.). Charlottesville: U. of Virginia Press, 1992.

Zysberg, André. *Marseille au temps des galères (1660–1748).* Marseille: Rivages, 1983.

————. *Les Galériens, Vies et destins de 60 000 forçats sur les galères de France 1680–1748.* Paris: Seuil, 1991.

Index

About the Contributors

Jean-Loup Amselle is director of research at the École des Hautes Études en Sciences Sociales (EHESS) where he directs the doctoral program in anthropology. He is editor-in-chief of the journal *Cahiers d'Etudes Africaines*. Among his publications are *Logiques métisses* (1990) translated in English as *Mestizo Logics* (1998), *Vers un Multiculturalisme français* (2001), translated in English as *Affirmative Exclusion* (2003), *Branchements* (2005), *Au Cœur de l'ethnie* (2005) in collaboration with Elikia M'Bokolo, and *L'Art de la friche* (2005).

André Benhaïm is assistant professor at Princeton University, specializing in twentieth-century French literature and culture, and in Francophone literature and culture from North Africa and the Mediterranean. His main research areas include questions of identity and representation, ethics, and aesthetics. He is the author of *Panim. Visages de Proust* (2006), and the editor of a collection of essays: *The Strange M. Proust* (forthcoming, 2008), and co-editor of a special issue of *Revue des Sciences Humaines* entitled "Petits coins. Lieux de Mémoire" (2001) and *Ecrivains de la Préhistoire* (2004). Currently, he is working on a book, *Passages of the Mediterranean. Tales of Travels and Transformations*.

Karl Ashoka Britto is associate professor of French and comparative literature at the University of California, Berkeley. He is the author of *Disorientation: France, Vietnam, and the Ambivalence of Interculturality* (2004), and he is currently working on a project that considers the ways in which certain bodies, including that of the colonized soldier, trouble colonial systems of signification.

Jocelyne Dakhlia is an historian of the Maghreb and Mediterranean Islam. Her most recent books are *L'Empire des passions: l'arbitraire politique en Islam* (2005), *Islamicités* (2005), and *La Langue franque méditerranéenne* (2008) (soon to be in press). Her current research interests focus on "Le Harem sultanien et la question du despotisme au Maroc (XVIIe et XVIIIe siècle)."

Assia Djebar is professor of Francophone literature at New York University and was elected member of l'Académie Française in June 2005. A novelist, translator, and filmmaker, Djebar has also published poetry, plays, short stories, and opera libretti, and has created two films. She is the author of numerous novels and the recipient of numerous literary prizes, including the Neustadt Prize. Her most recently translated novel is *The Tongue's Blood Does Not Run Dry* (2006).

Alec G. Hargreaves is director of the Winthrop-King Institute for Contemporary French and Francophone Studies at Florida State University. He has written extensively on North Africans in French. His recent publications include *Memory, Empire and Post-colonialism: Legacies of French Colonialism* (2005), and *Multi-Ethnic France: Immigration, Politics, Culture and Society* (2007).

Yvonne Hsieh is professor of French studies at the University of Victoria, Canada. She specializes in the perception and representation of other cultures in French literature. She is the author of *Victor Segalen's Literary Encounter with China: Chinese Moulds, Western Thoughts* (1988), *From Occupation to Revolution: China through the Eyes of Loti, Claudel, Segalen, and Malraux (1895–1933)* (1997), and *Eric-Emmanuel Schmitt ou la philosophie de l'ouverture* (2006), as well as a critical guide to Segalen's *Stèles* (2007).

Mireille Le Breton is a PhD student at Stanford University, specializing in twentieth-century French and Francophone literature and culture. Her research focuses on aesthetics and politics in the "Beur" literary and cinematic production.

Trevor Merrill is a PhD student in French and Francophone studies at UCLA. His research focuses on eighteenth-century fiction and contemporary French philosophy.

Elisabeth Mudimbe-Boyi is professor of French and comparative literature at Stanford University where she served as director of the Program in Modern Thought and Literature (2005-2008). She was the president of the African Literature Association (2003) and a member of the Modern Language Association Executive Committee. Her publications include *L'Oeuvre romanesque de Jacques-Stephen Alexis: Une écritute poétique, un engagement politique* (1992), *Essais sur les cultures en contact: Afrique, Amériques, Europe* (2006), and two edited volumes: *Beyond Dichotomies: Histories, Identities, Cultures, and the Challenge of Globalization* (2002) and *Remembering Africa* (2002).

Kathy Richman is assistant professor of French at the University of the Pacific and recently completed a Mellon Fellowship in the Humanities in the Department of French and Italian at Stanford University. Her research interests focus on the questions of altruism and authorship, particularly in the nineteenth-century novel in France. She previously worked on international development projects in Haiti, Madagascar, and Bolivia.

Mireille Rosello is professor of comparative analysis at the Universiteit van Amsterdam in the department of Literatuurwetenschap and the Amsterdam School of Cultural Analysis. Her most recent publications are *Postcolonial Hospitality: The Immigrant as Guest* (2001) and *France and the Maghreb: Performative Encounters* (2005) and in translation *Rencontres Méditerranéennes: Littératures et cultures France-Maghreb* (2006). She is currently working on migrant scripts and border constructions in the context of an ASCA project: "The Creolization of Europe."

Haun Saussy is Bird White Housum Professor of Comparative Literature at Yale University. He is currently working on a book with Paul Farmer, to be entitled *The Human Right to Health*.

Michel Serres is a philosopher and member of the Académie Française since 1991. He has written on philosophy and literature, as well as in philosophy of sciences. He is professor of philosophy and literature at Stanford University and is the author of more than twenty books. His recent publications include *Récits d'Humanisme* (2006), *L'Art des Ponts: homo pontifex* (2006), *Carpaccio: les esclaves libérés* (2007), and *Rameaux* (2007).

Tyler Stovall is professor of French history at the University of California, Berkeley. He has written several books and articles on the history of Modern France, including *Paris Noir: African Americans in the City of Light* (1996), *The Color of Liberty: Histories of Race in France* (2003), edited with Sue Peabody. He is currently working on a study of Caribbean migration to France.

Jennifer Lauren Williams has worked as research assistant for Assia Djebar the year of her election at the Académie française (2005). In collaboration with the author, she created in 2006 the official Assia Djebar's Website: "assiadjebar.net." Currently, she is writing her thesis on the figure of the couple in Assia Djebar's first fiction cycle, or on its after-effects, as she revisits the tetralogy of the "Algerian Quartet."